The

PERENNIAL

PHILOSOPHY

BOOKS BY ALDOUS HUXLEY

Novels
The Genius and the Goddess
Ape and Essence
Time Must Have a Stop
After Many a Summer Dies the
    Swan
Eyeless in Gaza
Point Counter Point
Those Barren Leaves
Antic Hay
Crome Yellow
Brave New World
Island

Essays and Belles Lettres
Brave New World Revisited
Tomorrow and Tomorrow and
    Tomorrow
Heaven and Hell
The Doors of Perception
The Devils of Loudun
Themes and Variations
Ends and Means
Texts and Pretexts
The Olive Tree
Music at Night
Vulgarity in Literature
Do What You Will
Proper Studies
Jesting Pilate
Along the Road
On the Margin

Essays New and Old
The Art of Seeing
The Perennial Philosophy
Science, Liberty and Peace

Short Stories
Collected Short Stories
Brief Candles
Two or Three Graces
Limbo
Little Mexican
Mortal Coils

Biography
Grey Eminence

Poetry
The Cicadas
Leda

Travel
Beyond the Mexique Bay

Drama
Mortal Coils—A Play
The World of Light
The Discovery, Adapted from
    Francis Sheridan

Selected Works
Rotunda
The World of Aldous Huxley

The
PERENNIAL
PHILOSOPHY

ALDOUS
HUXLEY

HARPER**PERENNIAL** 〇 MODERN**CLASSICS**

NEW YORK • LONDON • TORONTO • SYDNEY • NEW DELHI • AUCKLAND

HARPER**PERENNIAL**  MODERN**CLASSICS**

A hardcover edition of this book was published in 1945 by Harper & Brothers, Publishers.

P.S.™ is a trademark of HarperCollins Publishers.

HarperCollins books may be purchased for educational, business, or sales promotional use. For information, please e-mail the Special Markets Department at SPsales@harpercollins.com.

First Perennial Library edition published 1990.
First Perennial Classics edition published 2004.
First Harper Perennial Modern Classics edition published 2009.

Library of Congress Cataloging-in-Publication Data is available upon request.

ISBN 978-0-06-172494-7

24 25 26 27 28 LBC 36 35 34 33 32

Contents

Acknowledgements

For permission to use the following selections, grateful acknowledgement and thanks are extended to the following authors and publishers:

P. J. and A. E. Dobell: CENTURIES OF MEDITATION by Thomas Traherne

John Day: MONKEY, translated by Arthur Waley

E. P. Dutton & Co., Inc.: MUSINGS OF A CHINESE MYSTIC from THE WISDOM OF THE EAST SERIES, translated by Herbert Giles

Dwight Goddard Estate: A BUDDHIST BIBLE by Dwight Goddard

Harvard University Press: THE TRANSFORMATION OF NATURE IN ART by Ananda K. Coomaraswamy

Houghton Mifflin Company: THE WAY AND ITS POWER by Arthur Waley

The Macmillan Company: THE SPIRITUAL REFORMERS by Rufus Jones; MYSTICISM EAST AND WEST by Rudolph Otto; SONGS OF KABIR by Rabindranath Tagore

The Marcel Rodd Company: BHAGAVAD GITA, translated by Swami Prabhavananda and Christopher Isherwood

Newman Book Company: THE WORKS OF ST. JOHN OF THE CROSS, translated by Allison Piers from the Spanish of P. Silverio

R. A. Nicholson: MYSTICS OF ISLAM by R. A. Nicholson

Oxford University Press: THE PATH OF PURITY by Buddhaghosha; THE TIBETAN BOOK OF THE DEAD by W. Y. Evans-Wentz

Sheed & Ward: THE MYSTICAL THEOLOGY OF ST. BERNARD by Etienne Gilson

Introduction

PHILOSOPHIA PERENNIS—the phrase was coined by Leibniz; but the thing—the metaphysic that recognizes a divine Reality substantial to the world of things and lives and minds; the psychology that finds in the soul something similar to, or even identical with, divine Reality; the ethic that places man's final end in the knowledge of the immanent and transcendent Ground of all being—the thing is immemorial and universal. Rudiments of the Perennial Philosophy may be found among the traditionary lore of primitive peoples in every region of the world, and in its fully developed forms it has a place in every one of the higher religions. A version of this Highest Common Factor in all preceding and subsequent theologies was first committed to writing more than twenty-five centuries ago, and since that time the inexhaustible theme has been treated again and again, from the standpoint of every religious tradition and in all the principal languages of Asia and Europe. In the pages that follow I have brought together a number of selections from these writings, chosen mainly for their significance—because they effectively illustrated some particular point in the general system of the Perennial Philosophy—but also for their intrinsic beauty and memorableness. These selections are arranged under various heads and embedded, so to speak, in a commentary of my own, designed to illustrate and connect, to develop and, where necessary, to elucidate.

Knowledge is a function of being. When there is a change in the being of the knower, there is a corresponding change in the nature and amount of knowing. For example, the being of a child is transformed by growth and education into that of a man; among the results of this transformation is a revolutionary change in the way of knowing and the amount and character of the things known. As the individual grows up, his knowledge becomes more conceptual and systematic in form, and its factual, utilitarian content is enormously increased. But these gains are offset by a certain deterioration in the quality of immediate apprehension, a blunting and a loss of intuitive power. Or consider the change in his being which the scientist is able to induce mechanically by means of his instruments. Equipped with a spectroscope and a sixty-inch reflector an astronomer becomes, so far as eyesight is concerned, a superhuman creature; and, as we should naturally expect, the knowledge possessed by this superhuman creature is very different, both in quantity and quality, from that which can be acquired by a star-gazer with unmodified, merely human eyes.

Nor are changes in the knower's physiological or intellectual being the only ones to affect his knowledge. What we know depends also on what, as moral beings, we choose to make ourselves. "Practice," in the words of William James, "may change our theoretical horizon, and this in a twofold way: it may lead into new worlds and secure new powers. Knowledge we could never attain, remaining what we are, may be attainable in consequences of higher powers and a higher life, which we may morally achieve." To put the matter more succinctly, "Blessed are the pure in heart, for they shall see God." And the same idea has been expressed by the Sufi poet, Jalal-uddin Rumi, in terms of a scientific metaphor: "The astrolabe of the mysteries of God is love."

This book, I repeat, is an anthology of the Perennial Philosophy; but, though an anthology, it contans but few extracts from the writings of professional men of letters and, though illustrating a philosophy, hardly anything from the professional philosophers. The reason for this is very simple. The Perennial Philosophy is primarily concerned with the one, divine Reality substantial to the manifold world of things and lives and minds. But the nature of this one Reality is such that it cannot be directly and immediately apprehended except by those who have chosen to fulfil certain conditions, making themselves loving, pure in heart, and poor in spirit. Why should this be so? We do not know. It is just one of those facts which we have to accept, whether we like them or not and however implausible and unlikely they may seem. Nothing in our everyday experience gives us any reason for supposing that water is made up of hydrogen and oxygen; and yet when we subject water to certain rather drastic treatments, the nature of its constituent elements becomes manifest. Similarly, nothing in our everyday experience gives us much reason for supposing that the mind of the average sensual man has, as one of its constituents, something resembling, or identical with, the Reality substantial to the manifold world; and yet, when that mind is subjected to certain rather drastic treatments, the divine element, of which it is in part at least composed, becomes manifest, not only to the mind itself, but also, by its reflection in external behaviour, to other minds. It is only by making physical experiments that we can discover the intimate nature of matter and its potentialities. And it is only by making psychological and moral experiments that we can discover the intimate nature of mind and its potentialities. In the ordinary circumstances of average sensual life these potentialities of the mind remain latent and unmanifested. If we would realize them, we must fulfil certain conditions and obey certain rules, which experience has shown empirically to be valid.

In regard to few professional philosophers and men of letters is there any evidence that they did very much in the way of fulfilling the necessary conditions of direct spiritual knowledge. When poets or metaphysicians talk about the subject matter of the Perennial Philosophy, it is generally at second hand. But in every age there have been some men and women who chose to fulfil the conditions upon which alone, as a matter of brute empirical fact, such immediate knowledge can be had; and of these a few have left accounts of the Reality they were thus enabled to apprehend and have tried to relate, in one comprehensive system of thought, the given facts of this experience with the given facts of their other experiences. To such first-hand exponents of the Perennial Philosophy those who knew them have generally given the name of "saint" or "prophet," "sage" or "enlightened one." And it is mainly to these, because there is good reason for supposing that they knew what they were talking about, and not to the professional philosophers or men of letters, that I have gone for my selections.

In India two classes of scripture are recognized: the Shruti, or inspired writings which are their own authority, since they are the product of immediate insight into ultimate Reality; and the Smriti, which are based upon the Shruti and from them derive such authority as they have. "The Shruti," in Shankara's words, "depends upon direct perception. The Smriti plays a part analogous to induction, since, like induction, it derives its authority from an authority other than itself." This book, then, is an anthology, with explanatory comments, of passages drawn from the Shruti and Smriti of many times and places. Unfortunately, familiarity with traditionally hallowed writings tends to breed, not indeed contempt, but something which, for practical purposes, is almost as bad—namely a kind of reverential insensibility, a stupor of the spirit, an inward deafness to the meaning of the sacred words. For this reason, when selecting material to illustrate the doctrines of the Perennial Philosophy, as they were formulated in the West, I have gone almost always to sources other than the Bible. This Christian Smriti, from which I have drawn, is based upon the Shruti of the canonical books, but has the great advantage of being less well known and therefore more vivid and, so to say, more audible than they are. Moreover much of this Smriti is the work of genuinely saintly men and women, who have qualified themselves to know at first hand what they are talking about. Consequently it may be regarded as being itself a form of inspired and self-validating Shruti—and this in a much higher degree than many of the writings now included in the Biblical canon.

In recent years a number of attempts have been made to work out a system of empirical theology. But in spite of the subtlety and intellectual power of such writers as Sorley, Oman and Tennant, the effort has met with only a partial success. Even in the hands of its ablest exponents empirical theology is not particularly convincing. The reason, it seems to me, must be sought in the fact that the empirical theologians have confined their attention more or less exclusively to the experience of those whom the theologians of an older school called "the unregenerate"—that is to say, the experience of people who have not gone very far in fulfilling the necessary conditions of spiritual knowledge. But it is a fact, confirmed and re-confirmed during two or three thousand years of religious history, that the ultimate Reality is not clearly and immediately apprehended, except by those who have made themselves loving, pure in heart and poor in spirit. This being so, it is hardly surprising that a theology based upon the experience of nice, ordinary, unregenerate people should carry so little conviction. This kind of empirical theology is on precisely the same footing as an empirical astronomy, based upon the experience of naked-eye observers. With the unaided eye a small, faint smudge can be detected in the constellation of

Orion, and doubtless an imposing cosmological theory could be based upon the observation of this smudge. But no amount of such theorizing, however ingenious, could ever tell us as much about the galactic and extra-galactic nebulae as can direct acquaintance by means of a good telescope, camera and spectroscope. Analogously, no amount of theorizing about such hints as may be darkly glimpsed within the ordinary, unregenerate experience of the manifold world can tell us as much about divine Reality as can be directly apprehended by a mind in a state of detachment, charity and humility. Natural science is empirical; but it does not confine itself to the experience of human beings in their merely human and unmodified condition. Why empirical theologians should feel themselves obliged to submit to this handicap, goodness only knows. And of course, so long as they confine empirical experience within these all too human limits, they are doomed to the perpetual stultification of their best efforts. From the material they have chosen to consider, no mind, however brilliantly gifted, can infer more than a set of possibilities or, at the very best, specious probabilities. The self-validating certainty of direct awareness cannot in the very nature of things be achieved except by those equipped with the moral "astrolabe of God's mysteries." If one is not oneself a sage or saint, the best thing one can do, in the field of metaphysics, is to study the works of those who were, and who, because they had modified their merely human mode of being were capable of a more than merely human kind and amount of knowledge.

CHAPTER I

That Art Thou

IN STUDYING the Perennial Philosophy we can begin either at the bottom, with practice and morality; or at the top, with a consideration of metaphysical truths; or, finally, in the middle, at the focal point where mind and matter, action and thought have their meeting place in human psychology.

The lower gate is that preferred by strictly practical teachers —men who, like Gautama Buddha, have no use for speculation and whose primary concern is to put out in men's hearts the hideous fires of greed, resentment and infatuation. Through the upper gate go those whose vocation it is to think and speculate—the born philosophers and theologians. The middle gate gives entrance to the exponents of what has been called "spiritual religion"—the devout contemplatives of India, the Sufis of Islam, the Catholic mystics of the later Middle Ages, and, in the Protestant tradition, such men as Denk and Franck and Castellio, as Everard and John Smith and the first Quakers and William Law.

It is through this central door, and just because it is central, that we shall make our entry into the subject matter of this book. The psychology of the Perennial Philosophy has its source in metaphysics and issues logically in a characteristic way of life and system of ethics. Starting from this mid-point of doctrine, it is easy for the mind to move in either direction.

In the present section we shall confine our attention to but a single feature of this traditional psychology—the most important, the most emphatically insisted upon by all exponents of the Perennial Philosophy and, we may add, the least psychological. For the doctrine that is to be illustrated in this section belongs to autology rather than psychology—to the science, not of the personal ego, but of that eternal Self in the depth of particular, individualized selves, and identical with, or at least akin to, the divine Ground. Based upon the direct experience of those who have fulfilled the necessary conditions of such knowledge, this teaching is expressed most succinctly in the Sanskrit formula, *tat tvam asi* ("That art thou"); the Atman, or immanent eternal Self, is one with Brahman, the Absolute Principle of all existence; and the last end of every human being is to discover the fact for himself, to find out Who he really is.

> The more God is in all things, the more He is outside them. The more He is within, the more without.
>
> *Eckhart*

Only the transcendent, the completely other, can be immanent without being modified by the becoming of that in which it dwells. The Perennial Philosophy teaches that it is desirable and indeed necessary to know the spiritual Ground of things, not only within the soul, but also outside in the world and, beyond world and soul, in its transcendent otherness—"in heaven."

> Though GOD is everywhere present, yet He is only present to thee in the deepest and most central part of thy soul. The natural senses cannot possess God or unite thee to Him; nay, thy inward faculties of understanding, will and memory can only reach after God, but cannot be the place of his habitation in thee. But there is a root or depth of thee from whence all these faculties come forth, as lines from a centre, or as branches from the body of the tree. This depth is called the centre, the fund or bottom of the soul. This depth is the unity, the eternity —I had almost said the infinity—of thy soul; for it is so infinite that nothing can satisfy it or give it rest but the infinity of God.
>
> *William Law*

This extract seems to contradict what was said above; but the contradiction is not a real one. God within and God without —these are two abstract notions, which can be entertained by the understanding and expressed in words. But the facts to which these notions refer cannot be realized and experienced except in "the deepest and most central part of the soul." And this is true no less of God without than of God within. But though the two abstract notions have to be realized (to use a spatial metaphor) in the same place, the intrinsic nature of the realization of God within is qualitatively different from that of the realization of God without, and each in turn is different from that of the realization of the Ground as simultaneously within and without—as the Self of the perceiver and at the same time (in the words of the Bhagavad-Gita) as "That by which all this world is pervaded."

When Svetaketu was twelve years old he was sent to a teacher, with whom he studied until he was twenty-four. After learning all the Vedas, he returned home full of conceit in the belief that he was consummately well educated, and very censorious.

His father said to him, "Svetaketu, my child, you who are so full of your learning and so censorious, have you asked for that knowledge by which we hear the unhearable, by which we perceive what cannot be perceived and know what cannot be known?"

"What is that knowledge, sir?" asked Svetaketu.

His father replied, "As by knowing one lump of clay all that is made of clay is known, the difference being only in name, but the truth being that all is clay—so, my child, is that knowledge, knowing which we know all."

"But surely these venerable teachers of mine are ignorant of this knowledge; for if they possessed it they would have imparted it to me. Do you, sir, therefore give me that knowledge."

"So be it," said the father. . . . And he said, "Bring me a fruit of the nyagrodha tree."

"Here is one, sir."

"Break it."

"It is broken, sir."

"What do you see there?"

"Some seeds, sir, exceedingly small."

"Break one of these."

"It is broken, sir."

"What do you see there?"

"Nothing at all."

The father said, "My son, that subtle essence which you do not perceive there—in that very essence stands the being of the huge nyagrodha tree. In that which is the subtle essence all that exists has its self. That is the True, that is the Self, and thou, Svetaketu, art That."

"Pray, sir," said the son, "tell me more."

"Be it so, my child," the father replied; and he said, "Place this salt in water, and come to me tomorrow morning."

The son did as he was told.

Next morning the father said, "Bring me the salt which you put in the water."

The son looked for it, but could not find it; for the salt, of course, had dissolved.

The father said, "Taste some of the water from the surface of the vessel. How is it?"

"Salty."

"Taste some from the middle. How is it?"

"Salty."

"Taste some from the bottom. How is it?"

"Salty."

The father said, "Throw the water away and then come back to me again."

The son did so; but the salt was not lost, for salt exists for ever.

Then the father said, "Here likewise in this body of yours, my son, you do not perceive the True; but there in fact it is. In that which is the subtle essence, all that exists has its self. That is the True, that is the Self, and thou, Svetaketu, art That."

From the Chandogya Upanishad

The man who wishes to know the "That" which is "thou" may set to work in any one of three ways. He may begin by looking inwards into his own particular *thou* and, by a process of "dying to self"—self in reasoning, self in willing, self in feeling—come at last to a knowledge of the Self, the Kingdom of God that is within. Or else he may begin with the *thous* existing outside himself, and may try to realize their essential unity with God and, through God, with one another and with his own being. Or, finally (and this is doubtless the best way), he may seek to approach the ultimate That both from within and from without, so that he comes to realize God experimentally as at once the principle of his own *thou* and of all other *thous*, animate and inanimate. The completely illuminated human being knows, with Law, that God "is present in the deepest and most central part of his own soul"; but he is also and at the same time one of those who, in the words of Plotinus,

> see all things, not in process of becoming, but in Being, and see themselves in the other. Each being contains in itself the whole intelligible world. Therefore All is everywhere. Each is there All, and All is each. Man as he now is has ceased to be the All. But when he ceases to be an individual, he raises himself again and penetrates the whole world.

It is from the more or less obscure intuition of the oneness that is the ground and principle of all multiplicity that philosophy takes its source. And not alone philosophy, but natural science as well. All science, in Meyerson's phrase, is the reduction of multiplicities to identities. Divining the One within and beyond the many, we find an intrinsic plausibility in any explanation of the diverse in terms of a single principle.

The philosophy of the Upanishads reappears, developed and enriched, in the Bhagavad-Gita and was finally systematized, in the ninth century of our era, by Shankara. Shankara's teaching (simultaneously theoretical and practical, as is that of all true exponents of the Perennial Philosophy) is summarized in his versified treatise, *Viveka-Chudamani* ("The Crest-Jewel of Wisdom"). All the following passages are taken from this conveniently brief and untechnical work.

> The Atman is that by which the universe is pervaded, but which nothing pervades; which causes all things to shine, but which all things cannot make to shine. . . .

> The nature of the one Reality must be known by one's own clear spiritual perception; it cannot be known through a pandit (learned man). Similarly the form of the moon can only be known through one's own eyes. How can it be known through others?

> Who but the Atman is capable of removing the bonds of ignorance, passion and self-interested action? . . .

Liberation cannot be achieved except by the perception of the identity of the individual spirit with the universal Spirit. It can be achieved neither by Yoga (physical training), nor by Sankhya (speculative philosophy), nor by the practice of religious ceremonies, nor by mere learning. . . .

Disease is not cured by pronouncing the name of medicine, but by taking medicine. Deliverance is not achieved by repeating the word "Brahman," but by directly experiencing Brahman. . . .

The Atman is the Witness of the individual mind and its operations. It is absolute knowledge. . . .

The wise man is one who understands that the essence of Brahman and of Atman is Pure Consciousness, and who realizes their absolute identity. The identity of Brahman and Atman is affirmed in hundreds of sacred texts. . . .

Caste, creed, family and lineage do not exist in Brahman. Brahman has neither name nor form, transcends merit and demerit, is beyond time, space and the objects of sense-experience. Such is Brahman, and "thou art That." Meditate upon this truth within your consciousness.

Supreme, beyond the power of speech to express, Brahman may yet be apprehended by the eye of pure illumination. Pure, absolute and eternal Reality—such is Brahman, and "thou art That." Meditate upon this truth within your consciousness. . . .

Though One, Brahman is the cause of the many. There is no other cause. And yet Brahman is independent of the law of causation. Such is Brahman, and "thou art That." Meditate upon this truth within your consciousness. . . .

The truth of Brahman may be understood intellectually. But (even in those who so understand) the desire for personal separateness is deep-rooted and powerful, for it exists from beginningless time. It creates the notion, "I am the actor, I am he who experiences." This notion is the cause of bondage to conditional existence, birth and death. It can be removed only by the earnest effort to live constantly in union with Brahman. By the sages, the eradication of this notion and the craving for personal separateness is called Liberation.

It is ignorance that causes us to identify ourselves with the body, the ego, the senses, or anything that is not the Atman. He is a wise man who overcomes this ignorance by devotion to the Atman. . . .

When a man follows the way of the world, or the way of the flesh, or the way of tradition (i.e. when he believes in religious rites and the letter of the scriptures, as though they were intrinsically sacred), knowledge of Reality cannot arise in him.

The wise say that this threefold way is like an iron chain, binding the feet of him who aspires to escape from the prison-house of this world. He who frees himself from the chain achieves Deliverance.

Shankara

In the Taoist formulations of the Perennial Philosophy there is an insistence, no less forcible than in the Upanishads, the Gita and the writings of Shankara, upon the universal immanence of the transcendent spiritual Ground of all existence. What follows is an extract from one of the great classics of Taoist literature, the Book of Chuang Tzu, most of which seems to have been written around the turn of the fourth and third centuries B. C.

Do not ask whether the Principle is in this or in that; it is in all beings. It is on this account that we apply to it the epithets of supreme, universal, total. . . . It has ordained that all things should be limited, but is Itself unlimited, infinite. As to what pertains to manifestation, the Principle causes the succession of its phases, but is not this succession. It is the author of causes and effects, but is not the causes and effects. It is the author of condensations and dissipations (birth and death, changes of state), but is not itself condensations and dissipations. All proceeds from It and is under its influence. It is in all things, but is not identical with beings, for it is neither differentiated nor limited.

Chuang Tzu

From Taoism we pass to that Mahayana Buddhism which, in the Far East, came to be so closely associated with Taoism, borrowing and bestowing until the two came at last to be fused in what is known as Zen. The Lankavatara Sutra, from which the following extract is taken, was the scripture which the founder of Zen Buddhism expressly recommended to his first disciples.

Those who vainly reason without understanding the truth are lost in the jungle of the Vijnanas (the various forms of relative knowledge), running about here and there and trying to justify their view of ego-substance.

The self realized in your inmost consciousness appears in its purity; this is the Tathagata-garbha (literally, Buddha-womb), which is not the realm of those given over to mere reasoning. . . .

Pure in its own nature and free from the category of finite and infinite, Universal Mind is the undefiled Buddha-womb, which is wrongly apprehended by sentient beings.

Lankavatara Sutra

One Nature, perfect and pervading, circulates in all natures,
One Reality, all-comprehensive, contains within itself all realities.
The one Moon reflects itself wherever there is a sheet of water,
And all the moons in the waters are embraced within the one Moon.
The Dharma-body (the Absolute) of all the Buddhas enters into my own being.
And my own being is found in union with theirs. . . .
The Inner Light is beyond praise and blame;
Like space it knows no boundaries,
Yet it is even here, within us, ever retaining its serenity and fulness.

It is only when you hunt for it that you lose it;
You cannot take hold of it, but equally you cannot get
   rid of it,
And while you can do neither, it goes on its own way.
You remain silent and it speaks; you speak, and it is dumb;
The great gate of charity is wide open, with no obstacles
   before it.

Yung-chia Ta-shih

I am not competent, nor is this the place to discuss the doctrinal differences between Buddhism and Hinduism. Let it suffice to point out that, when he insisted that human beings are by nature "non-Atman," the Buddha was evidently speaking about the personal self and not the universal Self. The Brahman controversialists, who appear in certain of the Pali scriptures, never so much as mention the Vedanta doctrine of the identity of Atman and Godhead and the non-identity of ego and Atman. What they maintain and Gautama denies is the substantial nature and eternal persistence of the individual psyche. "As an unintelligent man seeks for the abode of music in the body of the lute, so does he look for a soul within the *skandhas* (the material and psychic aggregates, of which the individual mind-body is composed)." About the existence of the Atman that is Brahman, as about most other metaphysical matters, the Buddha declines to speak, on the ground that such discussions do not tend to edification or spiritual progress among the members of a monastic order, such as he had founded. But though it has its dangers, though it may become the most absorbing, because the most serious and noblest, of distractions, metaphysical thinking is unavoidable and finally necessary. Even the Hinayanists found this, and the later Mahayanists were to develop, in connection with the practice of their religion, a splendid and imposing system of cosmological, ethical and psychological thought. This system was based upon the postulates of a strict idealism and professed to dispense with the idea of God. But moral and spiritual experience was too strong for philosophical theory, and under the inspiration of direct experience, the writers of the Mahayana sutras found themselves using all their ingenuity to explain why the Tathagata and the Bodhisattvas display an infinite charity towards beings that do not really exist. At the same time they stretched the framework of subjective idealism so as to make room for Universal Mind; qualified the idea of soullessness with the doctrine that, if purified, the individual mind can identify itself with the Universal Mind or Buddha-womb; and, while maintaining godlessness, asserted that this realizable Universal Mind is the inner consciousness of the eternal Buddha and that the Buddha-mind is associated with "a great compassionate heart" which desires the liberation of every sentient being and bestows divine grace on all who make a serious effort to achieve man's final end. In a word, despite their inauspicious vocabulary, the best of the Mahayana sutras contain an authentic formulation of the Perennial Philosophy—a formulation which in some respects (as we shall see when we come to the section, "God in the World") is more complete than any other.

In India, as in Persia, Mohammedan thought came to be enriched by the doctrine that God is immanent as well as transcendent, while to Mohammedan practice were added the moral disciplines and "spiritual exercises," by means of which the soul is prepared for contemplation or the unitive knowledge of the Godhead. It is a significant historical fact that the poet-saint Kabir is claimed as a co-religionist both by Moslems and Hindus. The politics of those whose goal is beyond time are always pacific; it is the idolaters of past and future, of reactionary memory and Utopian dream, who do the persecuting and make the wars.

> Behold but One in all things; it is the second that leads you astray.
>
> *Kabir*

That this insight into the nature of things and the origin of good and evil is not confined exclusively to the saint, but is recognized obscurely by every human being, is proved by the very structure of our language. For language, as Richard Trench pointed out long ago, is often "wiser, not merely than the vulgar, but even than the wisest of those who speak it. Sometimes it locks up truths which were once well known, but have been forgotten. In other cases it holds the germs of truths which, though they were never plainly discerned, the genius of its framers caught a glimpse of in a happy moment of divination." For example, how significant it is that in the Indo-European languages, as Darmsteter has pointed out, the root meaning "two" should connote badness. The Greek prefix dys- (as in dyspepsia) and the Latin dis- (as in dishonorable) are both derived from "duo." The cognate bis- gives a pejorative sense to such modern French words as *bévue* ("blunder," literally "two-sight"). Traces of that "second which leads you astray" can be found in "dubious," "doubt" and *Zweifel*—for to doubt is to be double-minded. Bunyan has his Mr. Facing-both-ways, and modern American slang its "two-timers." Obscurely and unconsciously wise, our language confirms the findings of the mystics and proclaims the essential badness of division—a word, incidentally, in which our old enemy "two" makes another decisive appearance.

Here it may be remarked that the cult of unity on the political level is only an idolatrous *ersatz* for the genuine religion of unity on the personal and spiritual levels. Totalitarian regimes justify their existence by means of a philosophy of political monism, according to which the state is God on earth, unification under the heel of the divine state is salvation, and all means to such unification, however intrinsically wicked, are right and may be used without scruple. This political monism leads in practice to excessive privilege and power for the few and oppression for the many, to discontent at home and war abroad. But excessive privilege and power are standing temptations to pride, greed, vanity and cruelty; oppression results in fear and envy; war breeds hatred, misery and despair. All such negative emotions are fatal to the spiritual life. Only the pure in heart and poor in spirit can come to the unitive knowledge of God. Hence, the attempt to impose more unity upon societies than their individual members are ready for makes it psychologically almost impossible for those individuals to realize their unity with the divine Ground and with one another.

Among the Christians and the Sufis, to whose writings we now return, the concern is primarily with the human mind and its divine essence.

> My Me is God, nor do I recognize any other Me except my God Himself.
>
> *St. Catherine of Genoa*

> In those respects in which the soul is unlike God, it is also unlike itself.
>
> *St. Bernard*

I went from God to God, until they cried from me in me, "O thou I!"

Bayazid of Bistun

Two of the recorded anecdotes about this Sufi saint deserve to be quoted here. "When Bayazid was asked how old he was, he replied, 'Four years.' They said, 'How can that be?' He answered, 'I have been veiled from God by the world for seventy years, but I have seen Him during the last four years. The period during which one is veiled does not belong to one's life.'" On another occasion someone knocked at the saint's door and cried, "Is Bayazid here?" Bayazid answered, "Is anybody here except God?"

To gauge the soul we must gauge it with God, for the Ground of God and the Ground of the Soul are one and the same.

Eckhart

The spirit possesses God essentially in naked nature, and God the spirit.

Ruysbroeck

For though she sink all sinking in the oneness of divinity, she never touches bottom. For it is of the very essence of the soul that she is powerless to plumb the depths of her creator. And here one cannot speak of the soul any more, for she has lost her nature yonder in the oneness of divine essence. There she is no more called soul, but is called immeasurable being.

Eckhart

The knower and the known are one. Simple people imagine that they should see God, as if He stood there and they here. This is not so. God and I, we are one in knowledge.

Eckhart

"I live, yet not I, but Christ in me." Or perhaps it might be more accurate to use the verb transitively and say, "I live, yet not I; for it is the Logos who *lives me*"—lives me as an actor lives his part. In such a case, of course, the actor is always infinitely superior to the rôle. Where real life is concerned, there are no Shakespearean characters, there are only Addisonian Catos or, more often, grotesque Monsieur Perrichons and Charlie's Aunts mistaking themselves for Julius Caesar or the Prince of Denmark. But by a merciful dispensation it is always in the power of every *dramatis persona* to get his low, stupid lines pronounced and supernaturally transfigured by the divine equivalent of a Garrick.

> O my God, how does it happen in this poor old world that Thou art so great and yet nobody finds Thee, that Thou callest so loudly and nobody hears Thee, that Thou art so near and nobody feels Thee, that Thou givest Thyself to everybody and nobody knows Thy name? Men flee from Thee and say they cannot find Thee; they turn their backs and say they cannot see Thee; they stop their ears and say they cannot hear Thee.
>
> *Hans Denk*

Between the Catholic mystics of the fourteenth and fifteenth centuries and the Quakers of the seventeenth there yawns a wide gap of time made hideous, so far as religion is concerned, with interdenominational wars and persecutions. But the gulf was bridged by a succession of men, whom Rufus Jones, in the only accessible English work devoted to their lives and teachings, has called the "Spiritual Reformers." Denk, Franck, Castellio, Weigel, Everard, the Cambridge Platonists—in spite of the murdering and the madness, the apostolic succession remains unbroken. The truths that had been spoken in the *Theologia Germanica*—that book which Luther professed to love so much and from which, if we may judge from his career, he learned so singularly little—were being uttered once again by Englishmen during the Civil War and under the Cromwellian dictatorship. The mystical tradition, perpetuated by the Protestant Spiritual Reformers, had become diffused, as it were, in the religious atmosphere of the time when George Fox had his first great "opening" and knew by direct experience.

> that Every Man was enlightened by the Divine Light of Christ, and I saw it shine through all; And that they that believed in it came out of Condemnation and came

to the Light of Life, and became the Children of it; And that they that hated it and did not believe in it, were condemned by it, though they made a profession of Christ. This I saw in the pure Openings of Light, without the help of any Man, neither did I then know where to find it in the Scriptures, though afterwards, searching the Scriptures, I found it.

From Fox's Journal

The doctrine of the Inner Light achieved a clearer formulation in the writings of the second generation of Quakers. "There is," wrote William Penn, "something nearer to us than Scriptures, to wit, the Word in the heart from which all Scriptures come." And a little later Robert Barclay sought to explain the direct experience of *tat tvam asi* in terms of an Augustinian theology that had, of course, to be considerably stretched and trimmed before it could fit the facts. Man, he declared in his famous theses, is a fallen being, incapable of good, unless united to the Divine Light. This Divine Light is Christ within the human soul, and is as universal as the seed of sin. All men, heathen as well as Christian, are endowed with the Inward Light, even though they may know nothing of the outward history of Christ's life. Justification is for those who do not resist the Inner Light and so permit of a new birth of holiness within them.

Goodness needeth not to enter into the soul, for it is there already, only it is unperceived.

Theologia Germanica

When the Ten Thousand things are viewed in their oneness, we return to the Origin and remain where we have always been.

Sen T'sen

It is because we don't know Who we are, because we are unaware that the Kingdom of Heaven is within us, that we behave in the generally silly, the often insane, the sometimes criminal ways that are so characteristically human. We are saved, we are liberated and enlightened, by perceiving the hitherto unperceived good that is already within us, by returning to our eternal Ground and remaining where, without

knowing it, we have always been. Plato speaks in the same
sense when he says, in the *Republic*, that "the virtue of wisdom more than anything else contains a divine element which
always remains." And in the *Theaetetus* he makes the point,
so frequently insisted upon by those who have practised spiritual religion, that it is only by becoming Godlike that we can
know God—and to become Godlike is to identify ourselves
with the divine element which in fact constitutes our essential
nature, but of which, in our mainly voluntary ignorance, we
choose to remain unaware.

> They are on the way to truth who apprehend God by
> means of the divine, Light by the light.
>
> *Philo*

Philo was the exponent of the Hellenistic Mystery Religion
which grew up, as Professor Goodenough has shown, among
the Jews of the Dispersion, between about 200 B. C. and 100
A. D. Reinterpreting the Pentateuch in terms of a metaphysical
system derived from Platonism, Neo-Pythagoreanism and Stoicism, Philo transformed the wholly transcendental and almost
anthropomorphically personal God of the Old Testament into
the immanent-transcendent Absolute Mind of the Perennial
Philosophy. But even from the orthodox scribes and Pharisees
of that momentous century which witnessed, along with the
dissemination of Philo's doctrines, the first beginnings of
Christianity and the destruction of the Temple at Jerusalem,
even from the guardians of the Law we hear significantly
mystical utterances. Hillel, the great rabbi whose teachings
on humility and the love of God and man read like an earlier,
cruder version of some of the Gospel sermons, is reported to
have spoken these words to an assemblage in the courts of the
Temple. "If I am here," (it is Jehovah who is speaking
through the mouth of his prophet) "everyone is here. If I am
not here, no one is here."

> The Beloved is all in all; the lover merely veils Him;
> The Beloved is all that lives, the lover a dead thing.
>
> *Jalal-uddin Rumi*

> There is a spirit in the soul, untouched by time and flesh,
> flowing from the Spirit, remaining in the Spirit, itself

wholly spiritual. In this principle is God, ever verdant, ever flowering in all the joy and glory of His actual Self. Sometimes I have called this principle the Tabernacle of the soul, sometimes a spiritual Light, anon I say it is a Spark. But now I say that it is more exalted over this and that than the heavens are exalted above the earth. So now I name it in a nobler fashion. . . . It is free of all names and void of all forms. It is one and simple, as God is one and simple, and no man can in any wise behold it.

Eckhart

Crude formulations of some of the doctrines of the Perennial Philosophy are to be found in the thought-systems of the uncivilized and so-called primitive peoples of the world. Among the Maoris, for example, every human being is regarded as a compound of four elements—a divine eternal principle, known as the *toiora*; an ego, which disappears at death; a ghost-shadow, or psyche, which survives death; and finally a body. Among the Oglala Indians the divine element is called the *sican*, and this is regarded as identical with the *ton*, or divine essence of the world. Other elements of the self are the *nagi*, or personality, and *niya*, or vital soul. After death the *sican* is reunited with the divine Ground of all things, the *nagi* survives in the ghost world of psychic phenomena and the *niya* disappears into the material universe.

In regard to no twentieth-century "primitive" society can we rule out the possibility of influence by, or borrowing from, some higher culture. Consequently, we have no right to argue from the present to the past. Because many contemporary savages have an esoteric philosophy that is monotheistic with a monotheism that is sometimes of the "That art thou" variety, we are not entitled to infer offhand that neolithic or palaeolithic men held similar views.

More legitimate and more intrinsically plausible are the inferences that may be drawn from what we know about our own physiology and psychology. We know that human minds have proved themselves capable of everything from imbecility to Quantum Theory, from *Mein Kampf* and sadism to the sanctity of Philip Neri, from metaphysics to crossword puzzles, power politics and the *Missa Solemnis*. We also know that human minds are in some way associated with human brains, and we have fairly good reasons for supposing that there have been no considerable changes in the size and conformation of human brains for a good many thousands of years. Consequently it seems justifiable to infer that human minds in the remote past were capable of as many and as various kinds and degrees of activity as are minds at the present time.

It is, however, certain that many activities undertaken by some minds at the present time were not, in the remote past, undertaken by any minds at all. For this there are several obvious reasons. Certain thoughts are practically unthinkable except in terms of an appropriate language and within the framework of an appropriate system of classification. Where these necessary instruments do not exist, the thoughts in question are not expressed and not even conceived. Nor is this all: the incentive to develop the instruments of certain kinds of thinking is not always present. For long periods of history and prehistory it would seem that men and women, though perfectly capable of doing so, did not wish to pay attention to problems, which their descendants found absorbingly interesting. For example, there is no reason to suppose that, between the thirteenth century and the twentieth, the human mind underwent any kind of evolutionary change, comparable to the change, let us say, in the physical structure of the horse's foot during an incomparably longer span of geological time. What happened was that men turned their attention from certain aspects of reality to certain other aspects. The result, among other things, was the development of the natural sciences. Our perceptions and our understanding are directed, in large measure, by our will. We are aware of, and we think about, the things which, for one reason or another, we want to see and understand. Where there's a will there is always an intellectual way. The capacities of the human mind are almost indefinitely great. Whatever we will to do, whether it be to come to the unitive knowledge of the Godhead, or to manufacture self-propelled flame-throwers—that we are able to do, provided always that the willing be sufficiently intense and sustained. It is clear that many of the things to which modern men have chosen to pay attention were ignored by their predecessors. Consequently the very means for thinking clearly and fruitfully about those things remained uninvented, not merely during prehistoric times, but even to the opening of the modern era.

The lack of a suitable vocabulary and an adequate frame

of reference, and the absence of any strong and sustained desire to invent these necessary instruments of thought—here are two sufficient reasons why so many of the almost endless potentialities of the human mind remained for so long unactualized. Another and, on its own level, equally cogent reason is this: much of the world's most original and fruitful thinking is done by people of poor physique and of a thoroughly unpractical turn of mind. Because this is so, and because the value of pure thought, whether analytical or integral, has everywhere been more or less clearly recognized, provision was and still is made by every civilized society for giving thinkers a measure of protection from the ordinary strains and stresses of social life. The hermitage, the monastery, the college, the academy and the research laboratory; the begging bowl, the endowment, patronage and the grant of taxpayers' money—such are the principal devices that have been used by actives to conserve that rare bird, the religious, philosophical, artistic or scientific contemplative. In many primitive societies conditions are hard and there is no surplus wealth. The born contemplative has to face the struggle for existence and social predominance without protection. The result, in most cases, is that he either dies young or is too desperately busy merely keeping alive to be able to devote his attention to anything else. When this happens the prevailing philosophy will be that of the hardy, extraverted man of action.

All this sheds some light—dim, it is true, and merely inferential—on the problem of the perennialness of the Perennial Philosophy. In India the scriptures were regarded, not as revelations made at some given moment of history, but as eternal gospels, existent from everlasting to everlasting, inasmuch as coeval with man, or for that matter with any other kind of corporeal or incorporeal being possessed of reason. A similar point of view is expressed by Aristotle, who regards the fundamental truths of religion as everlasting and indestructible. There have been ascents and falls, periods (literally "roads around" or cycles) of progress and regress; but the great fact of God as the First Mover of a universe which partakes of His divinity has always been recognized. In the light of what we know about prehistoric man (and what we know amounts to nothing more than a few chipped stones, some paintings, drawings and sculptures) and of what we may legitimately infer from other, better documented fields of knowledge, what are we to think of these traditional doctrines? My own view is that they may be true. We know that born contemplatives in the realm both of analytic and of integral thought have turned up in fair numbers and at frequent intervals during recorded history. There is therefore every reason to suppose that they turned up before history was recorded. That many of these people died young or were unable to exercise their talents is certain. But a few of them must have survived. In this context it is highly significant that, among many contemporary primitives, two thought-patterns are found—an exoteric pattern for the unphilosophic many and an esoteric pattern (often monotheistic, with a belief in a God not merely of power, but of goodness and wisdom) for the initiated few. There is no reason to suppose that circumstances were any harder for prehistoric men than they are for many contemporary savages. But if an esoteric monotheism of the kind that seems to come natural to the born thinker is possible in modern savage societies, the majority of whose members accept the sort of polytheistic philosophy that seems to come natural to men of action, a similar esoteric doctrine might have been current in prehistoric societies. True, the modern esoteric doctrines may have been derived from higher cultures. But the significant fact remains that, if so derived, they yet had a meaning for certain members of the primitive society and were considered valuable enough to be carefully preserved. We have seen that many thoughts are unthinkable apart from an appropriate vocabulary and frame of reference. But the fundamental ideas of the Perennial Philosophy can be formulated in a very simple vocabulary, and the experiences to which the ideas refer can and indeed must be had immediately and apart from any vocabulary whatsoever. Strange openings and theophanies are granted to quite small children, who are often profoundly and permanently affected by these experiences. We have no reason to suppose that what happens now to persons with small vocabularies did not happen in remote antiquity. In the modern world (as Vaughan and Traherne and Wordsworth, among others, have told us) the child tends to grow out of his direct awareness of the one Ground of things; for the habit of analytical thought is fatal to the intuitions of integral thinking, whether on the "psychic" or the spiritual level. Psychic preoccupations may be and often are a major obstacle in the way of genuine spirituality. In primitive societies now (and, presumably, in the remote past) there is much preoccupation with, and a widespread talent for, psychic thinking. But a few people may have worked their way through psychic into genuinely spiritual experience—just as, even in modern industrialized societies, a few people work their way out of the prevailing preoccupation with matter and through the prevailing habits of analytical thought into the direct experience of the spiritual Ground of things.

Such, then, very briefly are the reasons for supposing that the historical traditions of oriental and our own classical antiquity may be true. It is interesting to find that at least one distinguished contemporary ethnologist is in agreement with Aristotle and the Vedantists. "Orthodox ethnology," writes Dr. Paul Radin in his *Primitive Man as Philosopher*, "has been nothing but an enthusiastic and quite uncritical attempt to apply the Darwinian theory of evolution to the facts of social experience." And he adds that "no progress in ethnology will be achieved until scholars rid themselves once and for all of the curious notion that everything possesses a history; until they realize that certain ideas and certain concepts are as ultimate for man, as a social being, as specific physiological reactions are ultimate for him, as a biological being." Among these ultimate concepts, in Dr. Radin's view, is that of monotheism. Such monotheism is often no more than the recognition of a single dark and numinous Power ruling the world. But it may sometimes be genuinely ethical and spiritual.

The nineteenth century's mania for history and prophetic Utopianism tended to blind the eyes of even its acutest thinkers to the timeless facts of eternity. Thus we find T. H. Green writing of mystical union as though it were an evolutionary process and not, as all the evidence seems to show, a state which man, as man, has always had it in his power to realize. "An animal organism, which has its history in time, gradually becomes the vehicle of an eternally complete consciousness, which in itself can have no history, but a history of the process by which the animal organism becomes its vehicle." But in actual fact it is only in regard to peripheral knowledge that there has been a genuine historical development. Without much lapse of time and much accumulation of skills and information, there can be but an imperfect knowledge of the material world. But direct awareness of the "eternally complete consciousness," which is the ground of the material world, is a possibility occasionally actualized by some human beings at almost any stage of their own personal development, from childhood to old age, and at any period of the race's history.

CHAPTER II

The Nature of the Ground

OUR starting point has been the psychological doctrine, "That art thou." The question that now quite naturally presents itself is a metaphysical one: What is the That to which the thou can discover itself to be akin?

To this the fully developed Perennial Philosophy has at all times and in all places given fundamentally the same answer. The divine Ground of all existence is a spiritual Absolute, ineffable in terms of discursive thought, but (in certain circumstances) susceptible of being directly experienced and realized by the human being. This Absolute is the God-without-form of Hindu and Christian mystical phraseology. The last end of man, the ultimate reason for human existence, is unitive knowledge of the divine Ground—the knowledge that can come only to those who are prepared to "die to self" and so make room, as it were, for God. Out of any given generation of men and women very few will achieve the final end of human existence; but the opportunity for coming to unitive knowledge will, in one way or another, continually be offered until all sentient beings realize Who in fact they are.

The Absolute Ground of all existence has a personal aspect. The activity of Brahman is Isvara, and Isvara is further manifested in the Hindu Trinity and, at a more distant remove, in the other deities or angels of the Indian pantheon. Analogously, for Christian mystics, the ineffable, attributeless Godhead is manifested in a Trinity of Persons, of whom it is possible to predicate such human attributes as goodness, wisdom, mercy and love, but in a supereminent degree.

Finally there is an incarnation of God in a human being, who possesses the same qualities of character as the personal God, but who exhibits them under the limitations necessarily

imposed by confinement within a material body born into the
world at a given moment of time. For Christians there has
been and, *ex hypothesi*, can be but one such divine incarnation; for Indians there can be and have been many. In
Christendom as well as in the East, contemplatives who follow
the path of devotion conceive of, and indeed directly perceive
the incarnation as a constantly renewed fact of experience.
Christ is for ever being begotten within the soul by the Father,
and the play of Krishna is the pseudo-historical symbol of an
everlasting truth of psychology and metaphysics—the fact
that, in relation to God, the personal soul is always feminine
and passive.

Mahayana Buddhism teaches these same metaphysical doctrines in terms of the "Three Bodies" of Buddha—the absolute Dharmakaya, known also as the Primordial Buddha, or
Mind, or the Clear Light of the Void; the Sambhogakaya,
corresponding to Isvara or the personal God of Judaism,
Christianity and Islam; and finally the Nirmanakaya, the
material body, in which the Logos is incarnated upon earth as
a living, historical Buddha.

Among the Sufis, Al Haqq, the Real, seems to be thought
of as the abyss of Godhead underlying the personal Allah,
while the Prophet is taken out of history and regarded as the
incarnation of the Logos.

Some idea of the inexhaustible richness of the divine nature
can be obtained by analysing, word by word, the invocation
with which the Lord's Prayer begins—"Our Father who art
in heaven." God is ours—ours in the same intimate sense that
our consciousness and life are ours. But as well as immanently
ours, God is also transcendently the personal Father, who
loves his creatures and to whom love and allegiance are owed
by them in return. "Our Father who *art*": when we come to
consider the verb in isolation, we perceive that the immanent-
transcendent personal God is also the immanent-transcendent
One, the essence and principle of all existence. And finally
God's being is "in heaven"; the divine nature is other than,
and incommensurable with, the nature of the creatures in
whom God is immanent. That is why we can attain to the
unitive knowledge of God only when we become in some
measure Godlike, only when we permit God's kingdom to
come by making our own creaturely kingdom go.

God may be worshipped and contemplated in any of his

aspects. But to persist in worshipping only one aspect to the exclusion of all the rest is to run into grave spiritual peril. Thus, if we approach God with the preconceived idea that He is exclusively the personal, transcendental, all-powerful ruler of the world, we run the risk of becoming entangled in a religion of rites, propitiatory sacrifices (sometimes of the most horrible nature) and legalistic observances. Inevitably so; for if God is an unapproachable potentate out there, giving mysterious orders, this kind of religion is entirely appropriate to the cosmic situation. The best that can be said for ritualistic legalism is that it improves conduct. It does little, however, to alter character and nothing of itself to modify consciousness.

Things are a great deal better when the transcendent, omnipotent personal God is regarded as also a loving Father. The sincere worship of such a God changes character as well as conduct, and does something to modify consciousness. But the complete transformation of consciousness, which is "enlightenment," "deliverance," "salvation," comes only when God is thought of as the Perennial Philosophy affirms Him to be—immanent as well as transcendent, supra-personal as well as personal—and when religious practices are adapted to this conception.

When God is regarded as exclusively immanent, legalism and external practices are abandoned and there is a concentration on the Inner Light. The dangers now are quietism and antinomianism, a partial modification of consciousness that is useless or even harmful, because it is not accompanied by the transformation of character which is the necessary prerequisite of a total, complete and spiritually fruitful transformation of consciousness.

Finally it is possible to think of God as an exclusively supra-personal being. For many persons this conception is too "philosophical" to provide an adequate motive for doing anything practical about their beliefs. Hence, for them, it is of no value.

It would be a mistake, of course, to suppose that people who worship one aspect of God to the exclusion of all the rest must inevitably run into the different kinds of trouble described above. If they are not too stubborn in their ready-made beliefs, if they submit with docility to what happens to them in the process of worshipping, the God who is both immanent and transcendent, personal and more than personal, may reveal Himself to them in his fulness. Nevertheless, the fact remains that it is easier for us to reach our goal if we are not handicapped by a set of erroneous or inadequate beliefs about the right way to get there and the nature of what we are looking for.

Who is God? I can think of no better answer than, He who is. Nothing is more appropriate to the eternity which God is. If you call God good, or great, or blessed, or wise, or anything else of this sort, it is included in these words, namely, He is.

St. Bernard

The purpose of all words is to illustrate the meaning of an object. When they are heard, they should enable the hearer to understand this meaning, and this according to the four categories of substance, of activity, of quality and of relationship. For example *cow* and *horse* belong to the category of substance. *He cooks* or *he prays* belongs to the category of activity. *White* and *black* belong to the category of quality. *Having money* or *possessing cows* belongs to the category of relationship. Now there is no class of substance to which the Brahman belongs, no common genus. It cannot therefore be denoted by words which, like "being" in the ordinary sense, signify a category of things. Nor can it be denoted by quality, for it is without qualities; nor yet by activity because it is without activity —"at rest, without parts or activity," according to the Scriptures. Neither can it be denoted by relationship, for it is "without a second" and is not the object of anything but its own self. Therefore it cannot be defined by word or idea; as the Scripture says, it is the One "before whom words recoil."

Shankara

It was from the Nameless that Heaven and Earth sprang; The named is but the mother that rears the ten thousand creatures, each after its kind.
Truly, "Only he that rids himself forever of desire can see the Secret Essences."
He that has never rid himself of desire can see only the Outcomes.

Lao Tzu

One of the greatest favours bestowed on the soul transiently in this life is to enable it to see so distinctly and to feel so profoundly that it cannot comprehend God at all. These souls are herein somewhat like the saints in heaven, where they who know Him most perfectly perceive most clearly that He is infinitely incomprehensible; for those who have the less clear vision do not perceive so clearly as do these others how greatly He transcends their vision.

St. John of the Cross

When I came out of the Godhead into multiplicity, then all things proclaimed, "There is a God" (the personal Creator). Now this cannot make me blessed, for hereby I realize myself as creature. But in the breaking through I am more than all creatures; I am neither God nor creature; I am that which I was and shall remain, now and for ever more. There I receive a thrust which carries me above all angels. By this thrust I become so rich that God is not sufficient for me, in so far as He is only God in his divine works. For in thus breaking through, I perceive what God and I are in common. There I am what I was. There I neither increase or decrease. For there I am the immovable which moves all things. Here man has won again what he is eternally and ever shall be. Here God is received into the soul.

Eckhart

The Godhead gave all things up to God. The Godhead is poor, naked and empty as though it were not; it has not, wills not, wants not, works not, gets not. It is God who has the treasure and the bride in him, the Godhead is as void as though it were not.

Eckhart

We can understand something of what lies beyond our experience by considering analogous cases lying within our experience. Thus, the relations subsisting between the world and God, and between God and the Godhead seem to be analogous, in some measure at least, to those that hold between the body (with its environment) and the psyche, and between the psyche and the spirit. In the light of what we know about the second—and what we know is not, unfortunately, very much—we may be able to form some not too hopelessly inadequate notions about the first.

Mind affects its body in four ways—subconsciously, through that unbelievably subtle physiological intelligence, which Driesch hypostatized under the name of the entelechy; consciously, by deliberate acts of will; subconsciously again, by the reaction upon the physical organism of emotional states having nothing to do with the organs or processes reacted upon; and, either consciously or subconsciously, in certain "supernormal" manifestations. Outside the body matter can be influenced by the mind in two ways—first, by means of the body and, second, by a "supernormal" process, recently studied under laboratory conditions and described as "the PK effect." Similarly, the mind can establish relations with other minds either indirectly, by willing its body to undertake symbolic activities, such as speech or writing; or "supernormally," by the direct approach of mind-reading, telepathy, extra-sensory perception.

Let us now consider these relationships a little more closely. In some fields the physiological intelligence works on its own initiative, as when it directs the never-ceasing processes of breathing, say, or assimilation. In others it acts at the behest of the conscious mind, as when we will to accomplish some action, but do not and cannot will the muscular, glandular, nervous and vascular means to the desired end. The apparently simple act of mimicry well illustrates the extraordinary nature of the feats performed by the physiological intelligence. When a parrot (making use, let us remember, of the beak, tongue and throat of a bird) imitates the sounds produced by the lips, teeth, palate and vocal cords of a man articulating words, what precisely happens? Responding in some as yet entirely uncomprehended way to the conscious mind's desire to imitate some remembered or immediately perceived event, the physiological intelligence sets in motion large numbers of muscles, co-ordinating their efforts with such exquisite skill that the result is a more or less perfect copy of the original. Working on its own level, the conscious mind not merely of a parrot, but of the most highly gifted of human beings, would find itself completely baffled by a problem of comparable complexity.

As an example of the third way in which our minds affect matter, we may cite the all-too-familiar phenomenon of "nervous indigestion." In certain persons symptoms of dyspepsia make their appearance when the conscious mind is troubled by such negative emotions as fear, envy, anger or hatred. These emotions are directed towards events or persons in the outer environment; but in some way or other they adversely affect the physiological intelligence and this derangement results, among other things, in "nervous indigestion." From tuberculosis and gastric ulcer to heart disease and even dental caries, numerous physical ailments have been found to be closely correlated with certain undesirable states of the conscious mind. Conversely, every physician knows that a calm and cheerful patient is much more likely to recover than one who is agitated and depressed.

Finally we come to such occurrences as faith healing and levitation—occurrences "supernormally" strange, but nevertheless attested by masses of evidence which it is hard to discount completely. Precisely how faith cures diseases (whether at Lourdes or in the hypnotist's consulting room), or how St. Joseph of Cupertino was able to ignore the laws of gravitation, we do not know. (But let us remember that we are no less ignorant of the way in which minds and bodies are related in the most ordinary of everyday activities.) In the same way we are unable to form any idea of the *modus operandi* of what Professor Rhine has called the PK effect. Nevertheless the fact that the fall of dice can be influenced by the mental states of certain individuals seems now to have been established beyond the possibility of doubt. And if the PK effect can be demonstrated in the laboratory and measured by statistical methods, then, obviously, the intrinsic credibility of the scattered anecdotal evidence for the direct influence of mind upon matter, not merely within the body, but outside in the external world, is thereby notably increased. The same is true of extra-sensory perception. Apparent examples of it are constantly turning up in ordinary life. But science is almost impotent to cope with the particular case, the isolated instance. Promoting their methodological ineptitude to the rank of a criterion of truth, dogmatic scientists have often branded everything beyond the pale of their limited competence as unreal and even impossible. But when tests for ESP can be repeated under standardized conditions, the subject comes under the jurisdiction of the law of probabilities and achieves (in the teeth of what passionate opposition!) a measure of scientific respectability.

Such, very baldly and briefly, are the most important things we know about mind in regard to its capacity to influence matter. From this modest knowledge about ourselves, what are we entitled to conclude in regard to the divine object of our nearly total ignorance?

First, as to creation: if a human mind can directly influence matter not merely within, but even outside its body, then a divine mind, immanent in the universe or transcendent to it, may be presumed to be capable of imposing forms upon a pre-existing chaos of formless matter, or even, perhaps, of thinking substance as well as forms into existence.

Once created or divinely informed, the universe has to be sustained. The necessity for a continuous re-creation of the world becomes manifest, according to Descartes, "when we consider the nature of time, or the duration of things; for this is of such a kind that its parts are not mutually dependent and never co-existent; and, accordingly, from the fact that we are now it does not necessarily follow that we shall be a moment afterwards, unless some cause, viz. that which first produced us, shall, as it were, continually reproduce us, that is, conserve us." Here we seem to have something analogous, on the cosmic level, to that physiological intelligence which, in men and the lower animals, unsleepingly performs the task of seeing that bodies behave as they should. Indeed, the physiological intelligence may plausibly be regarded as a special aspect of the general re-creating Logos. In Chinese phraseology it is the Tao as it manifests itself on the level of living bodies.

The bodies of human beings are affected by the good or bad states of their minds. Analogously, the existence at the heart of things of a divine serenity and good will may be regarded as one of the reasons why the world's sickness, though chronic, has not proved fatal. And if, in the psychic universe, there should be other and more than human consciousnesses obsessed by thoughts of evil and egotism and rebellion, this would account, perhaps, for some of the quite extravagant and improbable wickedness of human behaviour.

The acts willed by our minds are accomplished either through the instrumentality of the physiological intelligence and the body, or, very exceptionally, and to a limited extent, by direct supernormal means of the PK variety. Analogously the physical situations willed by a divine Providence may be arranged by the perpetually creating Mind that sustains the universe—in which case Providence will appear to do its work by wholly natural means; or else, very exceptionally, the divine Mind may act directly on the universe from the outside, as it were—in which case the workings of Providence and the gifts of grace will appear to be miraculous. Similarly, the divine Mind may choose to communicate with finite minds either by manipulating the world of men and things in ways, which the particular mind to be reached at that moment will find meaningful; or else there may be direct communication by something resembling thought transference.

In Eckhart's phrase, God, the creator and perpetual re-creator of the world, "becomes and disbecomes." In other words He is, to some extent at least, in time. A temporal God might have the nature of the traditional Hebrew God of the Old Testament; or He might be a limited deity of the kind described by certain philosophical theologians of the present century; or alternatively He might be an emergent God, starting unspiritually at Alpha and becoming gradually more divine as the aeons rolled on towards some hypothetical Omega. (Why the movement should be towards more and better rather than less and worse, upwards rather than downwards or in undulations, onwards rather than round and round, one really doesn't know. There seems to be no reason why a God who is exclusively temporal—a God who merely becomes and is ungrounded in eternity—should not be as completely at the mercy of time as is the individual mind apart from the spirit. A God who becomes is a God who also disbecomes, and it is the disbecoming which may ultimately prevail, so that the last state of emergent deity may be worse than the first.)

The ground in which the multifarious and time-bound psyche is rooted is a simple, timeless awareness. By making ourselves pure in heart and poor in spirit we can discover and be identified with this awareness. In the spirit we not only have, but are, the unitive knowledge of the divine Ground.

Analogously, God in time is grounded in the eternal now of the modeless Godhead. It is in the Godhead that things, lives and minds have their being; it is through God that they

have their becoming—a becoming whose goal and purpose
is to return to the eternity of the Ground.

> Meanwhile, I beseech you by the eternal and imperishable
> truth, and by my soul, consider; grasp the unheard-of.
> God and Godhead are as distinct as heaven and earth.
> Heaven stands a thousand miles above the earth, and
> even so the Godhead is above God. God becomes and
> disbecomes. Whoever understands this preaching, I wish
> him well. But even if nobody had been here, I must still
> have preached this to the poor-box.
>
> *Eckhart*

Like St. Augustine, Eckhart was to some extent the victim of
his own literary talents. *Le style c'est l'homme.* No doubt.
But the converse is also partly true. *L'homme c'est le style.*
Because we have a gift for writing in a certain way, we find
ourselves, in some sort, becoming our way of writing. We
mould ourselves in the likeness of our particular brand of
eloquence. Eckhart was one of the inventors of German prose,
and he was tempted by his new-found mastery of forceful
expression to commit himself to extreme positions—to be
doctrinally the image of his powerful and over-emphatic sentences. A statement like the foregoing would lead one to
believe that he despised what the Vedantists call the "lower
knowledge" of Brahman, not as the Absolute Ground of all
things, but as the personal God. In reality he, like the Vedantists, accepts the lower knowledge as genuine knowledge and
regards devotion to the personal God as the best preparation
for the unitive knowledge of the Godhead. Another point to
remember is that the attributeless Godhead of Vedanta, of
Mahayana Buddhism, of Christian and Sufi mysticism is the
Ground of all the qualities possessed by the personal God and
the Incarnation. "God is not good, I am good," says Eckhart
in his violent and excessive way. What he really meant was,
"I am just humanly good; God is supereminently good; the
Godhead *is*, and his 'isness' (*istigkeit*, in Eckhart's German)
contains goodness, love, wisdom and all the rest in their
essence and principle." In consequence, the Godhead is never,
for the exponent of the Perennial Philosophy, the mere Absolute of academic metaphysics, but something more purely
perfect, more reverently to be adored than even the personal

God or his human incarnation—a Being towards whom it is possible to feel the most intense devotion and in relation to whom it is necessary (if one is to come to that unitive knowledge which is man's final end) to practise a discipline more arduous and unremitting than any imposed by ecclesiastical authority.

There is a distinction and differentiation, according to our reason, between God and the Godhead, between action and rest. The fruitful nature of the Persons ever worketh in a living differentiation. But the simple Being of God, according to the nature thereof, is an eternal Rest of God and of all created things.

Ruysbroeck

(In the Reality unitively known by the mystic), we can speak no more of Father, Son and Holy Spirit, nor of any creature, but only one Being, which is the very substance of the Divine Persons. There were we all one before our creation, for this is our super-essence. There the Godhead is in simple essence without activity.

Ruysbroeck

The holy light of faith is so pure that, compared with it, particular lights are but impurities; and even ideas of the saints, of the Blessed Virgin, and the sight of Jesus Christ in his humanity are impediments in the way of the sight of God in His purity.

J. J. Olier

Coming as it does from a devout Catholic of the Counter-Reformation, this statement may seem somewhat startling. But we must remember that Olier (who was a man of saintly life and one of the most influential religious teachers of the seventeenth century) is speaking here about a state of consciousness, to which few people ever come. To those on the ordinary levels of being he recommends other modes of knowledge. One of his penitents, for example, was advised to read, as a corrective to St. John of the Cross and other exponents of pure mystical theology, St. Gertrude's revelations of the incarnate and even physiological aspects of the deity. In Olier's opinion, as in that of most directors of souls, whether Catholic or Indian, it was mere folly to recommend the worship of God-without-form to persons who are in a condition to understand only the personal and the incarnate aspects of the divine Ground. This is a perfectly sensible attitude, and we are justified in adopting a policy in accordance with it—provided always that we clearly remember that its adoption may be attended by certain spiritual dangers and disadvantages. The nature of these dangers and disadvantages will be illustrated and discussed in another section. For the present it will suffice to quote the warning words of Philo: "He who thinks that God has any quality and is not the One, injures not God, but himself."

> Thou must love God as not-God, not-Spirit, not-person, not-image, but as He is, a sheer, pure absolute One, sundered from all two-ness, and in whom we must eternally sink from nothingness to nothingness.
>
> *Eckhart*

What Eckhart describes as the pure One, the absolute not-God in whom we must sink from nothingness to nothingness is called in Mahayana Buddhism the Clear Light of the Void. What follows is part of a formula addressed by the Tibetan priest to a person in the act of death.

> O nobly born, the time has now come for thee to seek the Path. Thy breathing is about to cease. In the past thy teacher hath set thee face to face with the Clear Light; and now thou art about to experience it in its Reality in the *Bardo* state (the "intermediate state" immediately following death, in which the soul is judged—or rather judges itself by choosing, in accord with the character formed during its life on earth, what sort of an after-life it shall have). In this *Bardo* state all things are like the cloudless sky, and the naked, immaculate Intellect is like unto a translucent void without circumference or centre. At this moment know thou thyself and abide in that state. I too, at this time, am setting thee face to face.
>
> *The Tibetan Book of the Dead*

Going back further into the past, we find in one of the earliest Upanishads the classical description of the Absolute One as a Super-Essential No-Thing.

The significance of Brahman is expressed by *neti neti* (not so, not so); for beyond this, that you say it is not so, there is nothing further. Its name, however, is "the Reality of reality." That is to say, the senses are real, and the Brahman is their Reality.

Brhadaranyaka Upanishad

In other words, there is a hierarchy of the real. The manifold world of our everyday experience is real with a relative reality that is, on its own level, unquestionable; but this relative reality has its being within and because of the absolute Reality, which, on account of the incommensurable otherness of its eternal nature, we can never hope to describe, even though it is possible for us directly to apprehend it.

The extract which follows next is of great historical significance, since it was mainly through the "Mystical Theology" and the "Divine Names" of the fifth-century author who wrote under the name of Dionysius the Areopagite that mediaeval Christendom established contact with Neoplatonism and thus, at several removes, with the metaphysical thought and discipline of India. In the ninth century Scotus Erigena translated the two books into Latin and from that time forth their influence upon the philosophical speculations and the religious life of the West was wide, deep and beneficent. It was to the authority of the Areopagite that the Christian exponents of the Perennial Philosophy appealed, whenever they were menaced (and they were always being menaced) by those whose primary interest was in ritual, legalism and ecclesiastical organization. And because Dionysius was mistakenly identified with St. Paul's first Athenian convert, his authority was regarded as all but apostolic; therefore, according to the rules of the Catholic game, the appeal to it could not lightly be dismissed, even by those to whom the books meant less than nothing. In spite of their maddening eccentricity, the men and women who followed the Dionysian path had to be tolerated. And once left free to produce the fruits of the spirit, a number of them arrived at such a conspicuous degree of sanctity that it became impossible even for the heads of the Spanish Inquisition to condemn the tree from which such fruits had sprung.

The simple, absolute and immutable mysteries of divine Truth are hidden in the super-luminous darkness of that silence which revealeth in secret. For this darkness, though of deepest obscurity, is yet radiantly clear; and, though beyond touch and sight, it more than fills our unseeing minds with splendours of transcendent beauty. . . . We long exceedingly to dwell in this translucent darkness and, through not seeing and not knowing, to see Him who is beyond both vision and knowledge—by the very fact of neither seeing Him nor knowing Him. For this is truly to see and to know and, through the abandonment of all things, to praise Him who is beyond and above all things. For this is not unlike the art of those who carve a life-like image from stone; removing from around it all that impedes clear vision of the latent form, revealing its hidden beauty solely by taking away. For it is, as I believe, more fitting to praise Him by taking away than by ascription; for we ascribe attributes to Him, when we start from universals and come down through the intermediate to the particulars. But here we take away all things from Him going up from particulars to universals, that we may know openly the unknowable, which is hidden in and under all things that may be known. And we behold that darkness beyond being, concealed under all natural light.

Dionysius the Areopagite

The world as it appears to common sense consists of an indefinite number of successive and presumably causally connected events, involving an indefinite number of separate, individual things, lives and thoughts, the whole constituting a presumably orderly cosmos. It is in order to describe, discuss and manage this common-sense universe that human languages have been developed.

Whenever, for any reason, we wish to think of the world, not as it appears to common sense, but as a continuum, we find that our traditional syntax and vocabulary are quite inadequate. Mathematicians have therefore been compelled to invent radically new symbol-systems for this express purpose. But the divine Ground of all existence is not merely a continuum, it is also out of time, and different, not merely in degree, but in kind from the worlds to which traditional language and the languages of mathematics are adequate. Hence, in all expositions of the Perennial Philosophy, the frequency of paradox, of verbal extravagance, sometimes even of seeming blasphemy. Nobody has yet invented a Spiritual Calculus, in terms of which we may talk coherently about the divine Ground and of the world conceived as its manifestation. For the present, therefore, we must be patient with the linguistic eccentricities of those who are compelled to describe one order of experience in terms of a symbol-system, whose relevance is to the facts of another and quite different order.

So far, then, as a fully adequate expression of the Perennial Philosophy is concerned, there exists a problem in semantics that is finally insoluble. The fact is one which must be steadily borne in mind by all who read its formulations. Only in this way shall we be able to understand even remotely what is being talked about. Consider, for example, those negative definitions of the transcendent and immanent Ground of being. In statements such as Eckhart's, God is equated with nothing. And in a certain sense the equation is exact; for God is certainly no thing. In the phrase used by Scotus Erigena God is not a what; He is a That. In other words, the Ground can be denoted as being *there*, but not defined as having qualities. This means that discursive knowledge *about* the Ground is not merely, like all inferential knowledge, a thing at one remove, or even at several removes, from the reality of immediate acquaintance; it is and, because of the very nature of our language and our standard patterns of thought, it must be, paradoxical knowledge. Direct knowledge *of* the Ground cannot be had except by union, and union can be achieved only by the annihilation of the self-regarding ego, which is the barrier separating the "thou" from the "That."

CHAPTER III

Personality, Sanctity, Divine Incarnation

IN ENGLISH, words of Latin origin tend to carry overtones of intellectual, moral and aesthetic "classiness"—overtones which are not carried, as a rule, by their Anglo-Saxon equivalents. "Maternal," for instance, means the same as "motherly," "intoxicated" as "drunk"—but with what subtly important shades of difference! And when Shakespeare needed a name for a comic character, it was Sir Toby Belch that he chose, not Cavalier Tobias Eructation.

The word "personality" is derived from the Latin, and its upper partials are in the highest degree respectable. For some odd philological reason, the Saxon equivalent of "personality" is hardly ever used. Which is a pity. For if it were used—used as currently as "belch" is used for "eructation"—would people make such a reverential fuss about the thing connoted as certain English-speaking philosophers, moralists and theologians have recently done? "Personality," we are constantly being assured, is the highest form of reality, with which we are acquainted. But surely people would think twice about making or accepting this affirmation if, instead of "personality," the word employed had been its Teutonic synonym, "selfness." For "selfness," though it means precisely the same, carries none of the high-class overtones that go with "personality." On the contrary, its primary meaning comes to us embedded, as it were, in discords, like the note of a cracked bell. For, as all exponents of the Perennial Philosophy have constantly insisted, man's obsessive consciousness of, and insistence on being, a separate self is the final and most formidable obstacle to the unitive knowledge of God. To be a self is, for them, the original sin, and to die to self, in feeling, will and intellect, is the final and all-inclusive virtue. It is the memory of these utterances that calls up the unfavourable overtones with which the word "selfness" is associated. The all too favourable overtones of "personality" are evoked in part by its intrinsically solemn Latinity, but also by reminiscences of what has been said about the "persons" of the Trinity. But the persons of the Trinity have nothing in common with the flesh-and-blood persons of our everyday acquaintance—nothing, that is to say, except that indwelling Spirit, with which we ought and are intended to identify ourselves, but which most of us prefer to ignore in favour of our separate selfness. That this God-eclipsing and anti-spiritual selfness, should have been given the same name as is applied to the God who is a Spirit, is, to say the least of it, unfortunate. Like all such mistakes it is probably, in some obscure and subconscious way, voluntary and purposeful. We love our selfness; we want to be justified in our love; therefore we christen it with the same name as is applied by theologians to Father, Son and Holy Spirit.

But now thou askest me how thou mayest destroy this naked knowing and feeling of thine own being. For peradventure thou thinkest that if it were destroyed, all other hindrances were destroyed; and if thou thinkest thus, thou thinkest right truly. But to this I answer thee and I say, that without a full special grace full freely given by God, and also a full according ableness on thy part to receive this grace, this naked knowing and feeling of thy being may in nowise be destroyed. And this ableness is nought else but a strong and a deep ghostly sorrow. . . . All men have matter of sorrow; but most specially he feeleth matter of sorrow that knoweth and feeleth that he *is*. All other sorrows in comparison to this be but as it were game to earnest. For he may make sorrow earnestly that knoweth and feeleth not only what he is, but that he is. And whoso felt never this sorrow, let him make sorrow; for he hath never yet felt perfect sorrow. This sorrow, when it is had, cleanseth the soul, not only of sin, but also of pain that it hath deserved for sin; and also it maketh a soul able to receive that joy, the which reaveth from a man all knowing and feeling of his being.

This sorrow, if it be truly conceived, is full of holy desire; and else a man might never in this life abide it or bear it. For were it not that a soul were somewhat fed with a manner of comfort by his right working, he should not be able to bear that pain that he hath by the knowing and feeling of his being. For as oft as he would have a true knowing and a feeling of his God in purity of spirit (as it may be here), and then feeleth that he may not—for he findeth evermore his knowing and his feeling as it were occupied and filled with a foul stinking lump of himself, the which must always be hated and despised and forsaken, if he shall be God's perfect disciple, taught by Himself in the mount of perfction—so oft he goeth nigh mad for sorrow. . . .

This sorrow and this desire must every soul have and feel in itself (either in this manner or in another), as God vouchsafeth to teach his ghostly disciples according to his good will and their according ableness in body and in soul, in degree and disposition, ere the time be that they may perfectly be oned unto God in perfect charity—such as may be had here, if God vouchsafeth.

The Cloud of Unknowing

What is the nature of this "stinking lump" of selfness or personality, which has to be so passionately repented of and so completely died to, before there can be any "true knowing of God in purity of spirit"? The most meagre and non-committal hypothesis is that of Hume. "Mankind," he says, "are nothing but a bundle or collection of different perceptions, which succeed each other with an inconceivable rapidity and are in a perpetual flux and movement." An almost identical answer is given by the Buddhists, whose doctrine of *anatta* is the denial of any permanent soul, existing behind the flux of experience and the various psycho-physical *skandhas* (closely corresponding to Hume's "bundles"), which constitute the more enduring elements of personality. Hume and the Buddhists give a sufficiently realistic description of selfness in action; but they fail to explain how or why the bundles ever became bundles. Did their constituent atoms of experience come together of their own accord? And, if so, why, or by what means, and within what kind of a non-spatial universe? To give a plausible answer to these questions in terms of *anatta* is so difficult that we are forced to abandon the doctrine in favour of the notion that, behind the flux and within the bundles, there exists some kind of permanent soul, by which experience is organized and which in turn makes use of that organized experience to become a particular and unique personality. This is the view of the orthodox Hinduism, from which Buddhist thought parted company, and of almost all European thought from before the time of Aristotle to the present day. But whereas most contemporary thinkers make an attempt to describe human nature in terms of a dichotomy of interacting psyche and physique, or an inseparable wholeness of these two elements within particular embodied selves, all the exponents of the Perennial Philosophy make, in one form or another, the affirmation that man is a kind of trinity composed of body, psyche and spirit. Selfness or personality is a product of the first two elements. The third element (that *quidquid increatum et increabile*, as Eckhart called it) is akin to, or even identical with, the divine Spirit that is the Ground of all being. Man's final end, the purpose of his existence, is to love, know and be united with the immanent and transcendent Godhead. And this identification of self with spiritual not-self can be achieved only by "dying to" selfness and living to spirit.

What could begin to deny self, if there were not something in man different from self?

William Law

What is man? An angel, an animal, a void, a world, a nothing surrounded by God, indigent of God, capable of God, filled with God, if it so desires.

Bérulle

The separate creaturely life, as opposed to life in union with God, is only a life of various appetites, hungers and wants, and cannot possibly be anything else. God Himself cannot make a creature to be in itself, or in its own nature, anything else but a state of emptiness. The highest life that is natural and creaturely can go no higher than this; it can only be a bare capacity for goodness and cannot possibly be a good and happy life but by the life of God dwelling in and in union with it. And this is the twofold life that, of all necessity, must be united in every good and perfect and happy creature.

William Law

The Scriptures say of human beings that there is an outward man and along with him an inner man.

To the outward man belong those things that depend on the soul, but are connected with the flesh and are blended with it, and the co-operative functions of the several members, such as the eye, the ear, the tongue, the hand and so on.

The Scripture speaks of all this as the old man, the earthy man, the outward person, the enemy, the servant.

Within us all is the other person, the inner man, whom the Scripture calls the new man, the heavenly man, the young person, the friend, the aristocrat.

Eckhart

The seed of God is in us. Given an intelligent and hard-working farmer, it will thrive and grow up to God, whose seed it is; and accordingly its fruits will be God-nature. Pear seeds grow into pear trees, nut seeds into nut trees, and God seed into God.

Eckhart

The will is free and we are at liberty to identify our being either exclusively with our selfness and its interests, regarded as independent of indwelling Spirit and transcendent Godhead (in which case we shall be passively damned or actively fiendish), or exclusively with the divine within us and without (in which case we shall be saints), or finally with self at one moment or in one context and with spiritual not-self at other moments and in other contexts (in which case we shall be average citizens, too theocentric to be wholly lost, and too egocentric to achieve enlightenment and a total deliverance). Since human craving can never be satisfied except by the unitive knowledge of God and since the mind-body is capable of an enormous variety of experiences, we are free to identify ourselves with an almost infinite number of possible objects— with the pleasures of gluttony, for example, or intemperance, or sensuality; with money, power or fame; with our family, regarded as a possession or actually an extension and projection of our own selfness; with our goods and chattels, our hobbies, our collections; with our artistic or scientific talents; with some favourite branch of knowledge, some fascinating "special subject"; with our professions, our political parties, our churches; with our pains and illnesses; with our memories of success or misfortune, our hopes, fears and schemes for the future; and finally with the eternal Reality within which and by which all the rest has its being. And we are free, of course, to identify ourselves with more than one of these things simultaneously or in succession. Hence the quite astonishingly improbable combination of traits making up a complex personality. Thus a man can be at once the craftiest of politicians and the dupe of his own verbiage, can have a passion for brandy and money, and an equal passion for the poetry of George Meredith and under-age girls and his mother, for horse-racing and detective stories and the good of his country—the whole accompanied by a sneaking fear of hell-fire, a hatred of Spinoza and an unblemished record for Sunday church-going. A person born with one kind of psycho-physical constitution will be tempted to identify himself with one set of interests and passions, while a person with another kind of temperament will be tempted to make very different identifications. But these temptations (though extremely powerful, if the constitutional bias is strongly marked) do not have to be succumbed to; people can and do resist them, can and do refuse to identify themselves with what it would be all too easy and natural for them to be; can and do become better and quite other than their own selves. In this context the following brief article on "How Men Behave in Crisis" (published in a recent issue of *Harper's Magazine*) is highly significant. "A young psychiatrist, who went as a medical observer on five combat missions of the Eighth Air Force in England says that in times of great stress and danger men are likely to react quite uniformly, even though under normal circumstances, they differ widely in personality. He went on one mission, during which the B-17 plane and crew were so severely damaged that survival seemed impossible. He had already studied the "on the ground" personalities of the crew and had found that they represented a great diversity of human types. Of their behaviour in crisis he reported:

" 'Their reactions were remarkably alike. During the violent combat and in the acute emergencies that arose during it, they were all quietly precise on the interphone and decisive in action. The tail gunner, right waist gunner and navigator were severely wounded early in the fight, but all three kept at their duties efficiently and without cessation. The burden of emergency work fell on the pilot, engineer and ball turret gunner, and all functioned with rapidity, skilful effectiveness and no lost motion. The burden of the decisions, during, but particularly after the combat, rested essentially on the pilot and, in secondary details, on the co-pilot and bombardier. The decisions, arrived at with care and speed, were unquestioned once they were made, and proved excellent. In the period when disaster was momentarily expected, the alternative plans of action were made clearly and with no thought other than the safety of the entire crew. All at this point were quiet, unobtrusively cheerful and ready for anything. There was at no time paralysis, panic, unclear thinking, faulty or confused judgment, or self-seeking in any one of them.

" 'One could not possibly have inferred from their behaviour that this one was a man of unstable moods and that that one was a shy, quiet, introspective man. They all became outwardly calm, precise in thought and rapid in action.

" 'Such action is typical of a crew who know intimately what fear is, so that they can use, without being distracted by, its physiological concomitants; who are well trained, so that they can direct their action with clarity; and who have all the more than personal trust inherent in a unified team.' "

We see then that, when the crisis came, each of these young men forgot the particular personality, which he had built up out of the elements provided by his heredity and the environment in which he had grown up; that one resisted the normally irresistible temptation to identify himself with his mood of the moment, another the temptation to identify himself with his private day-dreams, and so on with the rest; and that all of them behaved in the same strikingly similar and wholly admirable way. It was as though the crisis and the preliminary training for crisis had lifted them out of their divergent personalities and raised them to the same higher level.

Sometimes crisis alone, without any preparatory training, is sufficient to make a man forget to be his customary self and become, for the time being, something quite different. Thus the most unlikely people will, under the influence of disaster, temporarily turn into heroes, martyrs, selfless labourers for the good of their fellows. Very often, too, the proximity of death produces similar results. For example, Samuel Johnson behaved in one way during almost the whole of his life and in quite another way during his last illness. The fascinatingly complex personality, in which six generations of Boswellians have taken so much delight—the learned boor and glutton, the kind-hearted bully, the superstitious intellectual, the convinced Christian who was a fetishist, the courageous man who was terrified of death—became, while he was actually dying, simple, single, serene and God-centred.

Paradoxical as it may seem, it is, for very many persons, much easier to behave selflessly in time of crisis than it is when life is taking its normal course in undisturbed tranquillity. When the going is easy, there is nothing to make us forget our precious selfness, nothing (except our own will to mortification and the knowledge of God) to distract our minds from the distractions with which we have chosen to be identified; we are at perfect liberty to wallow in our personality to our heart's content. And how we wallow! It is for this reason that all the masters of the spiritual life insist so strongly upon the importance of little things.

> God requires a faithful fulfilment of the merest trifle given us to do, rather than the most ardent aspiration to things to which we are not called.
>
> St. François de Sales

There is no one in the world who cannot arrive without difficulty at the most eminent perfection by fulfilling with love obscure and common duties.

J. P. de Caussade

Some people measure the worth of good actions only by their natural qualities or their difficulty, giving the preference to what is conspicuous or brilliant. Such men forget that Christian virtues, which are God's inspirations, should be viewed from the side of grace, not that of nature. The dignity and difficulty of a good action certainly affects what is technically called its accidental worth, but all its essential worth comes from love alone.

Jean Pierre Camus
(quoting St. François de Sales)

The saint is one who knows that every moment of our human life is a moment of crisis; for at every moment we are called upon to make an all-important decision—to choose between the way that leads to death and spiritual darkness and the way that leads towards light and life; between interests exclusively temporal and the eternal order; between our personal will, or the will of some projection of our personality, and the will of God. In order to fit himself to deal with the emergencies of his way of life, the saint undertakes appropriate training of mind and body, just as the soldier does. But whereas the objectives of military training are limited and very simple, namely, to make men courageous, cool-headed and co-operatively efficient in the business of killing other men, with whom, personally, they have no quarrel, the objectives of spiritual training are much less narrowly specialized. Here the aim is primarily to bring human beings to a state in which, because there are no longer any God-eclipsing obstacles between themselves and Reality, they are able to be aware continuously of the divine Ground of their own and all other beings; secondarily, as a means to this end, to meet all, even the most trivial circumstances of daily living without malice, greed, self-assertion or voluntary ignorance, but consistently with love and understanding. Because its objectives are not limited, because, for the lover of God, every moment is a moment of crisis, spiritual training is incomparably more difficult and searching than military training. There are many good soldiers, few saints.

We have seen that, in critical emergencies, soldiers specifically trained to cope with that kind of thing tend to forget the inborn and acquired idiosyncrasies with which they normally identify their being and, transcending selfness, to behave in the same, one-pointed, better-than-personal way. What is true of soldiers is also true of saints, but with this important difference—that the aim of spiritual training is to make people become selfless in *every* circumstance of life, while the aim of military training is to make them selfless only in certain very special circumstances and in relation to only certain classes of human beings. This could not be otherwise; for all that we are and will and do depends, in the last analysis, upon what we believe the Nature of Things to be. The philosophy that rationalizes power politics and justifies war and military training is always (whatever the official religion of the politicians and war makers) some wildly unrealistic doctrine of national, racial or ideological idolatry, having, as its inevitable corollaries, the notions of *Herrenvolk* and "the lesser breeds without the Law."

The biographies of the saints testify unequivocally to the fact that spiritual training leads to a transcendence of personality, not merely in the special circumstances of battle, but in all circumstances and in relation to all creatures, so that the saint "loves his enemies" or, if he is a Buddhist, does not even recognize the existence of enemies, but treats all sentient beings, sub-human as well as human, with the same compassion and disinterested good will. Those who win through to the unitive knowledge of God set out upon their course from the most diverse starting points. One is a man, another a woman; one a born active, another a born contemplative. No two of them inherit the same temperament and physical constitution, and their lives are passed in material, moral and intellectual environments that are profoundly dissimilar. Nevertheless, insofar as they are saints, insofar as they possess the unitive knowledge that makes them "perfect as their Father which is in heaven is perfect," they are all astonishingly alike. Their actions are uniformly selfless and they are constantly recollected, so that at every moment they know who they are and what is their true relation to the universe and its spiritual Ground. Of even plain average people it may be said that their name is Legion—much more so of exceptionally complex personalities, who identify themselves with a wide diversity of moods, cravings and opinions. Saints, on the contrary, are neither double-minded nor half-hearted, but single and, however great their intellectual gifts, profoundly simple. The multiplicity of Legion has given place to one-pointedness—not to any of those evil one-pointednesses of ambition or covetousness, or lust for power and fame, not even to any of the nobler, but still all too human one-pointednesses of art, scholarship and science, regarded as ends in themselves, but to the supreme, more than human one-pointedness that is the very being of those souls who consciously and consistently pursue man's final end, the knowledge of eternal Reality. In one of the Pali scriptures there is a significant anecdote about the Brahman Drona who, "seeing the Blessed One sitting at the foot of a tree, asked him, 'Are you a *deva?*' And the Exalted One answered, 'I am not.' 'Are you a *gandharva?*' 'I am not,' 'Are you a *yaksha?*' 'I am not.' 'Are you a man?' 'I am not a man.' On the Brahman asking what he might be, the Blessed One replied, 'Those evil influences, those cravings, whose non-destruction would have individualized me as a *deva*, a *gandharva*, a *yaksha* (three types of supernatural being), or a man, I have completely annihilated. Know therefore that I am Buddha.' "

Here we may remark in passing that it is only the one-pointed, who are truly capable of worshipping one God. Monotheism as a theory can be entertained even by a person whose name is Legion. But when it comes to passing from theory to practice, from discursive knowledge about to immediate acquaintance with the one God, there cannot be monotheism except where there is singleness of heart. Knowledge is in the knower according to the mode of the knower. Where the knower is poly-psychic the universe he knows by immediate experience is polytheistic. The Buddha declined to make any statement in regard to the ultimate divine Reality. All he would talk about was Nirvana, which is the name of the experience that comes to the totally selfless and one-pointed. To this same experience others have given the name of union with Brahman, with Al Haqq, with the immanent and transcendent Godhead. Maintaining, in this matter, the attitude of a strict operationalist, the Buddha would speak only of the spiritual experience, not of the metaphysical entity presumed by the theologians of other religions, as also of later Buddhism, to be the object and (since in contemplation the knower, the known and the knowledge are all one) at the same time the subject and substance of that experience.

> When a man lacks discrimination, his will wanders in all directions, after innumerable aims. Those who lack discrimination may quote the letter of the scripture; but they are really denying its inner truth. They are full of worldly desires and hungry for the rewards of heaven. They use beautiful figures of speech; they teach elaborate rituals, which are supposed to obtain pleasure and power for those who practice them. But, actually, they understand nothing except the law of Karma that chains men to rebirth.
>
> Those whose discrimination is stolen away by such talk grow deeply attached to pleasure and power. And so they are unable to develop that one-pointed concentration of the will, which leads a man to absorption in God.
>
> *Bhagavad Gita*

Among the cultivated and mentally active, hagiography is now a very unpopular form of literature. The fact is not at all surprising. The cultivated and the mentally active have an insatiable appetite for novelty, diversity and distraction. But the saints, however commanding their talents and whatever the nature of their professional activities, are all incessantly preoccupied with only one subject—spiritual Reality and the means by which they and their fellows can come to the unitive knowledge of that Reality. And as for their actions—these are as monotonously uniform as their thoughts; for in all circumstances they behave selflessly, patiently and with indefatigable charity. No wonder, then, if the biographies of such men and women remain unread. For one well educated person who knows anything about William Law there are two or three hundred who have read Boswell's life of his younger contemporary. Why? Because, until he actually lay dying, Johnson indulged himself in the most fascinating of multiple personalities; whereas Law, for all the superiority of his talents was almost absurdly simple and single-minded. Legion prefers to read about Legion. It is for this reason that, in the whole repertory of epic, drama and the novel there are hardly any representations of true theocentric saints.

O Friend, hope for Him whilst you live, know whilst you
live, understand whilst you live; for in life deliverance
abides.

If your bonds be not broken whilst living, what hope of
deliverance in death?

It is but an empty dream that the soul shall have union
with Him because it has passed from the body;

If He is found now, He is found then;

If not, we do but go to dwell in the City of Death.

Kabir

This figure in the form of a sun (the description is of the
engraved frontispiece to the first edition of *The Rule of
Perfection*) represents the will of God. The faces placed
here in the sun represent souls living in the divine will.
These faces are arranged in three concentric circles, show-
ing the three degrees of this divine will. The first, or
outermost degree signifies the souls of the active life; the
second, those of the life of contemplation; the third, those
of the life of supereminence. Outside the first circle are
many tools, such as pincers and hammers, denoting the
active life. But round the second circle we have placed
nothing at all, in order to signify that in this kind of contemplative life, without any other speculations or practices, one must follow the leading of the will of God.
The tools are on the ground and in shadow, inasmuch as
outward works are in themselves full of darkness. These
tools, however, are touched by a ray of the sun, to show
that works may be enlightened and illuminated by the
will of God.

The light of the divine will shines but little on the
faces of the first circle; much more on those of the second;
while those of the third, or innermost circle are resplend-
ent. The features of the first show up most clearly; the
second, less; the third, hardly at all. This signifies that the
souls of the first degree are much in themselves; those of
the second degree are less in themselves and more in God;
those in the third degree are almost nothing in themselves
and all in God, absorbed in his essential will. All these
faces have their eyes fixed on the will of God.

Benet of Canfield

It is in virtue of his absorption in God and just because he has not identified his being with the inborn and acquired elements of his private personality, that the saint is able to exercise his entirely non-coercive and therefore entirely beneficent influence on individuals and even on whole societies. Or, to be more accurate, it is because he has purged himself of selfness that divine Reality is able to use him as a channel of grace and power. "I live, yet not I, but Christ—the eternal Logos—liveth in me." True of the saint, this must *a fortiori* be true of the Avatar, or incarnation of God. If, insofar as he was a saint, St. Paul was "not I," then certainly Christ was "not I"; and to talk, as so many liberal churchmen now do, of worshipping "the personality of Jesus," is an absurdity. For, obviously, had Jesus remained content merely to have a personality, like the rest of us, he would never have exercised the kind of influence which in fact he did exercise, and it would never have occurred to anyone to regard him as a divine incarnation and to identify him with the Logos. That he came to be thought of as the Christ was due to the fact that he had passed beyond selfness and had become the bodily and mental conduit through which a more than personal, supernatural life flowed down into the world.

Souls which have come to the unitive knowledge of God, are, in Benet of Canfield's phrase, "almost nothing in themselves and all in God." This vanishing residue of selfness persists because, in some slight measure, they still identify their being with some innate psycho-physical idiosyncrasy, some acquired habit of thought or feeling, some convention or unanalyzed prejudice current in the social environment. Jesus was almost wholly absorbed in the esential will of God; but in spite of this, he may have retained some elements of selfness. To what extent there was any "I" associated with the more-than-personal, divine "Not-I," it is very difficult, on the basis of the existing evidence, to judge. For example, did Jesus interpret his experience of divine Reality and his own spontaneous inferences from that experience in terms of those fascinating apocalyptic notions current in contemporary Jewish circles? Some eminent scholars have argued that the doctrine of the world's imminent dissolution was the central core of his teaching. Others, equally learned, have held that it was attributed to him by the authors of the Synoptic Gospels, and that Jesus himself did not identify his experience and his theological thinking with locally popular opinions. Which party is right? Goodness knows. On this subject, as on so many others, the existing evidence does not permit of a certain and unambiguous answer.

The moral of all this is plain. The quantity and quality of the surviving biographical documents are such that we have no means of knowing what the residual personality of Jesus was really like. But if the Gospels tell us very little about the "I" which was Jesus, they make up for this deficiency by telling us inferentially, in the parables and discourses, a good deal about the spiritual "not-I," whose manifest presence in the mortal man was the reason why his disciples called him the Christ and identified him with the eternal Logos.

The biography of a saint or avatar is valuable only insofar as it throws light upon the means by which, in the circumstances of a particular human life, the "I" was purged away so as to make room for the divine "not-I." The authors of the Synoptic Gospels did not choose to write such a biography, and no amount of textual criticism or ingenious surmise can call it into existence. In the course of the last hundred years an enormous sum of energy has been expended on the attempt to make documents yield more evidence than in fact they contain. However regrettable may be the Synoptists' lack of interest in biography, and whatever objections may be raised against the theologies of Paul and John, there can still be no doubt that their instinct was essentially sound. Each in his own way wrote about the eternal "not-I" of Christ rather than the historical "I"; each in his own way stressed that element in the life of Jesus, in which, because it is more-than-personal, all persons can participate. (The nature of selfness is such that one person cannot be a part of another person. A self can contain or be contained by something that is either less or more than a self, it can never contain or be contained by a self.)

The doctrine that God can be incarnated in human form is found in most of the principal historic expositions of the Perennial Philosophy—in Hinduism, in Mahayana Buddhism, in Christianity and in the Mohammedanism of the Sufis, by whom the Prophet was equated with the eternal Logos.

> When goodness grows weak,
> When evil increases,
> I make myself a body.

In every age I come back
To deliver the holy,
To destroy the sin of the sinner,
To establish righteousness.

He who knows the nature
Of my task and my holy birth
Is not reborn
When he leaves this body;
He comes to Me.

Flying from fear,
From lust and anger,
He hides in Me,
His refuge and safety.
Burnt clean in the blaze of my being,
In Me many find home.

Bhagavad Gita

Then the Blessed One spoke and said: "Know, Vasetha,
that from time to time a Tathagata is born into the world,
a fully Enlightened One, blessed and worthy, abounding
in wisdom and goodness, happy with knowledge of the
worlds, unsurpassed as a guide to erring mortals, a teacher
of gods and men, a Blessed Buddha. He thoroughly understands this universe, as though he saw it face to face. . . .
The Truth does he proclaim both in its letter and in its
spirit, lovely in its origin, lovely in its progress, lovely
in its consummation. A higher life doth he make known
in all its purity and in all its perfectness.

Tevigga Sutta

Krishna is an incarnation of Brahman, Gautama Buddha of
what the Mahayanists called the Dharmakaya, Suchness, Mind,
the spiritual Ground of all being. The Christian doctrine of
the incarnation of the Godhead in human form differs from
that of India and the Far East inasmuch as it affirms that
there has been and can be only one Avatar.

What we do depends in large measure upon what we think,
and if what we do is evil, there is good empirical reason for
supposing that our thought patterns are inadequate to material. mental or spiritual reality. Because Christians believed

that there had been only one Avatar, Christian history has been disgraced by more and bloodier crusades, interdenominational wars, persecutions and proselytizing imperialism than has the history of Hinduism and Buddhism. Absurd and idolatrous doctrines, affirming the quasi-divine nature of sovereign states and their rulers, have led oriental, no less than Western, peoples into innumerable political wars; but because they have not believed in an exclusive revelation at one sole instant of time, or in the quasi-divinity of an ecclesiastical organization, oriental peoples have kept remarkably clear of the mass murder for religion's sake, which has been so dreadfully frequent in Christendom. And while, in this important respect, the level of public morality has been lower in the West than in the East, the levels of exceptional sanctity and of ordinary individual morality have not, so far as one can judge from the available evidence, been any higher. If the tree is indeed known by its fruits, Christianity's departure from the norm of the Perennial Philosophy would seem to be philosophically unjustifiable.

The Logos passes out of eternity into time for no other purpose than to assist the beings, whose bodily form he takes, to pass out of time into eternity. If the Avatar's appearance upon the stage of history is enormously important, this is due to the fact that by his teaching he points out, and by his being a channel of grace and divine power he actually is, the means by which human beings may transcend the limitations of history. The author of the Fourth Gospel affirms that the Word became flesh; but in another passage he adds that the flesh profiteth nothing—nothing, that is to say, in itself, but a great deal, of course, as a means to the union with immanent and transcendent Spirit. In this context it is very interesting to consider the development of Buddhism. "Under the forms of religious or mystical imagery," writes R. E. Johnston in his *Buddhist China*, "the Mahayana expresses the universal, whereas Hinayana cannot set itself free from the domination of historical fact." In the words of an eminent orientalist, Ananda K. Coomaraswamy, "The Mahayanist believer is warned—precisely as the worshipper of Krishna is warned in the Vaishnavite scriptures that the Krishna Lila is not a history, but a process for ever unfolded in the heart of man—that matters of historical fact are without religious significance" (except, we should add, insofar as they point to or themselves constitute the means—whether remote or proximate, whether political, ethical or spiritual—by which men may come to deliverance from selfness and the temporal order.)

In the West, the mystics went some way towards liberating Christianity from its unfortunate servitude to historic fact. (or, to be more accurate, to those various mixtures of contemporary record with subsequent inference and phantasy, which have, at different epochs, been accepted as historic fact). From the writings of Eckhart, Tauler and Ruysbroeck, of Boehme, William Law and the Quakers, it would be possible to extract a spiritualized and universalized Christianity, whose narratives should refer, not to history as it was, or as someone afterwards thought it ought to be, but to "processes forever unfolded in the heart of man." But unfortunately the influence of the mystics was never powerful enough to bring about a radical Mahayanist revolution in the West. In spite of them, Christianity has remained a religion in which the pure Perennial Philosophy has been overlaid, now more, now less, by an idolatrous preoccupation with events and things in time—events and things regarded not merely as useful means, but as ends, intrinsically sacred and indeed divine. Moreover such improvements on history as were made in the course of centuries were, most imprudently, treated as though they themselves were a part of history—a procedure which put a powerful weapon into the hands of Protestant and, later, of Rationalist controversialists. How much wiser it would have been to admit the perfectly avowable fact that, when the sternness of Christ the Judge had been unduly emphasized, men and women felt the need of personifying the divine compassion in a new form, with the result that the figure of the Virgin, mediatrix to the mediator, came into increased prominence. And when, in course of time, the Queen of Heaven was felt to be too awe-inspiring, compassion was re-personified in the homely figure of St. Joseph, who thus became mediator to the mediatrix to the mediator. In exactly the same way Buddhist worshippers felt that the historic Sakyamuni, with his insistence on recollectedness, discrimination and a total dying to self as the principal means of liberation, was too stern and too intellectual. The result was that the love and compassion which Sakyamuni had also inculcated came to be personified in Buddhas such as Amida and Maitreya—

divine characters completely removed from history, inasmuch as their temporal career was situated somewhere in the distant past or distant future. Here it may be remarked that the vast numbers of Buddhas and Bodhisattvas, of whom the Mahayanist theologians speak, are commensurate with the vastness of their cosmology. Time, for them, is beginningless, and the innumerable universes, every one of them supporting sentient beings of every possible variety, are born, evolve, decay and die, only to repeat the same cycle—again and again, until the final inconceivably remote consummation, when every sentient being in all the worlds shall have won to deliverance out of time into eternal Suchness or Buddhahood This cosmological background to Buddhism has affinities with the world picture of modern astronomy—especially with that version of it offered in the recently published theory of Dr. Weiszäcker regarding the formation of planets. If the Weiszäcker hypothesis is correct, the production of a planetary system would be a normal episode in the life of every star. There are forty thousand million stars in our own galactic system alone, and beyond our galaxy other galaxies, indefinitely. If, as we have no choice but to believe, spiritual laws governing consciousness are uniform throughout the whole planet-bearing and presumably life-supporting universe, then certainly there is plenty of room, and at the same time, no doubt, the most agonizing and desperate need, for those innumerable redemptive incarnations of Suchness, upon whose shining multitudes the Mahayanists love to dwell.

> For my part, I think the chief reason which prompted the invisible God to become visible in the flesh and to hold converse with men was to lead carnal men, who are only able to love carnally, to the healthful love of his flesh, and afterwards, little by little, to spiritual love.
>
> St. Bernard

St. Bernard's doctrine of "the carnal love of Christ" has been admirably summed up by Professor Étienne Gilson in his book, *The Mystical Theology of St Bernard.* "Knowledge of self already expanded into *social* carnal love of the neighbour, so like oneself in misery, is now a second time expanded into a carnal love of Christ, the model of compassion, since for our salvation He has become the Man of Sorrows. Here then is the place occupied in Cistercian mysticism by the meditation on the visible Humanity of Christ. It is but a beginning, but an absolutely necessary beginning. . . . Charity, of course, is essentially spiritual, and a love of this kind can be no more than its first moment. It is too much bound up with the senses, unless we know how to make use of it with prudence, and to lean on it only as something to be surpassed. In expressing himself thus, Bernard merely codified the teachings of his own experience; for we have it from him that he was much given to the practice of this sensitive love at the outset of his 'conversion'; later on he was to consider it an advance to have passed beyond it; not, that is to say, to have forgotten it, but to have added another, which outweighs it as the rational and spiritual outweigh the carnal. Nevertheless, this beginning is already a summit.

"This sensitive affection for Christ was always presented by St. Bernard as love of a relatively inferior order. It is so precisely on account of its sensitive character, for charity is of a purely spiritual essence. In right the soul should be able to enter directly into union, in virtue of its spiritual powers, with a God Who is pure spirit. The Incarnation, moreover, should be regarded as one of the consequences of man's transgression, so that love for the Person of Christ is, as a matter of fact, bound up with the history of a fall which need not, and should not, have happened. St. Bernard furthermore, and in several places, notes·that this affection cannot stand safely alone, but needs to be supported by what he calls 'science.' He had examples before him of the deviations into which even the most ardent devotion can fall, when it is not allied with, and ruled by, a sane theology."

Can the many fantastic and mutually incompatible theories of expiation and atonement, which have been grafted onto the Christian doctrine of divine incarnation, be regarded as indispensable elements in a "sane theology"? I find it difficult to imagine how anyone who has looked into a history of these notions, as expounded, for example, by the author of the Epistle to the Hebrews, by Athanasius and Augustine, by Anselm and Luther, by Calvin and Grotius, can plausibly answer this question in the affirmative. In the present context, it will be enough to call attention to one of the bitterest of all the bitter ironies of history. For the Christ of the Gospels, lawyers seemed further from the Kingdom of Heaven, more hopelessly impervious to Reality, than almost any other class of human beings except the rich. But Christian theology, especially that of the Western churches, was the product of minds imbued with Jewish and Roman legalism. In all too many instances the immediate insights of the Avatar and the theocentric saint were rationalized into a system, not by philosophers, but by speculative barristers and metaphysical jurists. Why should what Abbot John Chapman calls "the problem of *reconciling* (not merely uniting) Mysticism and Christianity" be so extremely difficult? Simply because so much Roman and Protestant thinking was done by those very lawyers whom Christ regarded as being peculiarly incapable of understanding the true Nature of Things. "The Abbot (Chapman is apparently referring to Abbot Marmion) says St John of the Cross is like a sponge full of Christianity. You can squeeze it all out, and the full mystical theory (in other words, the pure Perennial Philosophy) remains. Consequently for fifteen years or so I hated St John of the Cross and called him a Buddhist. I loved St Teresa and read her over and over again. She is first a Christian, only secondarily a mystic. Then I found I had wasted fifteen years, so far as prayer was concerned."

> Now see the meaning of these two sayings of Christ's. The one, "No man cometh unto the Father but by me," that is through my life. The other saying, "No man cometh unto me except the Father draw him"; that is, he does not take my life upon him and follow after me, except he is moved and drawn of my Father, that is, of the Simple and Perfect Good, of which St. Paul saith, 'When that which is perfect is come, that which is in part shall be done away."
>
> *Theologia Germanica*

In other words there must be imitation of Christ before there can be identification with the Father; and there must be essential identity or likeness between the human spirit and the God who is Spirit in order that the idea of imitating the earthly behaviour of the incarnate Godhead should ever cross anybody's mind. Christian theologians speak of the possibility of "deification," but deny that there is identity of substance between spiritual Reality and the human spirit. In Vedanta and Mahayana Buddhism, as also among the Sufis, spirit and Spirit are held to be the same substance; Atman is Brahman; That art thou.

> When not enlightened, Buddhas are no other than or-
> dinary beings; when there is enlightenment, ordinary
> beings at once turn into Buddhas.
>
> *Hui.Neng*

Every human being can thus become an Avatar by adoption, but not by his unaided efforts. He must be shown the way, and he must be aided by divine grace. That men and women may be thus instructed and helped, the Godhead assumes the form of an ordinary human being, who has to earn deliverance and enlightenment in the way that is prescribed by the divine Nature of Things—namely, by charity, by a total dying to self and a total, one-pointed awareness. Thus enlightened, the Avatar can reveal the way of enlightenment to others and help them actually to become what they already potentially are. *Tel qu'en Lui-même enfin l'éternité le change.* And of course the eternity which transforms us into Ourselves is not the experience of mere persistence after bodily death. There will be no experience of timeless Reality then, unless there is the same or a similar knowledge within the world of time and matter. By precept and by example, the Avatar teaches that this transforming knowledge is possible, that all sentient beings are called to it and that, sooner or later, in one way or another, all must finally come to it.

CHAPTER IV

God in the World

"THAT art thou": "Behold but One in all things"—God within and God without. There is a way to Reality in and through the soul, and there is a way to Reality in and through the world. Whether the ultimate goal can be reached by following either of these ways to the exclusion of the other is to be doubted. The third, best and hardest way is that which leads to the divine Ground simultaneously in the perceiver and in that which is perceived.

The Mind is no other than the Buddha, and Buddha is no other than sentient being. When Mind assumes the form of a sentient being, it has suffered no decrease; when it has become a Buddha, it has added nothing to itself.

Huang Po

All creatures have existed eternally in the divine essence, as in their exemplar. So far as they conform to the divine idea, all beings were, before their creation, one thing with the essence of God. (God creates into time what was and is in eternity.) Eternally, all creatures are God in God. . . . So far as they are in God, they are the same life, the same essence, the same power, the same One, and nothing less.

Suso

The image of God is found essentially and personally in all mankind. Each possesses it whole, entire and undivided, and all together not more than one alone. In this way we are all one, intimately united in our eternal image, which is the image of God and the source in us of all our life. Our created essence and our life are attached to it without mediation as to their eternal cause.

Ruysbroeck

God who, in his simple substance, is all everywhere equally, nevertheless, in efficacy, is in rational creatures in another way than in irrational, and in good rational creatures in another way than in the bad. He is in irrational creatures in such a way as not to be comprehended by them; by all rational ones, however, he can be comprehended through knowledge; but only by the good is he to be comprehended also through love.

St. Bernard

When is a man in mere understanding? I answer, "When a man sees one thing separated from another." And when is a man above mere understanding? That I can tell you: "When a man sees All in all, then a man stands beyond mere understanding."

Eckhart

There are four kinds of Dhyana (spiritual disciplines). What are these four? They are, first, the Dhyana practised by the ignorant; second, the Dhyana devoted to the examination of meaning; third, the Dhyana with Suchness for its object; fourth, the Dhyana of the Tathagatas (Buddhas).

What is meant by the Dhyana practised by the ignorant? It is the one resorted to by the Yogins who exercise themselves in the disciplines of Sravakas and Pratyeka-buddhas (contemplatives and 'solitary Buddhas' of the Hinayana school), who perceiving that there is no ego substance, that the body is a shadow and a skeleton which is transient, impure and full of suffering, persistently cling to these notions, which are regarded as just so and not otherwise, and who, starting from them, advance by stages until they reach the cessation, where there are no thoughts. This is called the Dhyana practised by the ignorant.

What then is the Dhyana devoted to the examination of meaning? It is the one practised by those who, having gone beyond the egolessness of things, beyond individuality and generality, beyond the untenability of such ideas as 'self,' 'other' and 'both,' which are held by the philosophers, proceed to examine and follow up the meaning of the various aspects of Bodhisattvahood. This is the Dhyana devoted to the examination of meaning.

What is the Dhyana with Tathata (or Suchness) as its object? When the Yogin recognizes that the discrimination of the two forms of egolessness is mere imagination and that where he establishes himself in the reality of Suchness there is no rising of discrimination—this I call the Dhyana with Suchness for its object.

What is the Dhyana of the Tathagata? When the Yogin, entering upon the stage of Tathagatahood and abiding in the triple bliss characterizing self-realization attained by noble wisdom, devotes himself for the sake of all beings to the accomplishment of incomprehensible works —this I call the Dhyana of the Tathagata.

Lankavatara Sutra

When followers of Zen fail to go beyond the world of their senses and thoughts, all their doings and movements

are of no significance. But when the senses and thoughts
are annihilated, all the passages to Universal Mind are
blocked, and no entrance then becomes possible. The
original Mind is to be recognized along with the working
of the senses and thoughts—only it does not belong to
them, nor yet is it independent of them. Do not build
up your views upon your senses and thoughts, do not
base your understanding upon your senses and thoughts;
but at the same time do not seek the Mind away from
your senses and thoughts, do not try to grasp Reality by
rejecting your senses and thoughts. When you are neither
attached to, nor detached from, them, then you enjoy
your perfect unobstructed freedom, then you have your
seat of enlightenment.

Huang-Po

Every individual being, from the atom up to the most highly
organized of living bodies and the most exalted of finite
minds may be thought of, in René Guénon's phrase, as a
point where a ray of the primordial Godhead meets one of
the differentiated, creaturely emanations of that same Godhead's creative energy. The creature, as creature, may be very
far from God, in the sense that it lacks the intelligence to
discover the nature of the divine Ground of its being. But
the creature in its eternal essence—as the meeting place of
creatureliness and primordial Godhead—is one of the infinite
number of points where divine Reality is wholly and eternally
present. Because of this, rational beings can come to the
unitive knowledge of the divine Ground, non-rational and
inanimate beings may reveal to rational beings the fulness of
God's presence within their material forms. The poet's or
the painter's vision of the divine in nature, the worshipper's
awareness of a holy presence in the sacrament, symbol or
image—these are not entirely subjective. True, such perceptions cannot be had by all perceivers, for knowledge is a
function of being; but the thing known is independent of the
mode and nature of the knower. What the poet and painter
see, and try to record for us, is actually there, waiting to be
apprehended by anyone who has the right kind of faculties.
Similarly, in the image or the sacramental object the divine
Ground is wholly present. Faith and devotion prepare the
worshipper's mind for perceiving the ray of Godhead at its

point of intersection with the particular fragment of matter before him. Incidentally, by being worshipped, such symbols become the centres of a field of force. The longings, emotions and imaginations of those who kneel and, for generations, have knelt before the shrine create, as it were, an enduring vortex in the psychic medium, so that the image lives with a secondary, inferior divine life projected on to it by its worshippers, as well as with the primary divine life which, in common with all other animate and inanimate beings, it possesses in virtue of its relation to the divine Ground. The religious experience of sacramentalists and image worshippers may be perfectly genuine and objective; but it is not always or necessarily an experience of God or the Godhead. It may be, and perhaps in most cases it actually is, an experience of the field of force generated by the minds of past and present worshippers and projected on to the sacramental object where it sticks, so to speak, in a condition of what may be called second-hand objectivity, waiting to be perceived by minds suitably attuned to it. How desirable this kind of experience really is will have to be discussed in another section. All that need be said here is that the iconoclast's contempt for sacraments and symbols, as being nothing but mummery with stocks and stones is quite unjustified.

> The workmen still in doubt what course to take,
> Whether I'd best a saint or hog-trough make,
> After debate resolved me for a saint;
> And so famed Loyola I represent.

The all too Protestant satirist forgot that God is in the hog trough no less than in the conventionally sacred image. "Lift the stone and you will find me," affirms the best known of the Oxyrhinchus Logia of Jesus, "cleave the wood, and I am there." Those who have personally and immediately realized the truth of this saying and, along with it, the truth of Brahmanism's "That art thou" are wholly delivered.

> The Sravaka (literally 'hearer,' the name given by Mahayana Buddhists to contemplatives of the Hinayana school) fails to perceive that Mind, as it is in itself, has no stages, no causation. Disciplining himself in the cause, he has attained the result and abides in the samadhi

(contemplation) of Emptiness for ever so many aeons. However enlightened in this way, the Sravaka is not at all on the right track. From the point of view of the Bodhisattva, this is like suffering the torture of hell. The Sravaka has buried himself in Emptiness and does not know how to get out of his quiet contemplation, for he has no insight into the Buddha-nature itself.

Mo Tsu

When Enlightenment is perfected, a Bodhisattva is free from the bondage of things, but does not seek to be delivered from things. Samsara (the world of becoming) is not hated by him, nor is Nirvana loved. When perfect Enlightenment shines, it is neither bondage nor deliverance.

Prunabuddha-sutra

The touch of Earth is always reinvigorating to the son of Earth, even when he seeks a supraphysical Knowledge. It may even be said that the supraphysical can only be really mastered in its fulness—to its heights we can always reach—when we keep our feet firmly on the physical. "Earth is His footing," says the Upanishad, whenever it images the Self that manifests in the universe.

Sri Aurobindo

"To its heights we can always come." For those of us who are still splashing about in the lower ooze, the phrase has a rather ironical ring. Nevertheless, in the light of even the most distant acquaintance with the heights and the fulness, it is possible to understand what its author means. To discover the Kingdom of God exclusively within oneself is easier than to discover it, not only there, but also in the outer world of minds and things and living creatures. It is easier because the heights within reveal themselves to those who are ready to exclude from their purview all that lies without. And though this exclusion may be a painful and mortificatory process, the fact remains that it is less arduous than the process of inclusion, by which we come to know the fulness as well as the heights of spiritual life. Where there is exclusive concentration on the heights within, temptations and distractions are avoided and there is a general denial and

suppression. But when the hope is to know God inclusively—
to realize the divine Ground in the world as well as in the
soul, temptations and distractions must not be avoided, but
submitted to and used as opportunities for advance; there
must be no suppression of outward-turning activities, but a
transformation of them so that they become sacramental.
Mortification becomes more searching and more subtle; there
is need of unsleeping awareness and, on the levels of thought,
feeling and conduct, the constant exercise of something like
an artist's tact and taste.

It is in the literature of Mahayana and especially of Zen
Buddhism that we find the best account of the psychology of
the man for whom Samsara and Nirvana, time and eternity,
are one and the same. More systematically perhaps than any
other religion, the Buddhism of the Far East teaches the way
to spiritual Knowledge in its fulness as well as in its heights,
in and through the world as well as in and through the soul.
In this context we may point to a highly significant fact,
which is that the incomparable landscape painting of China
and Japan was essentially a religious art, inspired by Taoism
and Zen Buddhism; in Europe, on the contrary, landscape
painting and the poetry of "nature worship" were secular
arts which arose when Christianity was in decline, and derived
little or no inspiration from Christian ideals.

> "Blind, deaf, dumb!
> Infinitely beyond the reach of imaginative contri-
> vances!"

In these lines Seccho has swept everything away for you—
what you see together with what you do not see, what you
hear together with what you do not hear, and what you
talk about together with what you cannot talk about.
All these are completely brushed off, and you attain the
life of the blind, deaf, and dumb. Here all your imaginations, contrivances and calculations are once and for all
put an end to; they are no more made use of. This is
where lies the highest point of Zen, this is where we have
true blindness, true deafness and true dumbness, each in
its artless and effectless aspect.

> "Above the heavens and below the heavens!
> How ludicrous, how disheartening!"

Here Seccho lifts up with one hand and with the other

puts down. Tell me what he finds to be ludicrous, what he finds to be disheartening. It is ludicrous that this dumb person is not dumb after all, that this deaf person is not after all deaf; it is disheartening that the one who is not at all blind is blind for all that, and that the one who is not at all deaf is deaf for all that.

"Li-lou does not know how to discriminate right colour."

Li-lou lived in the reign of the Emperor Huang. He is said to have been able to distinguish the point of a soft hair at a distance of one hundred paces. His eyesight was extraordinary. When the Emperor Huang took a pleasure cruise on the River Ch'ih, he dropped his precious jewel in the water and made Li fetch it up. But he failed. The Emperor made Ch'ih-kou search for it; but he also failed to find it. Later Hsiang-wang was ordered to get it, and he got it. Hence,

"When Hsiang-wang goes down, the precious gem shines most brilliantly;
But where Li-lou walks about, the waves rise even to the sky."

When we come to these higher spheres, even the eyes of Li-lou are incapable of discriminating the right colour.

"How can Shih-kuang recognize the mysterious tune?" Shih-kuang was the son of Ching-kuang of Chin in the province of Chiang under the Chou dynasty. His other name was Tzu-yeh. He could thoroughly distinguish the five sounds and the six notes; he could even hear the ants fighting on the other side of a hill. When Chin and Ch'u were at war, Shih-kuang could tell, just by softly fingering the strings of his lute, that the engagement would surely be unfavourable for Ch'u. In spite of his extraordinary sensitiveness Seccho declares that he is unable to recognize the mysterious tune. After all, one who is not at all deaf is really deaf. The most exquisite note in the higher spheres is beyond the hearing of Shih-kuang. Says Seccho, I am not going to be a Li-lou, nor a Shih-kuang; for

"What life can compare with this? Sitting quietly by the window,
I watch the leaves fall and the flowers bloom, as the seasons come and go."

When one reaches this stage of realization, seeing is

no-seeing, hearing is no-hearing, preaching is no-preaching. When hungry one eats, when tired one sleeps. Let the leaves fall, let the flowers bloom as they like. When the leaves fall, I know it is the autumn; when the flowers bloom, I know it is the spring.

Having swept everything clean before you, Seccho now opens a passage-way, saying:

"Do you understand, or not?

An iron bar without a hole!"

He has done all he could for you; he is exhausted—only able to turn round and present you with this iron bar without a hole. It is a most significant expression. Look and see with your own eyes! If you hesitate, you miss the mark for ever.

Yengo (the author of this commentary) now raised his staff and said, "Do you see?" He then struck his chair and said, "Do you hear?" Coming down from the chair, he said, "Was anything talked about?"

What precisely is the significance of that iron bar without a hole? I do not pretend to know. Zen has always specialized in nonsense as a means of stimulating the mind to go forward to that which is beyond sense; so perhaps the point of the bar resides precisely in its pointlessness and in our disturbed, bewildered reaction to that pointlessness.

In the root divine Wisdom is all-Brahman; in the stem she is all-Illusion; in the flower she is all-World; and in the fruit, all-Liberation.

Tantra Tattva

The Sravakas and the Pratyekabuddhas, when they reach the eighth stage of the Bodhisattva's discipline, become so intoxicated with the bliss of mental tranquillity that they fail to realize that the visible world is nothing but the Mind. They are still in the realm of individuation; their insight is not yet pure. The Bodhisattvas, on the other hand, are alive to their original vows, flowing out of the all-embracing love that is in their hearts. They do not enter into Nirvana (as a state separate from the world of becoming); they know that the visible world is nothing but a manifestation of Mind itself.

Condensed from the Lankavatara Sutra

A conscious being alone understands what is meant by
  moving;
To those not endowed with consciousness the moving is
  unintelligible.
If you exercise yourself in the practice of keeping your
  mind unmoved,
The immovable you gain is that of one who has no
  consciousness.

If you are desirous for the truly immovable,
The immovable is in the moving itself,
And this immovable is the truly immovable one.
There is no seed of Buddhahood where there is no con-
  sciousness.

Mark well how varied are the aspects of the immovable
  one,
And know that the first reality is immovable.
Only when this reality is attained
Is the true working of Suchness understood.

Hui Neng

These phrases about the unmoving first mover remind one of
Aristotle. But between Aristotle and the exponents of the
Perennial Philosophy within the great religious traditions
there is this vast difference: Aristotle is primarily concerned
with cosmology, the Perennial Philosophers are primarily concerned with liberation and enlightenment: Aristotle is content
to know about the unmoving mover, from the outside and
theoretically; the aim of the Perennial Philosophers is to
become directly aware of it, to know it unitively, so that they
and others may actually become the unmoving One. This
unitive knowledge can be knowledge in the heights, or knowledge in the fulness, or knowledge simultaneously in the
heights and the fulness. Spiritual knowledge exclusively in the
heights of the soul was rejected by Mahayana Buddhism as
inadequate. The similar rejection of quietism within the Christian tradition will be touched upon in the section, "Contemplation and Action." Meanwhile it is interesting to find
that the problem which aroused such acrimonious debate
throughout seventeenth-century Europe had arisen for the
Buddhists at a considerably earlier epoch. But whereas in
Catholic Europe the outcome of the battle over Molinos, Mme.

Guyon and Fénelon was to all intents and purposes the extinction of mysticism for the best part of two centuries, in Asia the two parties were tolerant enough to agree to differ. Hinayana spirituality continued to explore the heights within, while the Mahayanist masters held up the ideal not of the Arhat, but of the Bodhisattva, and pointed the way to spiritual knowledge in its fulness as well as in its heights. What follows is a poetical account, by a Zen saint of the eighteenth century, of the state of those who have realized the Zen ideal.

> Abiding with the non-particular which is in particulars,
> Going or returning, they remain for ever unmoved.
> Taking hold of the not-thought which lies in thoughts,
> In their every act they hear the voice of Truth.
> How boundless the sky of contemplation!
> How transparent the moonlight of the four-fold Wisdom!
> As the Truth reveals itself in its eternal tranquillity,
> This very earth is the Lotus-Land of Purity,
> And this body is the body of the Buddha.

Hakuin

Nature's intent is neither food, nor drink nor clothing, nor comfort, nor anything else from which God is left out. Whether you like it or not, whether you know it or not, secretly Nature seeks and hunts and tries to ferret out the track in which God may be found.

Eckhart

Any flea as it is in God is nobler than the highest of the angels in himself.

Eckhart

My inner man relishes things not as creatures but as the gift of God. But to my innermost man they savour not of God's gift, but of ever and aye.

Eckhart

Pigs eat acorns, but neither consider the sun that gave them life, nor the influence of the heavens by which they were nourished, nor the very root of the tree from whence they came.

Thomas Traherne

Your enjoyment of the world is never right till every morning you awake in Heaven; see yourself in your Father's palace; and look upon the skies, the earth and the air as celestial joys; having such a reverend esteem of all, as if you were among the Angels. The bride of a monarch, in her husband's chamber, hath no such causes of delight as you.

You never enjoy the world aright till the sea itself floweth in your veins, till you are clothed with the heavens and crowned with the stars; and perceive yourself to be the sole heir of the whole world, and more than so, because men are in it who are every one sole heirs as well as you. Till you can sing and rejoice and delight in God, as misers do in gold, and kings in sceptres, you can never enjoy the world.

Till your spirit filleth the whole world, and the stars are your jewels; till you are as familiar with the ways of God in all ages as with your walk and table; till you are intimately acquainted with that shady nothing out of which the world was made; till you love men so as to desire their happiness with a thirst equal to the zeal of your own; till you delight in God for being good to all; you never enjoy the world. Till you more feel it than your private estate, and are more present in the hemisphere, considering the glories and the beauties there, than in your own house; till you remember how lately you were made, and how wonderful it was when you came into it; and more rejoice in the palace of your glory than if it had been made today morning.

Yet further, you never enjoyed the world aright, till you so love the beauty of enjoying it, that you are covetous and earnest to persuade others to enjoy it. And so perfectly hate the abominable corruption of men in despising it that you had rather suffer the flames of hell than willingly be guilty of their error.

The world is a mirror of Infinite Beauty, yet no man sees it. It is a Temple of Majesty, yet no man regards it. It is a region of Light and Peace, did not men disquiet it. It is the Paradise of God. It is more to man since he is fallen than it was before. It is the place of Angels and the Gate of Heaven. When Jacob waked out of his dream, he said, God is here, and I wist it not. How dreadful is this

place! This is none other than the House of God and the
Gate of Heaven.

Thomas Traherne

Before going on to discuss the means whereby it is possible
to come to the fulness as well as the height of spiritual knowledge, let us briefly consider the experience of those who have
been privileged to "behold the One in all things," but have
made no efforts to perceive it within themselves. A great deal
of interesting material on this subject may be found in Buck's
Cosmic Consciousness. All that need be said here is that such
"cosmic consciousness" may come unsought and is in the
nature of what Catholic theologians call a "gratuitous grace."
One may have a gratuitous grace (the power of healing, for
example, or foreknowledge) while in a state of mortal sin, and
the gift is neither necessary to, nor sufficient for, salvation. At
the best such sudden accessions of "cosmic consciousness" as
are described by Buck are merely unusual invitations to further personal effort in the direction of the inner height as
well as the external fulness of knowledge. In a great many
cases the invitation is not accepted; the gift is prized for the
ecstatic pleasure it brings; its coming is remembered nostalgically and, if the recipient happens to be a poet, written about
with eloquence—as Byron, for example, wrote in a splendid
passage of *Childe Harold,* as Wordsworth wrote in *Tintern
Abbey* and *The Prelude.* In these matters no human being
may presume to pass definitive judgment upon another human
being; but it is at least permissible to say that, on the basis
of the biographical evidence, there is no reason to suppose
that either Wordsworth or Byron ever seriously did anything
about the theophanies they described; nor is there any evidence that these theophanies were of themselves sufficient to
transform their characters. That enormous egotism, to which
De Quincey and Keats and Haydon bear witness, seems to
have remained with Wordsworth to the end. And Byron was
as fascinatingly and tragi-comically Byronic after he had beheld the One in all things as he was before.

In this context it is interesting to compare Wordsworth with
another great nature lover and man of letters, St. Bernard.
"Let Nature be your teacher," says the first; and he goes on
to affirm that

One impulse from the vernal wood
Will tell you more of man,
Of moral evil and of good,
Than all the sages can.

St. Bernard speaks in what seems a similar strain. "What I know of the divine sciences and Holy Scripture, I learnt in woods and fields. I have had no other masters than the beeches and the oaks." And in another of his letters he says: "Listen to a man of experience: thou wilt learn more in the woods than in books. Trees and stones will teach thee more than thou canst acquire from the mouth of a magister." The phrases are similar; but their inner significance is very different. In Augustine's language, God alone is to be enjoyed; creatures are not to be enjoyed but used—used with love and compassion and a wondering, detached appreciation, as means to the knowledge of that which may be enjoyed. Wordsworth, like almost all other literary Nature-worshippers, preaches the enjoyment of creatures rather than their use for the attainment of spiritual ends—a use which, as we shall see, entails much self-discipline for the user. For Bernard it goes without saying that his correspondents are actively practising this self-discipline and that Nature, though loved and heeded as a teacher, is only being used as a means to God, not enjoyed as though she were God. The beauty of flowers and landscape is not merely to be relished as one "wanders lonely as a cloud" about the countryside, is not merely to be pleasurably remembered when one is lying "in vacant or in pensive mood" on the sofa in the library, after tea. The reaction must be a little more strenuous and purposeful. "Here, my brothers," says an ancient Buddhist author, "are the roots of trees, here are empty places; meditate." The truth is, of course, that the world is only for those who have deserved it; for, in Philo's words, "even though a man may be incapable of making himself worthy of the creator of the cosmos, yet he ought to try to make himself worthy of the cosmos. He ought to transform himself from being a man into the nature of the cosmos and become, if one may say so, a little cosmos." For those who have not deserved the world, either by making themselves worthy of its creator (that is to say, by non-attachment and a total self-naughting), or, less arduously, by making themselves worthy of the cosmos (by bringing order and a measure of unity to the manifold confusion of undisciplined human personality), the world is, spiritually speaking, a very dangerous place.

That Nirvana and Samsara are one is a fact about the nature of the universe; but it is a fact which cannot be fully realized or directly experienced, except by souls far advanced in spirituality. For ordinary, nice, unregenerate people to accept this truth by hearsay, and to act upon it in practice, is merely to court disaster. All the dismal story of antinomianism is there to warn us of what happens when men and women make practical applications of a merely intellectual and unrealized theory that all is God and God is all. And hardly less depressing than the spectacle of antinomianism is that of the earnestly respectable "well-rounded life" of good citizens who do their best to live sacramentally, but don't in fact have any direct acquaintance with that for which the sacramental activity really stands. Dr. Oman, in his *The Natural and the Supernatural*, writes at length on the theme that "reconciliation to the evanescent is revelation of the eternal"; and in a recent volume, *Science, Religion and the Future*, Canon Raven applauds Dr. Oman for having stated the principles of a theology, in which there could be no ultimate antithesis between nature and grace, science and religion, in which, indeed, the worlds of the scientist and the theologian are seen to be one and the same. All this is in full accord with Taoism and Zen Buddhism and with such Christian teachings as St. Augustine's *Ama et fac quod vis* and Father Lallemant's advice to theocentric contemplatives to go out and act in the world, since their actions are the only ones capable of doing any real good to the world. But what neither Dr. Oman nor Canon Raven makes sufficiently clear is that nature and grace, Samsara and Nirvana, perpetual perishing and eternity, are really and experientially one only to persons who have fulfilled certain conditions. *Fac quod vis* in the temporal world—but only when you have learnt the infinitely difficult art of loving God with all your mind and heart and your neighbor as yourself. If you haven't learnt this lesson, you will either be an antinomian eccentric or criminal or else a respectable well-rounded-lifer, who has left himself no time to understand either nature or grace. The Gospels are perfectly clear about the process by which, and by which alone, a man may gain the right to live in the world

as though he were at home in it: he must make a total denial
of selfhood, submit to a complete and absolute mortification.
At one period of his career, Jesus himself seems to have undertaken austerities, not merely of the mind, but of the body.
There is the record of his forty days' fast and his statement,
evidently drawn from personal experience, that some demons
cannot be cast out except by those who have fasted much
as well as prayed. (The Curé d'Ars, whose knowledge of
miracles and corporal penance was based on personal experience, insists on the close correlation between severe bodily
austerities and the power to get petitionary prayer answered
in ways that are sometimes supernormal.) The Pharisees re-
proached Jesus because he "came eating and drinking," and
associated with "publicans and sinners"; they ignored, or were
unaware of, the fact that this apparently worldly prophet had
at one time rivalled the physical austerities of John the Baptist
and was practising the spiritual mortifications which he consistently preached. The pattern of Jesus' life is essentially similar to that of the ideal sage, whose career is traced in the
"Oxherding Pictures," so popular among Zen Buddhists. The
wild ox, symbolizing the unregenerate self, is caught, made
to change its direction, then tamed and gradually transformed
from black to white. Regeneration goes so far that for a time
the ox is completely lost, so that nothing remains to be pic-
tured but the full-orbed moon, symbolizing Mind, Suchness,
the Ground. But this is not the final stage. In the end, the
herdsman comes back to the world of men, riding on the back
of his ox. Because he now loves, loves to the extent of being
identified with the divine object of his love, he can do what
he likes; for what he likes is what the Nature of Things likes.
He is found in company with wine-bibbers and butchers; he
and they are all converted into Buddhas. For him, there is
complete reconciliation to the evanescent and, through that
reconciliation, revelation of the eternal. But for nice ordinary
unregenerate people the only reconciliation to the evanescent
is that of indulged passions, of distractions submitted to and
enjoyed. To tell such persons that evanescence and eternity
are the same, and not immediately to qualify the statement,
is positively fatal—for, in practice, they are not the same except to the saint; and there is no record that anybody ever
came to sanctity, who did not, at the outset of his or her
career, behave as if evanescence and eternity, nature and grace,

were profoundly different and in many respects incompatible. As always, the path of spirituality is a knife-edge between abysses. On one side is the danger of mere rejection and escape, on the other the danger of mere acceptance and the enjoyment of things which should only be used as instruments or symbols. The versified caption which accompanies the last of the "Oxherding Pictures" runs as follows.

> Even beyond the ultimate limits there extends a passageway,
> By which he comes back to the six realms of existence.
> Every worldly affair is now a Buddhist work,
> And wherever he goes he finds his home air.
> Like a gem he stands out even in the mud,
> Like pure gold he shines even in the furnace.
> Along the endless road (of birth and death) he walks sufficient unto himself.
> In all circumstances he moves tranquil and unattached.

The means whereby man's final end is to be attained will be described and illustrated at length in the section on "Mortification and Non-attachment." This section, however, is mainly concerned with the disciplining of the will. But the disciplining of the will must have as its accompaniment a no less thorough disciplining of the consciousness. There has to be a conversion, sudden or otherwise, not merely of the heart, but also of the senses and of the perceiving mind. What follows is a brief account of this *metanoia*, as the Greeks called it, this total and radical "change of mind."

It is in the Indian and Far Eastern formulations of the Perennial Philosophy that this subject is most systematically treated. What is prescribed is a process of conscious discrimination between the personal self and the Self that is identical with Brahman, between the individual ego and the Buddha-womb or Universal Mind. The result of this discrimination is a more or less sudden and complete "revulsion" of consciousness, and the realization of a state of "no-mind," which may be described as the freedom from perceptual and intellectual attachment to the ego-principle. This state of "no-mind" exists, as it were, on a knife-edge between the carelessness of the average sensual man and the strained overeagerness of the zealot for salvation. To achieve it, one must walk delicately and, to maintain it, must learn to combine the most intense alertness with a tranquil and self-denying passivity, the most indomitable determination with a perfect submission to the leadings of the spirit. "When no-mind is sought after by a mind," says Huang Po, "that is making it a particular object of thought. There is only testimony of silence; it goes beyond thinking." In other words, we, as separate individuals, must not try to think it, but rather permit ourselves to be thought by it. Similarly, in the Diamond Sutra we read that if a Bodhisattva, in his attempt to realize Suchness, "retains the thought of an ego, a person, a separate being, or a soul, he is no longer a Bodhisattva." Al Ghazzali, the philosopher of Sufism, also stresses the need for intellectual humbleness and docility. "If the thought that he is effaced from self occurs to one who is in *fana* (a term roughly corresponding to Zen's 'no-mind,' or *mushin*), that is a defect. The highest state is to be effaced from effacement." There is an ecstatic effacement-from-effacement in the interior heights of the Atman-Brahman; and there is another, more comprehensive effacement-from-effacement, not only in the inner heights, but also in and through the world, in the waking, everyday knowledge of God in his fulness.

A man must become truly poor and as free from his own creaturely will as he was when he was born. And I tell you, by the eternal truth, that so long as you *desire* to fulfill the will of God and have any hankering after eternity and God, for just so long you are not truly poor. He alone has true spiritual poverty who wills nothing, knows nothing, desires nothing.

Eckhart

The Perfect Way knows no difficulties,
Except that it refuses to make preferences.
Only when freed from hate and love
Does it reveal itself fully and without disguise.

A tenth of an inch's difference,
And heaven and earth are set apart.
If you wish to see it before your own eyes,
Have no fixed thoughts either for or against it.

To set up what you like against what you dislike—
This is the disease of the mind.
When the deep meaning of the Way is not understood.
Peace of mind is disturbed to no purpose. . . .

Pursue not the outer entanglements,
Dwell not in the inner void;
Be serene in the oneness of things,
And dualism vanishes of itself.

When you strive to gain quiescence by stopping motion,
The quiescence so gained is ever in motion.
So long as you tarry in such dualism,
How can you realize oneness?

And when oneness is not thoroughly grasped,
Loss is sustained in two ways:
The denying of external reality is the assertion of it,
And the assertion of Emptiness (the Absolute) is the
   denying of it. . . .

Transformations going on in the empty world that con-
   fronts us
Appear to be real because of Ignorance.
Do not strive to seek after the True,
Only cease to cherish opinions.

The two exist because of the One;
But hold not even to this One.
When a mind is not disturbed,
The ten thousand things offer no offence. . . .

If an eye never falls asleep,
All dreams will cease of themselves;
If the Mind retains its absoluteness,
The ten thousand things are of one substance.

When the deep mystery of one Suchness is fathomed,
All of a sudden we forget the external entanglements;
When the ten thousand things are viewed in their oneness,
We return to the origin and remain where we have always
   been. . . .

One in all,
All in One—
If only this is realized,
No more worry about not being perfect!

When Mind and each believing mind are not divided,
And undivided are each believing mind and Mind,
This is where words fail,
For it is not of the past, present or future.

The Third Patriarch of Zen

Do what you are doing now, suffer what you are suffering
now; to do all this with holiness, nothing need be changed
but your hearts. Sanctity consists in *willing* what happens
to us by God's order.

de Caussade

The seventeenth-century Frenchman's vocabulary is very different from that of the seventh-century Chinaman's. But the
advice they give is fundamentally similar. Conformity to the
will of God, submission, docility to the leadings of the Holy
Ghost—in practice, if not verbally, these are the same as conformity to the Perfect Way, refusing to have preferences and
cherish opinions, keeping the eyes open so that dreams may
cease and Truth reveal itself.

The world inhabited by ordinary, nice, unregenerate people is mainly dull (so dull that they have to distract their
minds from being aware of it by all sorts of artificial "amuse-
ments"), sometimes briefly and intensely pleasurable, occasionally or quite often disagreeable and even agonizing. For those
who have deserved the world by making themselves fit to see
God within it as well as within their own souls, it wears a
very different aspect.

The corn was orient and immortal wheat, which never
should be reaped, nor was ever sown. I thought it had
stood from everlasting to everlasting. The dust and stones
of the street were as precious as gold. The gates at first
were the end of the world. The green trees, when I saw
them first through one of the gates, transported and
ravished me; their sweetness and unusual beauty made
my heart to leap, and almost mad with ecstasy, they were

such strange and wonderful things. The Men! O what venerable and reverend creatures did the aged seem! Immortal Cherubim! And young men glittering and sparkling angels, and maids strange seraphic pieces of life and beauty! Boys and girls tumbling in the street, and playing, were moving jewels. I knew not that they were born or should die. But all things abided eternally as they were in their proper places. Eternity was manifested in the light of the day, and something infinite behind everything appeared; which talked with my expectation and moved my desire. The city seemed to stand in Eden, or to be built in Heaven. The streets were mine, the temple was mine, the people were mine, their clothes and gold and silver were mine, as much as their sparkling eyes, fair skins and ruddy faces. The skies were mine, and so were the sun and moon and stars, and all the world was mine; and I the only spectator and enjoyer of it. . . . And so it was that with much ado I was corrupted and made to learn the dirty devices of the world. Which now I unlearn, and become as it were a little child again, that I may enter into the Kingdom of God.

Thomas Traherne

Therefore I give you still another thought, which is yet purer and more spiritual: In the Kingdom of Heaven all is in all, all is one, and all is ours.

Eckhart

The doctrine that God is in the world has an important practical corollary—the sacredness of Nature, and the sinfulness and folly of man's overweening efforts to be her master rather than her intelligently docile collaborator. Sub-human lives and even things are to be treated with respect and understanding, not brutally oppressed to serve our human ends.

The ruler of the Southern Ocean was Shu, the ruler of the Northern Ocean was Hu, and the ruler of the Centre was Chaos. Shu and Hu were continually meeting in the land of Chaos, who treated them very well. They consulted together how they might repay his kindness, and said: "Men all have seven orifices for the purpose of seeing, hearing, eating and breathing, while this ruler alone

has not a single one. Let us try to make them for him."
Accordingly they dug one orifice in him every day. At
the end of seven days Chaos died.

Chuang Tzu

In this delicately comic parable Chaos is Nature in the state
of *wu-wei*—non-assertion or equilibrium. Shu and Hu are
the living images of those busy persons who thought they
would improve on Nature by turning dry prairies into wheat
fields, and produced deserts; who proudly proclaimed the Conquest of the Air, and then discovered that they had defeated
civilization; who chopped down vast forests to provide the
newsprint demanded by that universal literacy which was to
make the world safe for intelligence and democracy, and got
wholesale erosion, pulp magazines and the organs of Fascist,
Communist, capitalist and nationalist propaganda. In brief,
Shu and Hu are devotees of the apocalyptic religion of Inevitable Progress, and their creed is that the Kingdom of
Heaven is outside you, and in the future. Chuang Tzu, on the
other hand, like all good Taoists, has no desire to bully Nature
into subserving ill-considered temporal ends, at variance with
the final end of men as formulated in the Perennial Philosophy. His wish is to work with Nature, so as to produce material and social conditions in which individuals may realize Tao
on every level from the physiological up to the spiritual.

Compared with that of the Taoists and Far Eastern Buddhists, the Christian attitude towards Nature has been curiously
insensitive and often downright domineering and violent. Taking their cue from an unfortunate remark in Genesis, Catholic
moralists have regarded animals as mere things which men
do right to exploit for their own ends. Like landscape painting,
the humanitarian movement in Europe was an almost completely secular affair. In the Far East both were essentially
religious.

The Greeks believed that *hubris* was always followed by
nemesis, that if you went too far you would get a knock on the
head to remind you that the gods will not tolerate insolence
on the part of mortal men. In the sphere of human relations,
the modern mind understands the doctrine of *hubris* and
regards it as mainly true. We wish pride to have a fall, and we
see that very often it does fall.

To have too much power over one's fellows, to be too rich,

too violent, too ambitious—all this invites punishment, and in the long run, we notice, punishment of one sort or another duly comes. But the Greeks did not stop there. Because they regarded Nature as in some way divine, they felt that it had to be respected and they were convinced that a hubristic lack of respect for Nature would be punished by avenging *nemesis*. In "The Persians," Aeschylus gives the reasons—the ultimate, metaphysical reasons—for the barbarians' defeat. Xerxes was punished for two offences—overweening imperialism directed against the Athenians, and overweening imperialism directed against Nature. He tried to enslave his fellow men, and he tried to enslave the sea, by building a bridge across the Hellespont.

> *Atossa*
> From shore to shore he bridged the Hellespont.
>
> *Ghost of Darius*
> What, could he chain the mighty Bosphorous?
>
> *Atossa*
> Even so, some god assisting his design.
>
> *Ghost of Darius*
> Some god of power to cloud his better sense.

Today we recognize and condemn the first kind of imperialism; but most of us ignore the existence and even the very possibility of the second. And yet the author of *Erewhon* was certainly not a fool, and now that we are paying the appalling price for our much touted "conquest of Nature" his book seems more than ever topical. And Butler was not the only nineteenth-century sceptic in regard to Inevitable Progress. A generation or more before him, Alfred de Vigny was writing about the new technological marvel of his days, the steam engine—writing in a tone very different from the enthusiastic roarings and trumpetings of his great contemporary, Victor Hugo.

> Sur le taureau de fer, qui fume, souffle et beugle,
> L'homme est monté trop tôt. Nul ne connaît encor
> Quels orages en lui porte ce rude aveugle,
> Et le gai voyageur lui livre son trésor.

And a little later in the same poem he adds,

> Tous se sont dit: "Allons," mais aucun n'est le maître
> D'un dragon mugissant qu'un savant a fait naître.
> Nous nous sommes joués à plus fort que nous tous.

Looking backwards across the carnage and the devastation, we can see that Vigny was perfectly right. None of those gay travellers, of whom Victor Hugo was the most vociferously eloquent, had the faintest notion where that first, funny little Puffing Billy was taking them. Or rather they had a very clear notion, but it happened to be entirely false. For they were convinced that Puffing Billy was hauling them at full speed towards universal peace and the brotherhood of man; while the newspapers which they were so proud of being able to read, as the train rumbled along towards its Utopian destination not more than fifty years or so away, were the guarantee that liberty and reason would soon be everywhere triumphant. Puffing Billy has now turned into a four-motored bomber loaded with white phosphorus and high explosives, and the free press is everywhere the servant of its advertisers, of a pressure group, or of the government. And yet, for some inexplicable reason, the travellers (now far from gay) still hold fast to the religion of Inevitable Progress—which is, in the last analysis, the hope and faith (in the teeth of all human experience) that one can get something for nothing. How much saner and more realistic is the Greek view that every victory has to be paid for, and that, for some victories, the price exacted is so high that it outweighs any advantage that may be obtained! Modern man no longer regards Nature as being in any sense divine and feels perfectly free to behave towards her as an overweening conqueror and tyrant. The spoils of recent technological imperialism have been enormous; but meanwhile *nemesis* has seen to it that we get our kicks as well as halfpence. For example, has the ability to travel in twelve hours from New York to Los Angeles given more pleasure to the human race than the dropping of bombs and fire has given pain? There is no known method of computing the amount of felicity or goodness in the world at large. What is obvious, however, is that the advantages accruing from recent technological advances—or, in Greek phraseology, from recent acts of *hubris* directed against Nature—are generally accompanied by corresponding disadvantages, that gains in one direction entail losses in other directions, and that we never get something except for something. Whether the net result of these elaborate credit and debit operations is a genuine Progress in virtue, happiness, charity and intelligence is something we can never definitely determine. It is because the reality of Progress can never be determined that the nineteenth and twentieth centuries have had to treat it as an article of religious faith. To the exponents of the Perennial Philosophy, the question whether Progress is inevitable or even real is not a matter of primary importance. For them, the important thing is that individual men and women should come to the unitive knowledge of the divine Ground, and what interests them in regard to the social environment is not its progressiveness or non-progressiveness (whatever those terms may mean), but the degree to which it helps or hinders individuals in their advance towards man's final end.

CHAPTER V

Charity

He that loveth not knoweth not God, for God is love.

I John: 4

By love may He be gotten and holden, but by thought never.

The Cloud of Unknowing

Whosoever studies to reach contemplation (i.e., unitive knowledge) should begin by searchingly enquiring of himself how much he loves. For love is the motive power of the mind (*machina mentis*), which draws it out of the world and raises it on high.

St. Gregory the Great

The astrolabe of the mysteries of God is love.

Jalal-uddin Rumi

Heavens, deal so still!
Let the superfluous and lust-dieted man
That slaves your ordinance, that will not see
Because he doth not feel, feel your power quickly.

Shakespeare

Love is infallible; it has no errors, for all errors are the
want of love.

William Law

We can only love what we know, and we can never know
completely what we do not love. Love is a mode of knowledge,
and when the love is sufficiently disinterested and sufficiently
intense, the knowledge becomes unitive knowledge and so
takes on the quality of infallibility. Where there is no disinterested love (or, more briefly, no charity), there is only
biased self-love, and consequently only a partial and distorted
knowledge both of the self and of the world of things, lives,
minds and spirit outside the self. The lust-dieted man "slaves
the ordinances of Heaven"—that is to say, he subordinates the
laws of Nature and the spirit to his own cravings. The result
is that "he does not feel" and therefore makes himself incapable of knowledge. His ignorance is ultimately voluntary;
if he cannot see, it is because "he will not see." Such voluntary
ignorance inevitably has its negative reward. Nemesis follows
hubris—sometimes in a spectacular way, as when the self-
blinded man (Macbeth, Othello, Lear) falls into the trap
which his own ambition or possessiveness or petulant vanity
has prepared for him; sometimes in a less obvious way, as in
the cases where power, prosperity and reputation endure to
the end but at the cost of an ever-increasing imperviousness
to grace and enlightenment, an ever completer inability to
escape, now or hereafter, from the stifling prison of selfness
and separateness. How profound can be the spiritual ignorance
by which such "enslavers of Heaven's ordinances" are punished is indicated by the behaviour of Cardinal Richelieu on
his death-bed. The priest who attended him urged the great
man to prepare his soul for its coming ordeal by forgiving
all his enemies. "I have never had any enemies," the Cardinal
replied with the calm sincerity of an ignorance which long
years of intrigue and avarice and ambition had rendered as

absolute as had been his political power, "save only those of the State." Like Napoleon, but in a different way, he was "feeling heaven's power," because he had refused to feel charity and therefore refused to know the whole truth about his own soul or anything else.

> Here on earth the love of God is better than the knowledge of God, while it is better to know inferior things than to love them. By knowing them we raise them, in a way, to our intelligence, whereas by loving them, we stoop towards them and may become subservient to them, as the miser to his gold.
>
> St. *Thomas Aquinas* (*paraphrased*)

This remark seems, at first sight, to be incompatible with what precedes it. But in reality St. Thomas is merely distinguishing between the various forms of love and knowledge. It is better to love-know God than just to know about God, without love, through the reading of a treatise on theology. Gold, on the other hand, should never be known with the miser's love, or rather concupiscence, but either abstractly, as the scientific investigator knows it, or else with the disinterested love-knowledge of the artist in metal, or of the spectator, who love-knows the goldsmith's work, not for its cash value, not for the sake of possessing it, but just because it is beautiful. And the same applies to all created things, lives and minds. It is bad to love-know them with self-centred attachment and cupidity; it is somewhat better to know them with scientific dispassion; it is best to supplement abstract knowledge-without-cupidity with true disinterested love-knowledge, having the quality of aesthetic delight, or of charity, or of both combined.

> We make an idol of truth itself; for truth apart from charity is not God, but his image and idol, which we must neither love nor worship.
>
> *Pascal*

By a kind of philological accident (which is probably no accident at all, but one of the more subtle expressions of man's deep-seated will to ignorance and spiritual darkness), the word "charity" has come, in modern English, to be synonymous with "almsgiving," and is almost never used in its original sense, as signifying the highest and most divine form of love. Owing to this impoverishment of our, at the best of times, very inadequate vocabulary of psychological and spiritual terms, the word "love" has had to assume an added burden. "God is love," we repeat glibly, and that we must "love our neighbours as ourselves"; but "love," unfortunately, stands for everything from what happens when, on the screen, two close-ups rapturously collide to what happens when a John Woolman or a Peter Claver feels a concern about Negro slaves, because they are temples of the Holy Spirit—from what happens when crowds shout and sing and wave flags in the *Sport-Palast* or the Red Square to what happens when a solitary contemplative becomes absorbed in the prayer of simple regard. Ambiguity in vocabulary leads to confusion of thought; and, in this matter of love, confusion of thought admirably serves the purpose of an unregenerate and divided human nature that is determined to make the best of both worlds—to say that it is serving God, while in fact it is serving Mammon, Mars or Priapus.

Systematically or in brief aphorism and parable, the masters of the spiritual life have described the nature of true charity and have distinguished it from the other, lower forms of love. Let us consider its principal characteristics in order. First, charity is disinterested, seeking no reward, nor allowing itself to be diminished by any return of evil for its good. God is to be loved for Himself, not for his gifts, and persons and things are to be loved for God's sake, because they are temples of the Holy Ghost. Moreover, since charity is disinterested, it must of necessity be universal.

> Love seeks no cause beyond itself and no fruit; it is its own fruit, its own enjoyment. I love because I love; I love in order that I may love. . . . Of all the motions and affections of the soul, love is the only one by means of which the creature, though not on equal terms, is able to treat with the Creator and to give back something resembling what has been given to it. . . . When God loves, he only desires to be loved, knowing that love will render all those who love Him happy.
>
> St. Bernard

> For as love has no by-ends, wills nothing but its own increase, so everything is as oil to its flame; it must have that which it wills and cannot be disappointed, because

everything (including unkindness on the part of those loved) naturally helps it to live in its own way and to bring forth its own work.

William Law

Those who speak ill of me are really my good friends.
When, being slandered, I cherish neither enmity nor preference,
There grows within me the power of love and humility, which is born of the Unborn.

Kung-chia Ta-shih

Some people want to see God with their eyes as they see a cow, and to love Him as they love their cow—for the milk and cheese and profit it brings them. This is how it is with people who love God for the sake of outward wealth or inward comfort. They do not rightly love God, when they love Him for their own advantage. Indeed, I tell you the truth, any object you have in your mind, however good, will be a barrier between you and the inmost Truth.

Eckhart

A beggar, Lord, I ask of Thee
More than a thousand kings could ask.
Each one wants something, which he asks of Thee.
I come to ask Thee to give me Thyself.

Ansari of Herat

I will have nothing to do with a love which would be for God or in God. This is a love which pure love cannot abide; for pure love is God Himself.

St. Catherine of Genoa

As a mother, even at the risk of her own life, protects her son, her only son, so let there be good will without measure between all beings. Let good will without measure prevail in the whole world, above, below, around, unstinted, unmixed with any feeling of differing or opposing interests. If a man remain steadfastly in this state of mind all the time he is awake, then is come to pass the saying, "Even in this world holiness has been found."

Metta Sutta

Learn to look with an equal eye upon all beings, seeing the one Self in all.

Srimad Bhagavatam

The second distinguishing mark of charity is that, unlike the lower forms of love, it is not an emotion. It begins as an act of the will and is consummated as a purely spiritual awareness, a unitive love-knowledge of the essence of its object.

Let everyone understand that real love of God does not consist in tear-shedding, nor in that sweetness and tenderness for which usually we long, just because they console us, but in serving God in justice, fortitude of soul and humility.

St. Teresa

The worth of love does not consist in high feelings, but in detachment, in patience under all trials for the sake of God whom we love.

St. John of the Cross

By love I do not mean any natural tenderness, which is more or less in people according to their constitution; but I mean a larger principle of the soul, founded in reason and piety, which makes us tender, kind and gentle to all our fellow creatures as creatures of God, and for his sake.

William Law

The nature of charity, or the love-knowledge of God, is defined by Shankara, the great Vedantist saint and philosopher of the ninth century, in the thirty-second couplet of his *Viveka-Chudamani*.

Among the instruments of emancipation the supreme is devotion. Contemplation of the true form of the real Self (the Atman which is identical with Brahman) is said to be devotion.

In other words, the highest form of the love of God is an immediate spiritual intuition, by which "knower, known and knowledge are made one." The means to, and earlier stages of, this supreme love-knowledge of Spirit by spirit are described by Shankara in the preceding verses of his philosophical poem, and consist in acts of a will directed towards the denial of selfness in thought, feeling and action, towards desirelessness and non-attachment or (to use the corresponding Christian term) "holy indifference," towards a cheerful acceptance of affliction, without self-pity and without thought of returning evil for evil, and finally towards unsleeping and one-pointed mindfulness of the Godhead who is at once transcendent and, because transcendent, immanent in every soul.

It is plain that no distinct object whatever that pleases the will can be God; and, for that reason, if the will is to be united with Him, it must empty itself, cast away every disorderly affection of the desire, every satisfaction it may distinctly have, high and low, temporal and spiritual, so that, purified and cleansed from all unruly satisfactions, joys and desires, it may be wholly occupied, with all its affections, in loving God. For if the will can in any way comprehend God and be united with Him, it cannot be through any capacity of the desire, but only by love; and as all the delight, sweetness and joy, of which the will is sensible, is not love, it follows that none of these pleasing impressions can be the adequate means of uniting the will to God. These adequate means consist in an act of the will. And because an act of the will is quite distinct from feeling, it is by an act that the will is united with God and rests in Him; that act is love. This union is never wrought by feeling or exertion of the desire; for these remain in the soul as aims and ends. It is only as motives of love that feelings can be of service, if the will is bent on going onwards, and for nothing else. . . .

He, then, is very unwise who, when sweetness and spiritual delight fail him, thinks for that reason that God has abandoned him; and when he finds them again, rejoices and is glad, thinking that he has in that way come to possess God.

More unwise still is he who goes about seeking for sweetness in God, rejoices in it, and dwells upon it; for in so doing he is not seeking after God with the will grounded in the emptiness of faith and charity, but only in spiritual sweetness and delight, which is a created thing, following herein in his own will and fond pleasure.

... It is impossible for the will to attain to the sweetness and bliss of the divine union otherwise than in detachment, in refusing to the desire every pleasure in the things of heaven and earth.

St. John of the Cross

Love (the sensible love of the emotions) does not unify. True, it unites in act; but it does not unite in essence.

Eckhart

The reason why sensible love even of the highest object cannot unite the soul to its divine Ground in spiritual essence is that, like all other emotions of the heart, sensible love intensifies that selfness, which is the final obstacle in the way of such union. "The damned are in eternal movement without any mixture of rest; we mortals, who are yet in this pilgrimage, have now movement, now rest. . . . Only God has repose without movement." Consequently it is only if we abide in the peace of God that passes all understanding that we can abide in the knowledge and love of God. And to the peace that passes understanding, we have to go by way of the humble and very ordinary peace which can be understood by everybody—peace between nations and within them (for wars and violent revolutions have the effect of more or less totally eclipsing God for the majority of those involved in them); peace between individuals and within the individual soul (for personal quarrels and private fears, loves, hates, ambitions and distractions are, in their petty way, no less fatal to the development of the spiritual life than are the greater calamities). We have to will the peace that it is within our power to get for ourselves and others, in order that we may be fit to receive that other peace, which is a fruit of the Spirit and the condition, as St. Paul implied, of the unitive knowledge-love of God.

It is by means of tranquillity of mind that you are able to transmute this false mind of death and rebirth into the clear Intuitive Mind and, by so doing, to realize the primal and enlightening Essence of Mind. You should make this your starting-point for spiritual practices. Having harmonized your starting-point with your goal, you will be able by right practice to attain your true end of perfect Enlightenment.

If you wish to tranquillize your mind and restore its original purity, you must proceed as you would do if you were purifying a jar of muddy water. You first let it stand, until the sediment settles at the bottom, when the water will become clear, which corresponds with the state of the mind before it was troubled by defiling passions. Then you carefully strain off the pure water. . . . When the mind becomes tranquillized and concentrated into perfect unity, then all things will be seen, not in their separateness, but in their unity, wherein there is no place for the passions to enter, and which is in full conformity with the mysterious and indescribable purity of Nirvana.

Surangama Sutra

This identity out of the One into the One and with the One is the source and fountainhead and breaking forth of glowing Love.

Eckhart

Spiritual progress, as we have had occasion to discover in several other contexts, is always spiral and reciprocal. Peace from distractions and emotional agitations is the way to charity; and charity, or unitive love-knowledge is the way to the higher peace of God. And the same is true of humility, which is the third characteristic mark of charity. Humility is a necessary condition of the highest form of love, and the highest form of love makes possible the consummation of humility in a total self-naughting.

Would you become a pilgrim on the road of Love?
The first condition is that you make yourself
humble as dust and ashes.

Ansari of Herat

I have but one word to say to you concerning love for your neighbour, namely that nothing save humility can mould you to it; nothing but the consciousness of your own weakness can make you indulgent and pitiful to that of others. You will answer, I quite understand that humility should produce forbearance towards others, but

how am I first to acquire humility? Two things combined
will bring that about; you must never separate them. The
first is contemplation of the deep gulf, whence God's all-
powerful hand has drawn you out, and over which he
ever holds you, so to say, suspended. The second is the
presence of that all-penetrating God. It is only in beholding and loving God that we can learn forgetfulness of
self, measure duly the nothingness which has dazzled us,
and accustom ourselves thankfully to decrease beneath
that great Majesty which absorbs all things. Love God
and you will be humble; love God and you will throw off
the love of self; love God and you will love all that He
gives you to love for love of Him.

Fénelon

Feelings, as we have seen, may be of service as motives of
charity; but charity as charity has its beginning in the will—
will to peace and humility in oneself, will to patience and
kindness towards one's fellow creatures, will to that disinterested love of God which "asks nothing and refuses nothing." But the will can be strengthened by exercise and confirmed by perseverance. This is very clearly brought out in
the following record—delightful for its Boswellian vividness
—of a conversation between the young Bishop of Belley and
his beloved friend and master, François de Sales.

I once asked the Bishop of Geneva what one must do to
attain perfection. "You must love God with all your
heart," he answered, "and your neighbour as yourself."

"I did not ask wherein perfection lies," I rejoined, "but
how to attain it." "Charity," he said again, "that is both
the means and the end, the only way by which we can
reach that perfection which is, after all, but Charity itself. . . . Just as the soul is the life of the body, so charity
is the life of the soul."

"I know all that," I said. "But I want to know *how* one
is to love God with all one's heart and one's neighbour as
oneself."

But again he answered, "We must love God with all
our hearts, and our neighbour as ourselves."

"I am no further than I was," I replied. "Tell me how
to acquire such love."

"The best way, the shortest and easiest way of loving God with all one's heart is to love him wholly and heartily!"

He would give no other answer. At last, however, the Bishop said, "There are many besides you who want me to tell them of methods and systems and secret ways of becoming perfect, and I can only tell them that the sole secret is a hearty love of God, and the only way of attaining that love is by loving. You learn to speak by speaking, to study by studying, to run by running, to work by working; and just so you learn to love God and man by loving. All those who think to learn in any other way deceive themselves. If you want to love God, go on loving Him more and more. Begin as a mere apprentice, and the very power of love will lead you on to become a master in the art. Those who have made most progress will continually press on, never believing themselves to have reached their end; for charity should go on increasing until we draw our last breath."

Jean Pierre Camus

The passage from what St. Bernard calls the "carnal love" of the sacred humanity to the spiritual love of the Godhead, from the emotional love that can only unite lover and beloved in act to the perfect charity which unifies them in spiritual substance, is reflected in religious practice as the passage from meditation, discursive and affective, to infused contemplation. All Christian writers insist that the spiritual love of the Godhead is superior to the carnal love of the humanity, which serves as introduction and means to man's final end in unitive love-knowledge of the divine Ground; but all insist no less strongly that carnal love is a necessary introduction and an indispensable means. Oriental writers would agree that this is true for many persons, but not for all, since there are some born contemplatives who are able to "harmonize their starting point with their goal" and to embark directly upon the Yoga of Knowledge. It is from the point of view of the born contemplative that the greatest of Taoist philosophers writes in the following passage.

Those men who in a special way regard Heaven as Father and have, as it were, a personal love for it, how much

more should they love what is above Heaven as Father!
Other men in a special way regard their rulers as better
than themselves and they, as it were, personally die for
them. How much more should they die for what is truer
than a ruler! When the springs dry up, the fish are all
together on dry land. They then moisten each other with
their dampness and keep each other wet with their slime.
But this is not to be compared with forgetting each other
in a river or lake.

Chuang Tzu

The slime of personal and emotional love is remotely similar
to the water of the Godhead's spiritual being, but of inferior
quality and (precisely because the love is emotional and therefore personal) of insufficient quantity. Having, by their voluntary ignorance, wrong-doing and wrong being, caused the
divine springs to dry up, human beings can do something to
mitigate the horrors of their situation by "keeping one another wet with their slime." But there can be no happiness
or safety in time and no deliverance into eternity, until they
give up thinking that slime is enough and, by abandoning
themselves to what is in fact their element, call back the
eternal waters. To those who seek first the Kingdom of God,
all the rest will be added. From those who, like the modern
idolaters of progress, seek first all the rest in the expectation
that (after the harnessing of atomic power and the next revolution but three) the Kingdom of God will be added, everything
will be taken away. And yet we continue to trust in progress,
to regard personal slime as the highest form of spiritual mois-
ture and to prefer an agonizing and impossible existence on
dry land to love, joy and peace in our native ocean.

The sect of lovers is distinct from all others;
Lovers have a religion and a faith all their own.

Jalal-uddin Rumi

The soul lives by that which it loves rather than in the
body which it animates. For it has not its life in the body,
but rather gives it to the body and lives in that which it
loves.

St. John of the Cross

Temperance is love surrendering itself wholly to Him who is its object; courage is love bearing all things gladly for the sake of Him who is its object; justice is love serving only Him who is its object, and therefore rightly ruling; prudence is love making wise distinctions between what hinders and what helps itself.

St. Augustine

The distinguishing marks of charity are disinterestedness, tranquillity and humility. But where there is disinterestedness there is neither greed for personal advantage nor fear for personal loss or punishment; where there is tranquillity, there is neither craving nor aversion, but a steady will to conform to the divine Tao or Logos on every level of existence and a steady awareness of the divine Suchness and what should be one's own relations to it; and where there is humility there is no censoriousness and no glorification of the ego or any projected alter-ego at the expense of others, who are recognized as having the same weaknesses and faults, but also the same capacity for transcending them in the unitive knowledge of God, as one has oneself. From all this it follows that charity is the root and substance of morality, and that where there is little charity there will be much avoidable evil. All this has been summed up in Augustine's formula: "Love, and do what you like." Among the later elaborations of the Augustinian theme we may cite the following from the writings of John Everard, one of those spiritually minded seventeenth-century divines whose teachings fell on the deaf ears of warring factions and, when the revolution and the military dictatorship were at an end, on the even deafer ears of Restoration clergymen and their successors in the Augustan age. (Just how deaf those ears could be we may judge by what Swift wrote of his beloved and morally perfect Houyhnhnms. The subject matter of their conversations, as of their poetry, consisted of such things as "friendship and benevolence, the visible operations of nature or ancient traditions; the bounds and limits of virtue, the unerring rules of reason." Never once do the ideas of God, or charity, or deliverance engage their minds. Which shows sufficiently clearly what the Dean of St. Patrick's thought of the religion by which he made his money.)

Turn the man loose who has found the living Guide within him, and then let him neglect the outward if he can! Just as you would say to a man who loves his wife with all tenderness, "You are at liberty to beat her, hurt her or kill her, if you want to."

John Everard

From this it follows that, where there is charity, there can be no coercion.

God forces no one, for love cannot compel, and God's service, therefore, is a thing of perfect freedom.

Hans Denk

But just because it cannot compel, charity has a kind of authority, a non-coercive power, by means of which it defends itself and gets its beneficent will done in the world—not always, of course, not inevitably or automatically (for individuals and, still more, organizations can be impenetrably armoured against divine influence), but in a surprisingly large number of cases.

Heaven arms with pity those whom it would not see destroyed.

Lao Tzu

"He abused me, he beat me, he defeated me, he robbed me"—in those who harbour such thoughts hatred will never cease.

"He abused me, he beat me, he defeated me, he robbed me"—in those who do not harbour such thoughts hatred will cease.

For hatred does not cease by hatred at any time—this is an old rule.

Dhammapada

Our present economic, social and international arrangements are based, in large measure, upon organized lovelessness. We begin by lacking charity towards Nature, so that instead of trying to co-operate with Tao or the Logos on the inanimate and subhuman levels, we try to dominate and exploit, we waste the earth's mineral resources, ruin its soil, ravage its forests, pour filth into its rivers and poisonous fumes into its air. From lovelessness in relation to Nature we advance to lovelessness in relation to art—a lovelessness so extreme that we have effectively killed all the fundamental or useful arts and set up various kinds of mass production by machines in their place. And of course this lovelessness in regard to art is at the same time a lovelessness in regard to the human beings who have to perform the fool-proof and grace-proof tasks imposed by our mechanical art-surrogates and by the interminable paper work connected with mass production and mass distribution. With mass-production and mass-distribution go mass-financing, and the three have conspired to expropriate ever-increasing numbers of small owners of land and productive equipment, thus reducing the sum of freedom among the majority and increasing the power of a minority to exercise a coercive control over the lives of their fellows. This coercively controlling minority is composed of private capitalists or governmental bureaucrats or of both classes of bosses acting in collaboration—and, of course, the coercive and therefore essentially loveless nature of the control remains the same, whether the bosses call themselves "company directors" or "civil servants." The only difference between these two kinds of oligarchical rulers is that the first derive more of their power from wealth than from position within a conventionally respected hierarchy, while the second derive more power from position than from wealth. Upon this fairly uniform groundwork of loveless relationships are imposed others, which vary widely from one society to another, according to local conditions and local habits of thought and feeling. Here are a few examples: contempt and exploitation of coloured minorities living among white majorities, or of coloured majorities governed by minorities of white imperialists; hatred of Jews, Catholics, Free Masons or of any other minority whose language, habits, appearance or religion happens to differ from those of the local majority. And the crowning superstructure of uncharity is the organized lovelessness of the relations between state and sovereign state—a lovelessness that expresses itself in the axiomatic assumption that it is right and natural for national organizations to behave like thieves and murderers, armed to the teeth and ready, at the first favourable opportunity, to steal and kill. (Just how axiomatic is this assumption about the nature of nationhood is shown by the history of Central America. So long as the arbitrarily delimited territories of Central America were called provinces of the Spanish colonial empire, there was peace between their inhabitants. But early in the nineteenth century the various administrative districts of the Spanish empire broke from their allegiance to the "mother country" and decided to become nations on the European model. Result: they immediately went to war with one another. Why? Because, by definition, a sovereign national state is an organization that has the right and duty to coerce its members to steal and kill on the largest possible scale.)

"Lead us not into temptation" must be the guiding principle of all social organization, and the temptations to be guarded against and, so far as possible, eliminated by means of appropriate economic and political arrangements are temptations against charity, that is to say, against the disinterested love of God, Nature and man. First, the dissemination and general acceptance of any form of the Perennial Philosophy will do something to preserve men and women from the temptation to idolatrous worship of things in time—church-worship, state-worship, revolutionary future-worship, humanistic self-worship, all of them essentially and necessarily opposed to charity. Next come decentralization, widespread private ownership of land and the means of production on a small scale, discouragement of monopoly by state or corporation, division of economic and political power (the only guarantee, as Lord Acton was never tired of insisting, of civil liberty under law). These social rearrangements would do much to prevent ambitious individuals, organizations and governments from being led into the temptation of behaving tyrannously; while co-operatives, democratically controlled professional organizations and town meetings would deliver the masses of the people from the temptation of making their decentralized individualism too rugged. But of course none of these intrinsically desirable reforms can possibly be carried out, so long as it is thought right and natural that sovereign states should prepare to make war on one another. For modern war cannot be waged except by countries with an over-developed capital goods industry; countries in which economic power is wielded either by the state or by a few monopolistic corporations which it is easy to tax and, if necessary, temporarily to nationalize; countries where the labouring masses, being without property, are rootless, easily transferable from one place to another, highly regimented by factory discipline. Any decentralized society of free, uncoerced small owners, with a properly balanced economy must, in a war-making world such as ours, be at the mercy of one whose production is highly mechanized and centralized, whose people are without property and therefore easily coercible, and whose economy is lop-sided. This is why the one desire of industrially undeveloped countries like Mexico and China is to become like Germany, or England, or the United States. So long as the organized lovelessness of war and preparation for war remains, there can be no mitigation, on any large, nation-wide or world-wide scale, of the organized lovelessness of our economic and political relationships. War and preparation for war are standing temptations to make the present bad, God-eclipsing arrangements of society progressively worse as technology becomes progressively more efficient.

CHAPTER VI

Mortification, Non-Attachment, Right Livelihood

> This treasure of the Kingdom of God has been hidden by time and multiplicity and the soul's own works, or briefly by its creaturely nature. But in the measure that the soul can separate itself from this multiplicity, to that extent it reveals within itself the Kingdom of God. Here the soul and the Godhead are one.
>
> *Eckhart*

"Our kingdom go" is the necessary and unavoidable corollary of "Thy kingdom come." For the more there is of self, the less there is of God. The divine eternal fulness of life can be gained only by those who have deliberately lost the partial, separative life of craving and self-interest, of egocentric thinking, feeling, wishing and acting. Mortification or deliberate dying to self is inculcated with an uncompromising firmness in the canonical writings of Christianity, Hinduism, Buddhism and most of the other major and minor religions of the world, and by every theocentric saint and spiritual reformer who has ever lived out and expounded the principles of the Perennial Philosophy. But this "self-naughting" is never (at least by anyone who knows what he is talking about) regarded as an end in itself. It possesses merely an instrumental value, as the indispensable means to something else. In the words of one whom we have often had occasion to cite in earlier sections, it is necessary for all of us to "learn the true nature and worth of all self-denials and mortifications."

As to their nature, considered in themselves, they have nothing of goodness or holiness, nor are any real part of our sanctification, they are not the true food or nourishment of the Divine Life in our souls, they have no quickening, sanctifying power in them; their only worth consists in this, that they remove the impediments of holiness, break down that which stands between God and us, and make way for the quickening, sanctifying spirit of God to operate on our souls, which operation of God is the one only thing that can raise the Divine Life in the soul, or help it to the smallest degree of real holiness or spiritual life. . . . Hence we may learn the reason why many people not only lose the benefit, but are even the worse for all their mortifications. It is because they mistake the whole nature and worth of them. They practice them for their own sakes, as things good in themselves; they think them to be real parts of holiness, and so rest in them and look no further, but grow full of self-esteem and self-admiration for their own progress in them. This makes them self-sufficient, morose, severe judges of all those that fall short of their mortifications. And thus their self-denials do only that for them which indulgences do for other people: they withstand and hinder the operation of God upon their souls, and instead of being really self-denials, they strengthen and keep up the kingdom of self.

William Law

The rout and destruction of the passions, while a good, is not the ultimate good; the discovery of Wisdom is the surpassing good. When this is found, all the people will sing.

Philo

Living in religion (as I can speak by experience) if one is not in a right course of prayer and other exercises between God and our soul, one's nature groweth much worse than ever it would have been, if one had lived in the world. For pride and self-love, which are rooted in the soul by sin, find means to strengthen themselves exceedingly in religion, if the soul is not in a course that may teach her and procure her true humility. For by the corrections and contradictions of the will (which cannot be avoided by any living in a religious community) I find my heart grown, as I may say, as hard as a stone; and nothing would have been able to soften it but by being put into a course of prayer, by which the soul tendeth towards God and learneth of Him the lesson of truly humbling herself.

Dame Gertrude More

Once, when I was grumbling over being obliged to eat meat and do no penance, I heard it said that sometimes there was more of self-love than desire of penance in such sorrow.

St. Teresa

That the mortified are, in some respects, often much worse than the unmortified is a commonplace of history, fiction and descriptive psychology. Thus, the Puritan may practice all the cardinal virtues—prudence, fortitude, temperance and chastity—and yet remain a thoroughly bad man; for, in all too many cases, these virtues of his are accompanied by, and indeed causally connected with, the sins of pride, envy, chronic anger and an uncharitableness pushed sometimes to the level of active cruelty. Mistaking the means for the end, the Puritan has fancied himself holy because he is stoically austere. But stoical austerity is merely the exaltation of the more creditable side of the ego at the expense of the less creditable. Holiness, on the contrary, is the total denial of the separative self, in its creditable no less than its discreditable aspects, and the abandonment of the will to God. To the extent that there is attachment to "I," "me," "mine," there is no attachment to, and therefore no unitive knowledge of, the divine Ground. Mortification has to be carried to the pitch of non-attachment or (in the phrase of St. François de Sales) "holy indifference"; otherwise it merely transfers self-will from one channel to another, not merely without decrease in the total volume of that self-will, but sometimes with an actual increase. As usual, the corruption of the best is the worst. The difference between the mortified, but still proud and self-centred stoic and the unmortified hedonist consists in this: the latter, being flabby, shiftless and at heart rather ashamed of himself, lacks the energy and the motive to do much harm except to his own body, mind and spirit; the former, because he has all the secondary virtues and looks down on those who are not like himself, is morally equipped to wish and to be able to do harm on the very largest scale and with a perfectly untroubled conscience. These are obvious facts; and yet, in the current religious jargon of our day the word "immoral" is reserved almost exclusively for the carnally self-indulgent. The covetous and the ambitious, the respectable toughs and those who cloak their lust for power and place under the right sort of idealistic cant, are not merely unblamed; they are even held up as models of virtue and godliness. The representatives of the organized churches begin by putting haloes on the heads of the people who do most to make wars and revolutions, then go on, rather plaintively, to wonder why the world should be in such a mess.

Mortification is not, as many people seem to imagine, a matter, primarily, of severe physical austerities. It is possible that, for certain persons in certain circumstances, the practice of severe physical austerities may prove helpful in advance towards man's final end. In most cases, however, it would seem that what is gained by such austerities is not liberation, but something quite different—the achievement of "psychic" powers. The ability to get petitionary prayer answered, the power to heal and work other miracles, the knack of looking into the future or into other people's minds—these, it would seem, are often related in some kind of causal connection with fasting, watching and the self-infliction of pain. Most of the great theocentric saints and spiritual teachers have admitted the existence of supernormal powers, only, however, to deplore them. To think that such *Siddhis*, as the Indians call them, have anything to do with liberation is, they say, a dangerous illusion. These things are either irrelevant to the main issue of life, or, if too much prized and attended to, an obstacle in the way of spiritual advance. Nor are these the only objections to physical austerities. Carried to extremes, they may be dangerous to health—and without health the steady persistence of effort required by the spiritual life is very difficult of achievement. And being difficult, painful and generally conspicuous, physical austerities are a standing temptation to vanity and the competitive spirit of record breaking. "When thou didst give thyself up to physical mortification, thou wast great, thou wast admired." So writes Suso of his own experiences—experiences which led him, just as Gautama Buddha had been led many centuries before, to give up his course of bodily penance. And St. Teresa remarks how much easier it is to impose great penances upon oneself than to suffer in patience, charity and humbleness the ordinary everyday crosses of family life (which did not prevent her, incidentally, from practising, to the very day of her death, the most excruciating forms of self-torture. Whether these austerities really helped her to come to the unitive knowledge of God, or whether they were prized and persisted in because of the psychic powers they helped to develop, there is no means of determining).

Our dear Saint (François de Sales) disapproved of immoderate fasting. He used to say that the spirit could not endure the body when overfed, but that, if underfed, the body could not endure the spirit.

Jean Pierre Camus

When the will, the moment it feels any joy in sensible things rises upwards in that joy to God, and when sensible things move it to pray, it should not neglect them, it should make use of them for so holy an exercise; because sensible things, in these conditions, subserve the end for which God created them, namely to be occasions for making Him better known and loved.

St. John of the Cross

He who is not conscious of liberty of spirit among the things of sense and sweetness—things which should serve as motives to prayer—and whose will rests and feeds upon them, ought to abstain from the use of them; for to him they are a hindrance on the road to God.

St. John of the Cross

One man may declare that he cannot fast; but can he declare that he cannot love God? Another may affirm that he cannot preserve virginity or sell all his goods in order to give the price to the poor; but can he tell me that he cannot love his enemies? All that is necessary is to look into one's own heart; for what God asks of us is not found at a great distance.

St. Jerome

Anybody who wishes to do so can get all, and indeed more than all, the mortification he wants out of the incidents of ordinary, day-to-day living, without ever resorting to harsh bodily penance. Here are the rules laid down by the author of *Holy Wisdom* for Dame Gertrude More.

First, that she should do all that belonged to her to do by any law, human or Divine. Secondly, that she was to refrain from doing those things that were forbidden her by human or Divine Law, or by Divine inspiration. Thirdly, that she should bear with as much patience or resignation as possible all crosses and contradictions to her natural will, which were inflicted by the hand of God. Such, for instance, were aridities, temptations, afflictions or bodily pain, sickness and infirmity; or again, the loss of friends or want of necessaries and comforts. All this was to be endured patiently, whether the crosses came direct from God or by means of His creatures. . . . These indeed were mortifications enough for Dame Gertrude, or for any other soul, and there was no need for anyone to advise or impose others.

Augustine Baker

To sum up, that mortification is the best which results in the elimination of self-will, self-interest, self-centred thinking, wishing and imagining. Extreme physical austerities are not likely to achieve this kind of mortification. But the acceptance of what happens to us (apart, of course, from our own sins) in the course of daily living *is* likely to produce this result. If specific exercises in self-denial are undertaken, they should be inconspicuous, non-competitive and uninjurious to health. Thus, in the matter of diet, most people will find it sufficiently mortifying to refrain from eating all the things which the experts in nutrition condemn as unwholesome. And where social relations are concerned, self-denial should take the form, not of showy acts of would-be humility, but of control of the tongue and the moods—in refraining from saying anything uncharitable or merely frivolous (which means, in practice, refraining from about fifty per cent of ordinary conversation), and in behaving calmly and with quiet cheerfulness when external circumstances or the state of our bodies predisposes us to anxiety, gloom or an excessive elation.

> When a man practises charity in order to be reborn in heaven, or for fame, or reward, or from fear, such charity can obtain no pure effect.
>
> *Sutra on the Distinction and Protection of the Dharma*

> When Prince Wen Wang was on a tour of inspection in Tsang, he saw an old man fishing. But his fishing was not real fishing, for he did not fish in order to catch fish, but to amuse himself. So Wen Wang wished to employ him in the administration of government, but feared lest his own ministers, uncles and brothers might object. On the other hand, if he let the old man go, he could not bear to think of the people being deprived of such an influence.
>
> *Chuang Tzu*

> God, if I worship Thee in fear of hell, burn me in hell. And if I worship Thee in hope of Paradise, exclude me from Paradise; but if I worship Thee for Thine own sake, withhold not Thine everlasting Beauty.
>
> *Rabi'a*

Rabi'a, the Sufi woman-saint, speaks, thinks and feels in terms of devotional theism; the Buddhist theologian, in terms of impersonal moral Law; the Chinese philosopher, with characteristic humour, in terms of politics; but all three insist on the need for non-attachment to self-interest—insist on it as strongly as does Christ when he reproaches the Pharisees for their egocentric piety, as does the Krishna of the Bhagavad Gita, when he tells Arjuna to do his divinely ordained duty without personal craving for, or fear of, the fruits of his actions.

St. Ignatius Loyola was once asked what his feelings would be if the Pope were to suppress the Company of Jesus. "A quarter of an hour of prayer," he answered, "and I should think no more about it."

This is, perhaps, the most difficult of all mortifications—to achieve a "holy indifference" to the temporal success or failure of the cause to which one has devoted one's best energies. If it triumphs, well and good; and if it meets defeat, that also is well and good, if only in ways that, to a limited and time-bound mind, are here and now entirely incomprehensible.

By a man without passions I mean one who does not permit good or evil to disturb his inward economy, but rather falls in with what happens and does not add to the sum of his mortality.

Chuang Tzu

The fitting disposition for union with God is not that the soul should understand, feel, taste or imagine anything on the subject of the nature of God, or any other thing whatever, but should remain in that pureness and love which is perfect resignation and complete detachment from all things for God alone.

St. John of the Cross

Disquietude is always vanity, because it serves no good. Yes, even if the whole world were thrown into confusion and all things in it, disquietude on that account would be vanity.

St. John of the Cross

Sufficient not only unto the day, but also unto the place, is the evil thereof. Agitation over happenings which we are powerless to modify, either because they have not yet occurred, or else are occurring at an inaccessible distance from us, achieves nothing beyond the inoculation of here and now with the remote or anticipated evil that is the object of our distress. Listening four or five times a day to newscasters and commentators, reading the morning papers and all the weeklies and monthlies—nowadays, this is described as "taking an intelligent interest in politics." St. John of the Cross would have called it indulgence in idle curiosity and the cultivation of disquietude for disquietude's sake.

I want very little, and what I do want I have very little wish for. I have hardly any desires, but if I were to be born again, I should have none at all. We should ask nothing and refuse nothing, but leave ourselves in the arms of divine Providence without wasting time in any desire, except to will what God wills of us.

St. François de Sales

Push far enough towards the Void,
Hold fast enough to Quietness,
And of the ten thousand things none but can be worked
    on by you.
I have beheld them, whither they go back.
See, all things howsoever they flourish
Return to the root from which they grew.
This return to the root is called Quietness;
Quietness is called submission to Fate;
What has submitted to Fate becomes part of the always-so;
To know the always-so is to be illumined;
Not to know it means to go blindly to disaster.

Lao Tzu

I wish I could join the 'Solitaries' (on Caldey Island), instead of being Superior and having to write books. But I don't wish to have what I wish, of course.

Abbot John Chapman

We must not wish anything other than what happens from moment to moment, all the while, however, exercising ourselves in goodness.

St. Catherine of Genoa

In the practice of mortification as in most other fields, advance is along a knife-edge. On one side lurks the Scylla of egocentric austerity, on the other the Charybdis of an uncaring quietism. The holy indifference inculcated by the exponents of the Perennial Philosophy is neither stoicism nor mere passivity. It is rather an active resignation. Self-will is renounced, not that there may be a total holiday from willing, but that the divine will may use the mortified mind and body as its instrument for good. Or we may say, with Kabir, that "the devout seeker is he who mingles in his heart the double currents of love and detachment, like the mingling of the streams of Ganges and Jumna." Until we put an end to particular attachments, there can be no love of God with the whole heart, mind and strength and no universal charity towards all creatures for God's sake. Hence the hard sayings in the Gospels about the need to renounce exclusive family ties. And if the Son of Man has nowhere to lay his head, if the Tathagata and the Bodhisattvas "have their thoughts awakened to the nature of Reality without abiding in anything whatever," this is because a truly Godlike love which, like the sun, shines equally upon the just and the unjust, is impossible to a mind imprisoned in private preferences and aversions.

The soul that is attached to anything, however much good there may be in it, will not arrive at the liberty of divine union. For whether it be a strong wire rope or a slender and delicate thread that holds the bird, it matters not, if it really holds it fast; for, until the cord be broken, the bird cannot fly. So the soul, held by the bonds of human affections, however slight they may be, cannot, while they last, make its way to God.

St. John of the Cross

There are some who are newly delivered from their sins and so, though they are resolved to love God, they are still novices and apprentices, soft and weak. . . . They love a number of superfluous, vain and dangerous things at the same time as Our Lord. Though they love God above all things, they yet continue to take pleasure in many things which they do not love according to God, but besides Him—things such as slight inordinations in word, gesture, clothing, pastimes and frivolities.

St. François de Sales

There are souls who have made some progress in divine love, and have cut off all the love they had for dangerous things; yet they still have dangerous and superfluous loves, because they love what God wills them to love, but with

excess and too tender and passionate a love. . . . The love
of our relations, friends and benefactors is itself according
to God, but we may love them excessively; as also our
vocations, however spiritual they be; and our devotional
exercises (which we should yet love very greatly) may be
loved inordinately, when we set them above obedience
and the more general good, or care for them as an end,
when they are only means.

St. François de Sales

The goods of God, which are beyond all measure, can
only be contained in an empty and solitary heart.

St. John of the Cross

Suppose a boat is crossing a river and another boat, an
empty one, is about to collide with it. Even an irritable
man would not lose his temper. But suppose there was
someone in the second boat. Then the occupant of the
first would shout to him to keep clear. And if he did not
hear the first time, nor even when called to three times,
bad language would inevitably follow. In the first case
there was no anger, in the second there was—because in
the first case the boat was empty, in the second it was
occupied. And so it is with man. If he could only pass
empty through life, who would be able to injure him?

Chuang Tzu

When the heart weeps for what it has lost, the spirit
laughs for what it has found.

Anonymous Sufi Aphorism

It is by losing the egocentric life that we save the hitherto
latent and undiscovered life which, in the spiritual part of
our being, we share with the divine Ground. This new-found
life is "more abundant" than the other, and of a different and
higher kind. Its possession is liberation into the eternal, and
liberation is beatitude. Necessarily so; for the Brahman, who
is one with the Atman, is not only Being and Knowledge, but
also Bliss, and, after Love and Peace, the final fruit of the
Spirit is Joy. Mortification is painful, but that pain is one of
the pre-conditions of blessedness. This fact of spiritual experience is sometimes obscured by the language in which it is
described. Thus, when Christ says that the Kingdom of

Heaven cannot be entered except by those who are as little children, we are apt to forget (so touching are the images evoked by the simple phrase) that a man cannot become childlike unless he chooses to undertake the most strenuous and searching course of self-denial. In practice the command to become as little children is identical with the command to lose one's life. As Traherne makes clear in the beautiful passage quoted in the section on "God in the World," one cannot know created Nature in all its essentially sacred beauty, unless one first unlearns the dirty devices of adult humanity. Seen through the dung-coloured spectacles of self-interest, the universe looks singularly like a dung-heap; and as, through long wearing, the spectacles have grown on to the eyeballs, the process of "cleansing the doors of perception" is often, at any rate in the earlier stages of the spiritual life, painfully like a surgical operation. Later on, it is true, even self-naughting may be suffused with the joy of the Spirit. On this point the following passage from the fourteenth-century *Scale of Perfection* is illuminating.

Many a man hath the virtues of humility, patience and charity towards his neighbours, only in the reason and will, and hath no spiritual delight nor love in them; for ofttimes he feeleth grudging, heaviness and bitterness for to do them, but yet nevertheless he doth them, but 'tis only by stirring of reason for dread of God. This man hath these virtues in reason and will, but not the love of them in affection. But when, by the grace of Jesus and by ghostly and bodily exercise, reason is turned into light and will into love, then hath he virtues in affection; for he hath so gnawn on the bitter bark or shell of the nut that at length he hath broken it and now feeds on the kernel; that is to say, the virtues which were first heavy for to practise are now turned into a very delight and savour.

Walter Hilton

As long as I am this or that, or have this or that, I am not all things and I have not all things. Become pure till you neither are nor have either this or that; then you are omnipresent and, being neither this nor that, are all things.

Eckhart

The point so dramatically emphasized by Eckhart in these lines is one that has often been made by the moralists and psychologists of the spiritual life. It is only when we have renounced our preoccupation with "I," "me," "mine" that we can truly possess the world in which we live. Everything is ours, provided that we regard nothing as our property. And not only is everything ours; it is also everybody else's.

> True love in this differs from dross and clay,
>   That to divide is not to take away.

There can be no complete communism except in the goods of the spirit and, to some extent also, of the mind, and only when such goods are possessed by men and women in a state of non-attachment and self-denial. Some degree of mortification, it should be noted, is an indispensable prerequisite for the creation and enjoyment even of merely intellectual and aesthetic goods. Those who choose the profession of artist, philosopher, or man of science, choose, in many cases, a life of poverty and unrewarded hard work. But these are by no means the only mortifications they have to undertake. When he looks at the world, the artist must deny his ordinary human tendency to think of things in utilitarian, self-regarding terms. Similarly, the critical philosopher must mortify his common-sense, while the research worker must steadfastly resist the temptations to over-simplify and think conventionally, and must make himself docile to the leadings of mysterious Fact. And what is true of the creators of aesthetic and intellectual goods is also true of the enjoyers of such goods, when created. That these mortifications are by no means trifling has been shown again and again in the course of history. One thinks, for example, of the intellectually mortified Socrates and the hemlock with which his unmortified compatriots rewarded him. One thinks of the heroic efforts that had to be made by Galileo and his contemporaries to break with the Aristotelian convention of thought, and the no less heroic efforts that have to be made today by any scientist who believes that there is more in the universe than can be discovered by employing the time-hallowed recipes of Descartes. Such mortifications have their reward in a state of consciousness that corresponds, on a lower level, to spiritual beatitude. The artist—and the philosopher and the man of science are also artists—knows the bliss of aesthetic contemplation, discovery and non-attached possession.

The goods of the intellect, the emotions and the imagination are real goods; but they are not the final good, and when we treat them as ends in themselves, we fall into idolatry. Mortification of will, desire and action is not enough; there must also be mortification in the fields of knowing, thinking, feeling and fancying.

> Man's intellectual faculties are by the Fall in a much worse state than his animal appetites and want a much greater self-denial. And when own will, own understanding and own imagination have their natural strength indulged and gratified, and are made seemingly rich and honourable with the treasures acquired from a study of the *Belles Lettres*, they will just as much help poor fallen man to be like-minded with Christ as the art of cookery, well and duly studied, will help a professor of the Gospel to the spirit and practise of Christian abstinence.
>
> *William Law*

Because it was German and spelt with a *K*, *Kultur* was an object, during the first World War, of derisive contempt. All this has now been changed. In Russia, Literature, Art and Science have become the three persons of a new humanistic Trinity. Nor is the cult of Culture confined to the Soviet Union. It is practised by a majority of intellectuals in the capitalist democracies. Clever, hard-boiled journalists, who write about everything else with the condescending cynicism of people who know all about God, Man and the Universe, and have seen through the whole absurd caboodle, fairly fall over themselves when it comes to Culture. With an earnestness and enthusiasm that are, in the circumstances, unutterably ludicrous, they invite us to share their positively religious emotions in the face of High Art, as represented by the latest murals or civic centres; they insist that so long as Mrs. X. goes on writing her inimitable novels and Mr. Y. his more than Coleridgean criticism, the world, in spite of all appearances to the contrary, makes sense. The same overvaluation of Culture, the same belief that Art and Literature are ends in themselves and can flourish in isolation from a reasonable and realistic philosophy of life, have even invaded the schools and colleges. Among "advanced" educationists there are many people who seem to think that all will be well, so long as adolescents are permitted to "express themselves," and small children are encouraged to be "creative" in the art class. But, alas, plasticine and self-expression will not solve the problems of education. Nor will technology and vocational guidance; nor the classics and the Hundred Best Books. The following criticisms of education were made more than two and a half centuries ago; but they are as relevant today as they were in the seventeenth century.

> He knoweth nothing as he ought to know, who thinks he knoweth anything without seeing its place and the manner how it relateth to God, angels and men, and to all the creatures in earth, heaven and hell, time and eternity.
>
> *Thomas Traherne*

> Nevertheless some things were defective too (at Oxford under the Commonwealth). There was never a tutor that did professly teach Felicity, though that be the mistress of all the other sciences. Nor did any of us study these things but as *aliens*, which we ought to have studied as our own enjoyments. We studied to inform our knowledge, but knew not for what end we studied. And for lack of aiming at a certain end, we erred in the manner.
>
> *Thomas Traherne*

In Traherne's vocabulary "felicity" means "beatitude," which is identical in practice with liberation, which, in its turn, is the unitive knowledge of God in the heights within and in the fulness without as well as within.

What follows is an account of the intellectual mortifications which must be practised by those whose primary concern is with the knowledge of the Godhead in the interior heights of the soul.

> Happy is the man who, by continually effacing all images and through introversion and the lifting up of his mind to God, at last forgets and leaves behind all such hindrances. For by such means only, he operates inwardly, with his naked, pure, simple intellect and affections, about

the most pure and simple object, God. Therefore see that thy whole exercise about God within thee may depend wholly and only on that naked intellect, affection and will. For indeed, this exercise cannot be discharged by any bodily organ, or by the external senses, but only by that which constitutes the essence of man—understanding and love. If, therefore, thou desirest a safe stair and short path to arrive at the end of true bliss, then, with an intent mind, earnestly desire and aspire after continual cleanness of heart and purity of mind. Add to this a constant calm and tranquillity of the senses, and a recollecting of the affections of the heart, continually fixing them above. Work to simplify the heart, that being immovable and at peace from any invadi g vain phantasms, thou mayest always stand fast in the Lord within thee, to that degree as if thy soul had already entered the always present now of eternity—that is, the state of the deity. To mount to God is to enter into oneself. For he who so mounts and enters and goes above and beyond himself, he truly mounts up to God. The mind must then raise itself above itself and say, "He who above all I need is above all I know." And so carried into the darkness of the mind, gathering itself into that all-sufficient good, it learns to stay at home and with its whole affection it cleaves and becomes habitually fixed in the supreme good within. Thus continue, until thou becomest immutable and dost arrive at that true life which is God Himself, perpetually, without any vicissitude of space or time, reposing in that inward quiet and secret mansion of the deity.

Albertus Magnus (?)

Some men love knowledge and discernment as the best and most excellent of all things. Behold, then knowledge and discernment come to be loved more than that which is discerned; for the false natural light loveth its knowledge and powers, which are itself, more than what is known. And were it possible that this false natural light should understand the simple Truth, as it is in God and in truth, it still would not lose its own property, that is, it could not depart from itself and its own things.

Theologia Germanica

The relationship between moral action and spiritual knowledge is circular, as it were, and reciprocal. Selfless behaviour makes possible an accession of knowledge, and the accession of knowledge makes possible the performance of further and more genuinely selfless actions, which in their turn enhance the agent's capacity for knowing. And so on, if all goes well and there is perfect docility and obedience, indefinitely. The process is summed up in a few lines of the Maitrayana Upanishad. A man undertakes right action (which includes, of course, right recollectedness and right meditation), and this enables him to catch a glimpse of the Self that underlies his separate individuality. "Having seen his own self as the Self, he becomes selfless (and therefore acts selflessly) and in virtue of selflessness he is to be conceived as unconditioned. This is the highest mystery, betokening emancipation; through selflessness he has no part in pleasure or pain (in other words, he enters a state of non-attachment or holy indifference), but achieves absoluteness" (or as Albertus Magnus phrases it, "becomes immutable and arrives at that true life which is God Himself").

When mortification is perfect, its most characteristic fruit is simplicity.

> A simple heart will love all that is most precious on earth, husband or wife, parent or child, brother or friend, without marring its singleness; external things will have no attraction save inasmuch as they lead souls to Him; all exaggeration or unreality, affectation and falsehood must pass away from such a one, as the dews dry up before the sunshine. The single motive is to please God, and hence arises total indifference as to what others say and think, so that words and actions are perfectly simple and natural, as in his sight only. Such Christian simplicity is the very perfection of interior life—God, his will and pleasure, its sole object.
>
> N. Grou

And here is a more extended account of the matter by one of the greatest masters of psychological analysis.

> In the world, when people call anyone simple, they generally mean a foolish, ignorant, credulous person. But

real simplicity, so far from being foolish, is almost sub-
lime. All good men like and admire it, are conscious of
sinning against it, observe it in others and know what it
involves; and yet they could not precisely define it. I
should say that simplicity is an uprightness of soul which
prevents self-consciousness. It is not the same as sincerity,
which is a much humbler virtue. Many people are sincere
who are not simple. They say nothing but what they
believe to be true, and do not aim at appearing anything
but what they are. But they are for ever thinking about
themselves, weighing their every word and thought, and
dwelling upon themselves in apprehension of having done
too much or too little. These people are sincere but they
are not simple. They are not at their ease with others, nor
others with them. There is nothing easy, frank, unrestrained or natural about them. One feels that one would
like less admirable people better, who were not so stiff.

To be absorbed in the world around and never turn
a thought within, as is the blind condition of some who
are carried away by what is pleasant and tangible, is one
extreme as opposed to simplicity. And to be self-absorbed
in all matters, whether it be duty to God or man, is the
other extreme, which makes a person wise in his own
conceit—reserved, self-conscious, uneasy at the least thing
which disturbs his inward self-complacency. Such false
wisdom, in spite of its solemnity, is hardly less vain and
foolish than the folly of those who plunge headlong into
worldly pleasures. The one is intoxicated by his outward
surroundings, the other by what he believes himself to be
doing inwardly; but both are in a state of intoxication,
and the last is a worse state than the first, because it seems
to be wise, though it is not really, and so people do not
try to be cured. Real simplicity lies in a *juste milieu*
equally free from thoughtlessness and affectation, in which
the soul is not overwhelmed by externals, so as to be
unable to reflect, nor yet given up to the endless refine-
ments, which self-consciousness induces. That soul which
looks where it is going without losing time arguing over
every step, or looking back perpetually, possesses true
simplicity. Such simplicity is indeed a great treasure. How
shall we attain to it? I would give all I possess for it; it is
the costly pearl of Holy Scripture.

The first step, then, is for the soul to put away outward things and look within so as to know its own real interest; so far all is right and natural; thus much is only a wise self-love, which seeks to avoid the intoxication of the world.

In the next step the soul must add the contemplation of God, whom it fears, to that of self. This is a faint approach to the real wisdom, but the soul is still greatly self-absorbed: it is not satisfied with fearing God; it wants to be certain that it does fear him and fears lest it fear him not, going round in a perpetual circle of self-consciousness. All this restless dwelling on self is very far from the peace and freedom of real love; but that is yet in the distance; the soul must needs go through a season of trial, and were it suddenly plunged into a state of rest, it would not know how to use it.

The third step is that, ceasing from a restless self-contemplation, the soul begins to dwell upon God instead, and by degrees forgets itself in Him. It becomes full of Him and ceases to feed upon self. Such a soul is not blinded to its own faults or indifferent to its own errors; it is more conscious of them than ever, and increased light shows them in plainer form, but this self-knowledge comes from God, and therefore it is not restless or uneasy.

Fénelon

How admirably acute and subtle this is! One of the most extraordinary, because most gratuitous, pieces of twentieth-century vanity is the assumption that nobody knew anything about psychology before the days of Freud. But the real truth is that most modern psychologists understand human beings less well than did the ablest of their predecessors. Fénelon and La Rochefoucauld knew all about the surface rationalization of deep, discreditable motives in the subconscious, and were fully aware that sexuality and the will to power were, all too often, the effective forces at work under the polite mask of the *persona*. Machiavelli had drawn Pareto's distinction between "residues" and "derivations"—between the real, self-interested motives for political action and the fancy theories, principles and ideals in terms of which such action is explained and justified to the credulous public. Like Buddha's and St. Augustine's, Pascal's view of human virtue and rationality could not have been more realistically low. But all these men, even La Rochefoucauld, even Machiavelli, were aware of certain facts which twentieth-century psychologists have chosen to ignore—the fact that human nature is tripartite, consisting of a spirit as well as of a mind and body; the fact that we live on the border-line between two worlds, the temporal and the eternal, the physical-vital-human and the divine; the fact that, though nothing in himself, man is "a nothing surrounded by God, indigent of God, capable of God and filled with God, if he so desires."

The Christian simplicity, of which Grou and Fénelon write, is the same thing as the virtue so much admired by Lao Tzu and his successors. According to these Chinese sages, personal sins and social maladjustments are all due to the fact that men have separated themselves from their divine source and live according to their own will and notions, not according to Tao—which is the Great Way, the Logos, the Nature of Things, as it manifests itself on every plane from the physical, up through the animal and the mental, to the spiritual. Enlightenment comes when we give up self-will and make ourselves docile to the workings of Tao in the world around us and in our own bodies, minds and spirits. Sometimes the Taoist philosophers write as though they believed in Rousseau's Noble Savage, and (being Chinese and therefore much more concerned with the concrete and the practical than with the merely speculative) they are fond of prescribing methods by which rulers may reduce the complexity of civilization and so preserve their subjects from the corrupting influences of man-made and therefore Tao-eclipsing conventions of thought, feeling and action. But the rulers who are to perform this task for the masses must themselves be sages; and to become a sage, one must get rid of all the rigidities of unregenerate adulthood and become again as a little child. For only that which is soft and docile is truly alive; that which conquers and outlives everything is that which adapts itself to everything, that which always seeks the lowest place—not the hard rock, but the water that wears away the everlasting hills. The simplicity and spontaneity of the perfect sage are the fruits of mortification—mortification of the will and, by recollectedness and meditation, of the mind. Only the most highly disciplined artist can recapture, on a higher level, the spontaneity of the child with its first paint-box. Nothing is more difficult than to be simple.

> "May I ask," said Yen Hui, "in what consists the fasting of the heart?"
>
> "Cultivate unity," replied Confucius. "You do your hearing, not with your ears, but with your mind; not with your mind, but with your very soul. But let the hearing stop with the ears. Let the working of the mind stop with itself. Then the soul will be a negative existence, passively responsive to externals. In such a negative existence, only Tao can abide. And that negative state is the fasting of the heart."
>
> "Then," said Yen Hui, "the reason I could not get the use of this method is my own individuality. If I could get the use of it, my individuality would have gone. Is this what you mean by the negative state?"
>
> "Exactly so," replied the Master. "Let me tell you. If you can enter the domain of this prince (a bad ruler whom Yen Hui was ambitious to reform) without offending his *amour propre*, cheerful if he hears you, passive if he does not; without science, without drugs, simply living there in a state of complete indifference—you will be near success. . . . Look at that window. Through it an empty room becomes bright with scenery; but the landscape stops outside. In this sense you may use your ears and eyes to communicate within, but shut out all wisdom (in the sense of conventional, copybook maxims) from your mind. This is the method for regenerating all creation."

> *Chuang Tzu*

Mortification may be regarded, in this context, as the process of study, by which we learn at last to have unstudied reactions to events—reactions in harmony with Tao, Suchness, the Will of God. Those who have made themselves docile to the divine Nature of Things, those who respond to circumstances, not with craving and aversion, but with the love that permits them to do spontaneously what they like; those who can truthfully say, Not I, but God in me—such men and women are compared by the exponents of the Perennial Philosophy to children, to fools and simpletons, even sometimes, as in the following passage, to drunkards.

> A drunken man who falls out of a cart, though he may suffer, does not die. His bones are the same as other people's; but he meets his accident in a different way. His spirit is in a condition of security. He is not conscious of riding in the cart; neither is he conscious of falling out of it. Ideas of life, death, fear and the like cannot penetrate his breast; and so he does not suffer from contact with objective existence. If such security is to be got from wine, how much more is it to be got from God?
>
> *Chuang Tzu*

It is by long obedience and hard work that the artist comes to unforced spontaneity and consummate mastery. Knowing that he can never create anything on his own account, out of the top layers, so to speak, of his personal consciousness, he submits obediently to the workings of "inspiration"; and knowing that the medium in which he works has its own self-nature, which must not be ignored or violently overriden, he makes himself its patient servant and, in this way, achieves perfect freedom of expression. But life is also an art, and the man who would become a consummate artist in living must follow, on all the levels of his being, the same procedure as that by which the painter or the sculptor or any other craftsman comes to his own more limited perfection.

> Prince Hui's cook was cutting up a bullock. Every blow of his knife, every heave of his shoulders, every tread of his foot, every *whshh* of rent flesh, every *chhk* of the chopper, was in perfect harmony—rhythmical like the Dance of the Mulberry Grove, simultaneous like the chords of the Ching Shou.
>
> "Well done!" cried the Prince. "Yours is skill indeed."
>
> "Sire," replied the cook, "I have always devoted myself to Tao. It is better than skill. When I first began to cut up bullocks, I saw before me simply whole bullocks. After three years' practice I saw no more whole animals. And now I work with my mind and not with my eye. When my senses bid me stop, but my mind urges me on, I fall back upon eternal principles. I follow such openings or cavities

as there may be, according to the natural constitution of the animal. I do not attempt to cut through joints, still less through large bones.

"A good cook changes his chopper once a year—because he cuts. An ordinary cook, once a month—because he hacks. But I have had this chopper nineteen years, and though I have cut up many thousands of bullocks, its edge is as if fresh from the whetstone. For at the joints there are always interstices, and the edge of a chopper being without thickness, it remains only to insert that which is without thickness into such an interstice. By these means the interstice will be enlarged, and the blade will find plenty of room. It is thus that I have kept my chopper for nineteen years, as though fresh from the whetstone.

"Nevertheless, when I come upon a hard part, where the blade meets with a difficulty, I am all caution. I fix my eyes on it. I stay my hand, and gently apply the blade, until with a *hwah* the part yields like earth crumbling to the ground. Then I withdraw the blade and stand up and look around; and at last I wipe my chopper and put it carefully away."

"Bravo!" cried the Prince. "From the words of this cook I have learnt how to take care of my life."

                                                            Chuang Tzu

In the first seven branches of his Eightfold Path the Buddha describes the conditions that must be fulfilled by anyone who desires to come to that right contemplation which is the eighth and final branch. The fulfilment of these conditions entails the undertaking of a course of the most searching and comprehensive mortification—mortification of intellect and will, craving and emotion, thought, speech, action and, finally, means of livelihood. Certain professions are more or less completely incompatible with the achievement of man's final end; and there are certain ways of making a living which do so much physical and, above all, so much moral, intellectual and spiritual harm that, even if they could be practised in a non-attached spirit (which is generally impossible), they would still have to be eschewed by anyone dedicated to the task of liberating, not only himself, but others. The exponents of the Perennial Philosophy are not content to avoid and forbid the practice of criminal professions, such as brothel-keeping, forgery, racketeering and the like; they also avoid themselves, and warn others against, a number of ways of livelihood commonly regarded as legitimate. Thus, in many Buddhist societies, the manufacture of arms, the concoction of intoxicating liquors and the wholesale purveying of butcher's meat were not, as in contemporary Christendom, rewarded by wealth, peerages and political influence; they were deplored as businesses which, it was thought, made it particularly difficult for their practitioners and for other members of the communities in which they were practised to achieve enlightenment and liberation. Similarly, in mediaeval Europe, Christians were forbidden to make a living by the taking of interest on money or by cornering the market. As Tawney and others have shown, it was only after the Reformation that coupon-clipping, usury and gambling in stocks and commodities became respectable and received ecclesiastical approval.

For the Quakers, soldiering was and is a form of wrong livelihood—war being, in their eyes, anti-Christian, not so much because it causes suffering as because it propagates hatred, puts a premium on fraud and cruelty, infects whole societies with anger, fear, pride and uncharitableness. Such passions eclipse the Inner Light, and therefore the wars by which they are aroused and intensified, must be regarded, whatever their immediate political outcome, as crusades to make the world safe for spiritual darkness.

It has been found, as a matter of experience, that it is dangerous to lay down detailed and inflexible rules for right livelihood—dangerous, because most people see no reason for being righteous overmuch and consequently respond to the imposition of too rigid a code by hypocrisy or open rebellion. In the Christian tradition, for example, a distinction is made between the precepts, which are binding on all and sundry, and the counsels of perfection, binding only upon those who feel drawn towards a total renunciation of "the world." The precepts include the ordinary moral code and the commandment to love God with all one's heart, strength and mind, and one's neighbour as oneself. Some of those who make a serious effort to obey this last and greatest commandment find that they cannot do so whole-heartedly, unless they follow the counsels and sever all connections with the world. Nevertheless it is possible for men and women to achieve that "perfection," which is deliverance into the unitive knowledge of God, without abandoning the married state and without selling all they have and giving the price to the poor. Effective poverty (possessing no money) is by no means always affective poverty (being indifferent to money). One man may be poor, but desperately concerned with what money can buy, full of cravings, envy and bitter self-pity. Another may have money, but no attachment to money or the things, powers and privileges that money can buy. "Evangelical poverty" is a combination of effective with affective poverty; but a genuine poverty of spirit is possible even in those who are not effectively poor. It will be seen, then, that the problems of right livelihood, in so far as they lie outside the jurisdiction of the common moral code, are strictly personal. The way in which any individual problem presents itself and the nature of the appropriate solution depend upon the degree of knowledge, moral sensibility and spiritual insight achieved by the individual concerned. For this reason no universally applicable rules can be formulated except in the most general terms. "Here are my three treasures," says Lao Tzu. "Guard and keep them! The first is pity, the second frugality, the third refusal to be foremost of all things under heaven." And when Jesus is asked by a stranger to settle a dispute between himself and his brother over an inheritance, he refuses (since he does not know the circumstances) to be a judge in the case and merely utters a general warning against covetousness.

> Ga-San instructed his adherents one day: "Those who speak against killing, and who desire to spare the lives of all conscious beings are right. It is good to protect even animals and insects. But what about those persons who kill time, what about those who destroy wealth, and those who murder the economy of their society? We should not overlook them. Again, what of the one who preaches without enlightenment? He is killing Buddhism."
>
> *From "One Hundred and One Zen Stories"*

Once the noble Ibrahim, as he sat on his throne,
Heard a clamour and noise of cries on the roof,
Also heavy footsteps on the roof of his palace.
He said to himself, "Whose heavy feet are these?"
He shouted from the window, "Who goes there?"

> The guards, filled with confusion, bowed their heads,
>   saying,
> "It is we, going the rounds in search."
> He said, "What seek ye?" They said, "Our camels."
> He said, "Who ever searched for camels on a housetop?"
> They said, "We follow thy example,
> Who seekest union with God, while sitting on a throne."
>
>   *Jalal-uddin Rumi*

Of all social, moral and spiritual problems that of power is the most chronically urgent and the most difficult of solution. Craving for power is not a vice of the body, consequently knows none of the limitations imposed by a tired or satiated physiology upon gluttony, intemperance and lust. Growing with every successive satisfaction, the appetite for power can manifest itself indefinitely, without interruption by bodily fatigue or sickness. Moreover, the nature of society is such that the higher a man climbs in the political, economic or religious hierarchy, the greater are his opportunities and resources for exercising power. But climbing the hierarchical ladder is ordinarily a slow process, and the ambitious rarely reach the top till they are well advanced in life. The older he grows, the more chances does the power lover have for indulging his besetting sin, the more continuously is he subjected to temptations and the more glamorous do those temptations become. In this respect his situation is profoundly different from that of the debauchee. The latter may never voluntarily leave his vices, but at least, as he advances in years, he finds his vices leaving him; the former neither leaves his vices nor is left by them. Instead of bringing to the power lover a merciful respite from his addictions, old age is apt to intensify them by making it easier for him to satisfy his cravings on a larger scale and in a more spectacular way. That is why, in Acton's words, "all great men are bad." Can we therefore be surprised if political action, undertaken, in all too many cases, not for the public good, but solely or at least primarily to gratify the power lusts of bad men, should prove so often either self-stultifying or downright disastrous?

"*L'état c'est moi*," says the tyrant; and this is true, of course, not only of the autocrat at the apex of the pyramid, but of all the members of the ruling minority through whom he governs and who are, in fact, the real rulers of the nation. Moreover, so long as the policy which gratifies the power lusts of the ruling class is successful, and so long as the price of success is not too high, even the masses of the ruled will feel that the state is themselves—a vast and splendid projection of the individual's intrinsically insignificant ego. The little man can satisfy his lust for power vicariously through the activities of the imperialistic state, just as the big man does; the difference between them is one of degree, not of kind.

No infallible method for controlling the political manifestations of the lust for power has ever been devised. Since power is of its very essence indefinitely expansive, it cannot be checked except by colliding with another power. Hence, any society that values liberty, in the sense of government by law rather than by class interest or personal decree, must see to it that the power of its rulers is divided. National unity means national servitude to a single man and his supporting oligarchy. Organized and balanced disunity is the necessary condition of liberty. His Majesty's Loyal Opposition is the loyalest, because the most genuinely useful section of any liberty-loving community. Furthermore, since the appetite for power is purely mental and therefore insatiable and impervious to disease or old age, no community that values liberty can afford to give its rulers long tenures of office. The Carthusian Order, which was "never reformed because never deformed," owed its long immunity from corruption to the fact that its abbots were elected for periods of only a single year. In ancient Rome the amount of liberty under law was in inverse ratio to the length of the magistrates' terms of office. These rules for controlling the lust for power are very easy to formulate, but very difficult, as history shows, to enforce in practice. They are particularly difficult to enforce at a period like the present, when time-hallowed political machinery is being rendered obsolete by rapid technological change and when the salutary principle of organized and balanced disunity requires to be embodied in new and more appropriate institutions.

Acton, the learned Catholic historian, was of opinion that all great men are bad; Rumi, the Persian poet and mystic, thought that to seek for union with God while occupying a throne was an undertaking hardly less senseless than looking for camels among the chimney pots. A slightly more optimistic note is sounded by St. François de Sales, whose views on the matter were recorded by his Boswellizing disciple, the young Bishop of Belley.

> "*Mon Père*," I said one day, "how is it possible for those who are themselves high in office to practice the virtue of obedience?"
>
> François de Sales replied, "They have greater and more excellent ways of doing so than their inferiors."
>
> As I did not understand this reply, he went on to say, "Those who are bound by obedience are usually subject to one superior only. . . . But those who are themselves superiors have a wider field for obedience, even while they command; for if they bear in mind that it is God who has placed them over other men, and gives them the rule they have, they will exercise it out of obedience to God, and thus, even while commanding, they will obey. Moreover there is no position so high but that it is subject to a spiritual superior in what concerns the conscience and the soul. But there is a yet higher point of obedience to which all superiors may aspire, even that to which St. Paul alludes, when he says, 'Though I be free from all men, yet have I made myself servant unto all.' It is by such universal obedience to everyone that we become 'all things to all men'; and serving everyone for Our Lord's sake, we esteem all to be our superiors."
>
> In accordance with this rule, I have often observed how François de Sales treated everyone, even the most insignificant persons who approached him, as though he were the inferior, never repulsing anyone, never refusing to enter into conversation, to speak or to listen, never betraying the slightest sign of weariness, impatience and annoyance, however importunate or ill-timed the interruption. To those who asked him why he thus wasted his time his constant reply was, "It is God's will; it is what He requires of me; what more need I ask? While I am doing this, I am not required to do anything else. God's Holy Will is the centre from which all we do must radiate; all else is mere weariness and excitement."
>
> *Jean Pierre Camus*

We see, then, that a "great man" can be good—good enough even to aspire to unitive knowledge of the divine Ground—

provided that, while exercising power, he fulfills two conditions. First, he must deny himself all the personal advantages
of power and must practise the patience and recollectedness
without which there cannot be love either of man or God.
And, second, he must realize that the accident of possessing
temporal power does not give him spiritual authority, which
belongs only to those seers, living or dead, who have achieved
a direct insight into the Nature of Things. A society, in which
the boss is mad enough to believe himself a prophet, is a
society doomed to destruction. A viable society is one in which
those who have qualified themselves to see indicate the goals
to be aimed at, while those whose business it is to rule respect
the authority and listen to the advice of the seers. In theory,
at least, all this was well understood in India and, until the
Reformation, in Europe, where "no position was so high but
that it was subject to a spiritual superior in what concerned
the conscience and the soul." Unfortunately the churches tried
to make the best of both worlds—to combine spiritual authority with temporal power, wielded either directly or at one
remove, from behind the throne. But spiritual authority can
be exercised only by those who are perfectly disinterested and
whose motives are therefore above suspicion. An ecclesiastical
organization may call itself the Mystical Body of Christ; but if
its prelates are slave-holders and the rulers of states, as they
were in the past, or if the corporation is a large-scale capitalist,
as is the case today, no titles, however honorific, can conceal the
fact that, when it passes judgment, it does so as an interested
party with some political or economic axe to grind. True, in
matters which do not directly concern the temporal powers of
the corporation, individual churchmen can be, and have actually proved themselves, perfectly disinterested—consequently
can possess, and have possessed, genuine spiritual authority.
St. Philip Neri's is a case in point. Possessing absolutely no
temporal power, he yet exercised a prodigious influence over
sixteenth-century Europe. But for that influence, it may be
doubted whether the efforts of the Council of Trent to reform
the Roman church from within would have met with much
success.

In actual practice how many great men have ever fulfilled,
or are ever likely to fulfil, the conditions which alone render
power innocuous to the ruler as well as to the ruled? Obviously,
very few. Except by saints, the problem of power is finally

insoluble. But since genuine self-government is possible only in very small groups, societies on a national or super-national scale will always be ruled by oligarchical minorities, whose members come to power because they have a lust for power. This means that the problem of power will always arise and, since it cannot be solved except by people like François de Sales, will always make trouble. And this, in its turn, means that we cannot expect the large-scale societies of the future to be much better than were the societies of the past during the brief periods when they were at their best.

CHAPTER VII

Truth

> Why dost thou prate of God? Whatever thou sayest of Him is untrue.
>
> *Eckhart*

IN RELIGIOUS literature the word "truth" is used indiscriminately in at least three distinct and very different senses. Thus, it is sometimes treated as a synonym for "fact," as when it is affirmed that God is Truth—meaning that He is the primordial Reality. But this is clearly not the meaning of the word in such a phrase as "worshipping God in spirit and in truth." Here, it is obvious, "truth" signifies direct apprehension of spiritual Fact, as opposed to second-hand knowledge *about* Reality, formulated in sentences and accepted on authority or because an argument from previously granted postulates was logically convincing. And finally there is the more ordinary meaning of the word, as in such a sentence as, "This statement is the truth," where we mean to assert that the verbal symbols of which the statement is composed correspond to the facts to which it refers. When Eckhart writes that "whatever thou sayest of God is untrue," he is not affirming that all theological statements are false. Insofar as there can be any correspondence between human symbols and divine Fact, some theological statements are as true as it is possible for us to make them. Himself a theologian, Eckhart would certainly have admitted this. But besides being a theologian, Eckhart was a mystic. And being a mystic, he understood very vividly what the modern semanticist is so busily (and, also, so unsuccessfully) trying to drum into contemporary minds—namely, that words are not the same as things and that a knowledge of words about facts is in no sense equivalent to a direct and immediate apprehension of the facts themselves. What Eckhart actually asserts is this: whatever one may say about God can never in any circumstances be the "truth" in the first two meanings of that much abused and ambiguous word. By implication St. Thomas Aquinas was saying exactly the same thing when, after his experience of infused contemplation, he refused to go on with his theological work, declaring that everything he had written up to that time was as mere straw compared with the immediate knowledge, which had been vouchsafed to him. Two hundred years earlier, in Bagdad, the great Mohammedan theologian, Al Ghazzali, had similarly turned from the consideration of truths about God to the contemplation and direct apprehension of Truth-the-Fact, from the purely intellectual discipline of the philosophers to the moral and spiritual discipline of the Sufis.

The moral of all this is obvious. Whenever we hear or read about "truth," we should always pause long enough to ask ourselves in which of the three senses listed above the word is, at the moment, being used. By taking this simple precaution (and to take it is a genuinely virtuous act of intellectual honesty), we shall save ourselves a great deal of disturbing and quite unnecessary mental confusion.

> Wishing to entice the blind,
> The Buddha playfully let words escape from his golden
>   mouth;
> Heaven and earth are filled, ever since, with entangling
>   briars.
>
> *Dai-o Kokushi*

> There is nothing true anywhere,
> The True is nowhere to be found.
> If you say you see the True,
> This seeing is not the true one.
> When the True is left to itself,

There is nothing false in it, for it is Mind itself.
When Mind in itself is not liberated from the false,
There is nothing true; nowhere is the True to be found.

Hui Neng

The truth indeed has never been preached by the Buddha,
seeing that one has to realize it within oneself.

Sutralamkara

The further one travels, the less one knows.

Lao Tzu

"Listen to this!" shouted Monkey. "After all the trouble
we had getting here from China, and after you specially
ordered that we were to be given the scriptures, Ananda
and Kasyapa made a fraudulent delivery of goods. They
gave us blank copies to take away; I ask you, what is the
good of that to us?"

"You needn't shout," said the Buddha smiling. ". . . As
a matter of fact, it is such blank scrolls as these that are
the true scriptures. But I quite see that the people of
China are too foolish and ignorant to believe this, so there
is nothing for it but to give them copies with some writing on."

Wu Ch'êng-ên

The philosophers indeed are clever enough, but wanting
in wisdom;
As to the others, they are either ignorant or puerile!
They take an empty fist as containing something real and
the pointing finger as the object pointed at.
Because the finger is adhered to as though it were the
Moon, all their efforts are lost.

Yoka Daishi

What is known as the teaching of the Buddha is not the
teaching of the Buddha.

Diamond Sutra

"What is the ultimate teaching of Buddhism?"
"You won't understand it until you have it."

Shih-t'ou

The subject matter of the Perennial Philosophy is the nature of eternal, spiritual Reality; but the language in which it must be formulated was developed for the purpose of dealing with phenomena in time. That is why, in all these formulations, we find an element of paradox. The nature of Truth-the-Fact cannot be described by means of verbal symbols that do not adequately correspond to it. At best it can be hinted at in terms of *non sequiturs* and contradictions.

To these unavoidable paradoxes some spiritual writers have chosen to add deliberate and calculated enormities of language—hard sayings, exaggerations, ironic or humorous extravagances, designed to startle and shock the reader out of that self-satisfied complacency which is the original sin of the intellect. Of this second kind of paradox the masters of Taoism and Zen Buddhism were particularly fond. The latter, indeed, made use of paralogisms and even of nonsense as a device for "taking the kingdom of heaven by violence." Aspirants to the life of perfection were encouraged to practice discursive meditation on some completely non-logical formula. The result was a kind of *reductio ad absurdum* of the whole self-centred and world-centred discursive process, a sudden breaking through from "reason" (in the language of scholastic philosophy) to intuitive "intellect," capable of a genuine insight into the divine Ground of all being. This method strikes us as odd and eccentric; but the fact remains that it worked to the extent of producing in many persons the final *metanoia*, or transformation of consciousness and character.

Zen's use of almost comic extravagance to emphasize the philosophic truths it regarded as most important is well illustrated in the first of the extracts cited above. We are not intended seriously to imagine that an Avatar preaches in order to play a practical joke on the human race. But meanwhile what the author has succeeded in doing is to startle us out of our habitual complacency about the home-made verbal universe in which we normally do most of our living. Words are not facts, and still less are they the primordial Fact. If we take them too seriously, we shall lose our way in a forest of entangling briars. But if, on the contrary, we don't take them seriously enough, we shall remain unaware that there is a way to lose or a goal to be reached. If the Enlightened did not preach, there would be no deliverance for anyone. But because human minds and human languages are what they are, this necessary and indispensable preaching is beset with dangers. The history of all the religions is similar in one important respect; some of their adherents are enlightened and delivered, because they have chosen to react appropriately to the words which the founders have let fall; others achieve a partial salvation by reacting with partial appropriateness; yet others harm themselves and their fellows by reacting with a total inappropriateness—either ignoring the words altogether or, more often, taking them too seriously and treating them as though they were identical with the Fact to which they refer.

That words are at once indispensable and, in many cases, fatal has been recognized by all the exponents of the Perennial Philosophy. Thus, Jesus spoke of himself as bringing into the world something even worse than briars—a sword. St. Paul distinguished between the letter that kills and the spirit that gives life. And throughout the centuries that followed, the masters of Christian spirituality have found it necessary to harp again and again upon a theme which has never been outdated because *homo loquax*, the talking animal, is still as naïvely delighted by his chief accomplishment, still as helplessly the victim of his own words, as he was when the Tower of Babel was being built. Recent years have seen the publication of numerous works on semantics and of an ocean of nationalistic, racialistic and militaristic propaganda. Never have so many capable writers warned mankind against the dangers of wrong speech—and never have words been used more recklessly by politicians or taken more seriously by the public. The fact is surely proof enough that, under changing forms, the old problems remain what they always were—urgent, unsolved and, to all appearances, insoluble.

> All that the imagination can imagine and the reason conceive and understand in this life is not, and cannot be, a proximate means of union with God.
>
> *St. John of the Cross*

> Jejune and barren speculations may unfold the plicatures of Truth's garment, but they cannot discover her lovely face.
>
> *John Smith, the Platonist*

In all faces is shown the Face of faces, veiled and in a riddle. Howbeit, unveiled it is not seen, until, above all faces, a man enter into a certain secret and mystic silence, where there is no knowing or concept of a face. This mist, cloud, darkness or ignorance, into which he that seeketh thy Face entereth, when he goeth beyond all knowledge or concept, is the state below which thy Face cannot be found, except veiled; but that very darkness revealeth thy Face to be there beyond all veils. Hence I observe how needful it is for me to enter into the darkness and to admit the coincidence of opposites, beyond all the grasp of reason, and there to seek the Truth, where impossibility meeteth us.

Nicholas of Cusa

As the Godhead is nameless, and all naming is alien to Him, so also the soul is nameless; for it is here the same as God.

Eckhart

God being, as He is, inaccessible, do not rest in the consideration of objects perceptible to the senses and comprehended by the understanding. This is to be content with what is less than God; so doing, you will destroy the energy of the soul, which is necessary for walking with Him.

St. John of the Cross

To find or know God in reality by any outward proofs, or by anything but by God Himself made manifest and self-evident in you, will never be your case either here or hereafter. For neither God, nor heaven, nor hell, nor the devil, nor the flesh, can be any otherwise knowable in you or by you but by their own existence and manifestation in you. And all pretended knowledge of any of these things, beyond and without this self-evident sensibility of their birth within you, is only such knowledge of them as the blind man hath of the light that hath never entered into him.

William Law

What follows is a summary by an eminent scholar of the Indian doctrines concerning *jnana*, the liberating knowledge of Brahman or the divine Ground.

Jnana is eternal, is general, is necessary and is not a personal knowledge of this man or that man. It is there, as knowledge in the *Atman* itself, and lies there hidden under all *avidya* (ignorance)—irremovable, though it may be obscured, unprovable, because self-evident, needing no proof, because itself giving to all proof the ground of possibility. These sentences come near to Eckhart's "knowledge" and to the teaching of Augustine on the Eternal Truth in the soul which, itself immediately certain, is the ground of all certainty and is a possession, not of A or B, but of "the soul."

Rudolf Otto

The science of aesthetics is not the same as, nor even a proximate means to, the practice and appreciation of the arts. How can one learn to have an eye for pictures, or to become a good painter? Certainly not by reading Benedetto Croce. One learns to paint by painting, and one learns to appreciate pictures by going to picture galleries and looking at them.

But this is not to say that Croce and his fellows have wasted their time. We should be grateful to them for their labours in building up a system of thought, by means of which the immediately apprehended significance and value of art can be assessed in the light of general knowledge, related to other facts of experience and, in this way and to this extent, "explained."

What is true of aesthetics is also true of theology. Theological speculation is valuable insofar as it enables those who have had immediate experience of various aspects of God to form intelligible ideas about the nature of the divine Ground, and of their own experience of the Ground in relation to other experiences. And when a coherent system of theology has been worked out, it is useful insofar as it convinces those who study it that there is nothing inherently self-contradictory about the postulate of the divine Ground and that, for those who are ready to fulfill certain conditions, the postulate may become a realized Fact. In no circumstances, however, can the study of theology or the mind's assent to theological propositions take the place of what Law calls "the birth of God within." For theory is not practice, and words are not the things for which they stand.

Theology as we know it has been formed by the great mystics, especially St Augustine and St Thomas. Plenty of other great theologians—especially St Gregory and St Bernard, even down to Suarez—would not have had such insight without mystic super-knowledge.

Abbot John Chapman

Against this we must set Dr. Tennant's view—namely, that religious experience is something real and unique, but does not add anything to the experiencer's knowledge of ultimate Reality and must always be interpreted in terms of an idea of God derived from other sources. A study of the facts would suggest that both these opinions are to some degree correct. The facts of mystical insight (together with the facts of what is taken to be historic revelation) are rationalized in terms of general knowledge and become the basis of a theology. And, reciprocally, an existing theology in terms of general knowledge exercises a profound influence upon those who have undertaken the spiritual life, causing them, if it is low, to be content with a low form of experience, if it is high, to reject as inadequate the experience of any form of reality having characteristics incompatible with those of the God described in the books. Thus mystics make theology, and theology makes mystics.

A person who gives assent to untrue dogma, or who pays all his attention and allegiance to one true dogma in a comprehensive system, while neglecting the others (as many Christians concentrate exclusively on the humanity of the Second Person of the Trinity and ignore the Father and the Holy Ghost), runs the risk of limiting in advance his direct apprehension of Reality. In religion as in natural science, experience is determined only by experience. It is fatal to prejudge it, to compel it to fit the mould imposed by a theory which either does not correspond to the facts at all, or corresponds to only some of the facts. "Do not strive to seek after the true," writes a Zen master, "only cease to cherish opinions." There is only one way to cure the results of belief in a false or incomplete theology and it is the same as the only known way of passing from belief in even the truest theology to knowledge or primordial Fact—selflessness, docility, openness to the datum of Eternity. Opinions are things which we make and can therefore understand, formulate and argue about. But "to rest in the consideration of objects perceptible to the sense or comprehended by the understanding is to be content," in the words of St. John of the Cross, "with what is less than God." Unitive knowledge of God is possible only to those who "have ceased to cherish opinions"—even opinions that are as true as it is possible for verbalized abstractions to be.

> Up then, noble soul! Put on thy jumping shoes which are intellect and love, and overleap the worship of thy mental powers, overleap thine understanding and spring into the heart of God, into his hiddenness where thou art hidden from all creatures.
>
> *Eckhart*

> With the lamp of word and discrimination one must go beyond word and discrimination and enter upon the path of realization.
>
> *Lankavatara Sutra*

The word "intellect" is used by Eckhart in the scholastic sense of immediate intuition. "Intellect and reason," says Aquinas, "are not two powers, but distinct as the perfect from the imperfect. . . . The intellect means, an intimate penetration of truth; the reason, enquiry and discourse." It is by following, and then abandoning, the rational and emotional path of "word and discrimination" that one is enabled to enter upon the intellectual or intuitive "path of realization." And yet, in spite of the warnings pronounced by those who, through selflessness, have passed from letter to spirit and from theory to immediate knowledge, the organized Christian churches have persisted in the fatal habit of mistaking means for ends. The verbal statements of theology's more or less adequate rationalizations of experience have been taken too seriously and treated with the reverence that is due only to the Fact they are intended to describe. It has been fancied that souls are saved if assent is given to what is locally regarded as the correct formula, lost if it is withheld. The two words, *filioque*, may not have been the sole cause of the schism between the Eastern and Western churches; but they were unquestionably the pretext and *casus belli*.

The overvaluation of words and formulae may be regarded as a special case of that overvaluation of the things of time, which is so fatally characteristic of historic Christianity. To know Truth-as-Fact and to know it unitively, "in spirit and in truth-as-immediate-apprehension"—this is deliverance, in this "standeth our eternal life." To be familiar with the verbalized truths, which symbolically correspond to Truth-as-Fact insofar as it can be known in, or inferred from, truth-as-immediate-apprehension, or truth-as-historic-revelation—this is not salvation, but merely the study of a special branch of philosophy. Even the most ordinary experience of a thing or event in time can never be fully or adequately described in words. The experience of seeing the sky or having neuralgia is incommunicable; the best we can do is to say "blue" or "pain," in the hope that those who hear us may have had experiences similar to our own and so be able to supply their own version of the meaning. God, however, is not a thing or event in time, and the time-bound words which cannot do justice even to temporal matters are even more inadequate to the intrinsic nature and our own unitive experience of that which belongs to an incommensurably different order. To suppose that people can be saved by studying and giving assent to formulae is like supposing that one can get to Timbuctoo by poring over a map of Africa. Maps are symbols, and even the best of them are inaccurate and imperfect symbols. But to anyone who really wants to reach a given destination, a map is indispensably useful as indicating the direction in which the traveller should set out and the roads which he must take.

In later Buddhist philosophy words are regarded as one of the prime determining factors in the creative evolution of human beings. In this philosophy five categories of being are recognized—Name, Appearance, Discrimination, Right Knowledge, Suchness. The first three are related for evil, the last two for good. Appearances are discriminated by the sense organs, then reified by naming, so that words are taken for things and symbols are used as the measure of reality. According to this view, language is a main source of the sense of separateness and the blasphemous idea of individual self-sufficiency, with their inevitable corollaries of greed, envy, lust for power, anger and cruelty. And from these evil passions there springs the necessity of an indefinitely protracted and repeated separate existence under the same, self-perpetuated conditions of craving and infatuation. The only escape is through a creative act of the will, assisted by Buddha-grace, leading through selflessness to Right Knowledge, which consists, among other things, in a proper appraisal of Names, Appearances and Discrimination. In and through Right Knowledge, one emerges from the infatuating delusion of "I," "me," "mine," and, resisting the temptation to deny the world in a state of premature and one-sided ecstasy, or to affirm it by living like the average sensual man, one comes at last to the transfiguring awareness that *samsara* and *nirvana* are one, to the unitive apprehension of pure Suchness—the ultimate Ground, which can only be indicated, never adequately described in verbal symbols.

In connection with the Mahayanist view that words play an important and even creative part in the evolution of unregenerate human nature, we may mention Hume's arguments against the reality of causation. These arguments start from the postulate that all events are "loose and separate" from one another and proceed with faultless logic to a conclusion that makes complete nonsense of all organized thought or purposive action. The fallacy, as Professor Stout has pointed out, lies in the preliminary postulate. And when we ask ourselves what it was that induced Hume to make this odd and quite unrealistic assumption that events are "loose and separate," we see that his only reason for flying in the face of immediate experience was the fact that things and happenings are symbolically represented in our thought by nouns, verbs and adjectives, and that these words are, in effect, "loose and separate" from one another in a way which the events and things they stand for quite obviously are not. Taking words as the measure of things, instead of using things as the measure of words, Hume imposed the discrete and, so to say, *pointilliste* pattern of language upon the continuum of actual experience —with the impossibly paradoxical results with which we are all familiar. Most human beings are not philosophers and care not at all for consistency in thought or action. Thus, in some circumstances they take it for granted that events are not "loose and separate," but co-exist or follow one another within the organized and organizing field of a cosmic whole. But on other occasions, where the opposite view is more nearly in accord with their passions or interests, they adopt, all unconsciously, the Humian position and treat events as though they were as independent of one another and the rest of the world as the words by which they are symbolized. This is generally true of all occurrences involving "I," "me," "mine." Reifying the "loose and separate" names, we regard the things as also loose and separate—not subject to law, not involved in the network of relationships, by which in fact they are so obviously bound up with their physical, social and spiritual environment. We regard as absurd the idea that there is no causal process in nature and no organic connection between events and things in the lives of other people; but at the same time we accept as axiomatic the notion that our own sacred ego is "loose and separate" from the universe, a law unto itself above the moral *dharma* and even, in many respects, above the natural law of causality. Both in Buddhism and Catholicism, monks and nuns were encouraged to avoid the personal pronoun and to speak of themselves in terms of circumlocutions that clearly indicated their real relationship with the cosmic reality and their fellow creatures. The precaution was a wise one. Our responses to familiar words are conditioned reflexes. By changing the stimulus, we can do something to change the response. No Pavlov bell, no salivation; no harping on words like "me" and "mine," no purely automatic and unreflecting egotism. When a monk speaks of himself, not as "I," but as "this sinner" or "this unprofitable servant," he tends to stop taking his "loose and separate" selfhood for granted, and makes himself aware of his real, organic relationship with God and his neighbours.

In practice words are used for other purposes than for making statements about facts. Very often they are used rhetorically, in order to arouse the passions and direct the will towards some course of action regarded as desirable. And sometimes, too, they are used poetically—that is to say, they are used in such a way that, besides making a statement about real or imaginary things and events, and besides appealing rhetorically to the will and the passions, they cause the reader to be aware that they are beautiful. Beauty in art or nature is a matter of relationships between things not in themselves intrinsically beautiful. There is nothing beautiful, for example, about the vocables, "time," or "syllable." But when they are used in such a phrase as "to the last syllable of recorded time," the relationship between the sound of the component words, between our ideas of the things for which they stand, and between the overtones of association with which each word and the phrase as a whole are charged, is apprehended, by a direct and immediate intuition, as being beautiful.

About the rhetorical use of words nothing much need be said. There is rhetoric for good causes and there is rhetoric for bad causes—rhetoric which is tolerably true to facts as well as emotionally moving, and rhetoric which is unconsciously or deliberately a lie. To learn to discriminate between the different kinds of rhetoric is an essential part of intellectual morality; and intellectual morality is as necessary a pre-condition of the spiritual life as is the control of the will and the guard of heart and tongue.

We have now to consider a more difficult problem. How should the poetical use of words be related to the life of the spirit? (And, of course, what applies to the poetical use of words applies equally to the pictorial use of pigments, the musical use of sounds, the sculptural use of clay or stone—in a word, to all the arts.)

"Beauty is truth, truth, beauty." But unfortunately Keats failed to specify in which of its principal meanings he was using the word "truth." Some critics have assumed that he was using it in the third of the senses listed at the opening of this section, and have therefore dismissed the aphorism as nonsensical. $Zn + H_2SO_4 = ZnSO_4 + H_2$. This is a truth in the third sense of the word—and, manifestly, this truth is not identical with beauty. But no less manifestly Keats was not talking about this kind of "truth." He was using the word primarily in its first sense, as a synonym for "fact," and secondarily with the significance attached to it in the Johannine phrase, "to worship God in truth." His sentence, therefore, carries two meanings. "Beauty is the Primordial Fact, and the Primordial Fact is Beauty, the principle of all particular beauties"; and "Beauty is an immediate experience, and this immediate experience is identical with Beauty-as-Principle, Beauty-as-Primordial-Fact." The first of these statements is fully in accord with the doctrines of the Perennial Philosophy. Among the trinities in which the ineffable One makes itself manifest is the trinity of the Good, the True, and the Beautiful. We perceive beauty in the harmonious intervals between the parts of a whole. In this context the divine Ground might be paradoxically defined as Pure Interval, independent of what is separated and harmonized within the totality.

With Keats's statement in its secondary meaning the exponents of the Perennial Philosophy would certainly disagree. The experience of beauty in art or in nature may be qualitatively akin to the immediate, unitive experience of the divine Ground or Godhead; but it is not the same as that experience, and the particular beauty-fact experienced, though partaking in some sort of the divine nature, is at several removes from the Godhead. The poet, the nature lover, the aesthete are granted apprehensions of Reality analogous to those vouchsafed to the selfless contemplative; but because they have not troubled to make themselves perfectly selfless, they are incapable of knowing the divine Beauty in its fulness, as it is in itself. The poet is born with the capacity of arranging words in such a way that something of the quality of the graces and inspirations he has received can make itself felt to other human beings in the white spaces, so to speak, between the lines of his verse. This is a great and precious gift; but if the poet remains content with his gift, if he persists in worshipping the beauty in art and nature without going on to make himself capable, through selflessness, of apprehending Beauty as it is in the divine Ground, then he is only an idolater. True, his idolatry is among the highest of which human beings are capable; but an idolatry, none the less, it remains.

> The experience of beauty is pure, self-manifested, compounded equally of joy and consciousness, free from admixture of any other perception, the very twin brother of mystical experience, and the very life of it is supersensuous wonder. . . . It is enjoyed by those who are competent thereto, in identity, just as the form of God is itself the joy with which it is recognized.
>
> *Visvanatha*

What follows is the last composition of a Zen nun, who had been in her youth a great beauty and an accomplished poetess.

> Sixty-six times have these eyes beheld the changing scenes of Autumn.
> I have said enough about moonlight,
> Ask me no more.
> Only listen to the voice of pines and cedars, when no wind stirs.
>
> *Ryo-Nen*

The silence under windless trees is what Mallarmé would call a *creux néant musicien*. But whereas the music for which the poet listened was merely aesthetic and imaginative, it was to pure Suchness that the self-naughted contemplative was laying herself open. "Be still and know that I am God."

> This truth is to be lived, it is not to be merely pronounced with the mouth. . . .
> There is really nothing to argue about in this teaching;
> Any arguing is sure to go against the intent of it.
> Doctrines given up to controversy and argumentation lead of themselves to birth and death.
>
> *Hui Neng*

Away, then, with the fictions and workings of discursive reason, either for or against Christianity! They are only the wanton spirit of the mind, whilst ignorant of God and insensible of its own nature and condition. Death and life are the only things in question; life is God living and working in the soul; death is the soul living and working according to the sense and reason of bestial flesh and blood. Both this life and this death are of their own growth, growing from their own seed within us, not as busy reason talks and directs, but as the heart turns either to the one or to the other.

> *William Law*

> Can I explain the Friend to one for whom He is no Friend?
>
> *Jalal-uddin Rumi*

> When a mother cries to her sucking babe, "Come, O son, I am thy mother!"
> Does the child answer, "O mother, show a proof
> That I shall find comfort in taking thy milk"?
>
> *Jalal-uddin Rumi*

Great truths do not take hold of the hearts of the masses. And now, as all the world is in error, how shall I, though I know the true path, how shall I guide? If I know that I cannot succeed and yet try to force success, this would be but another source of error. Better then to desist and strive no more. But if I do not strive, who will?

Chuang Tzu

Between the horns of Chuang Tzu's dilemma there is no way but that of love, peace and joy. Only those who manifest their possession, in however small a measure, of the fruits of the Spirit can persuade others that the life of the spirit is worth living. Argument and controversy are almost useless; in many cases, indeed, they are positively harmful. But this, of course, is a thing that clever men with a gift for syllogisms and sarcasm, find it peculiarly hard to admit. Milton, no doubt, genuinely believed that he was working for truth, righteousness and the glory of God by exploding in torrents of learned scurrility against the enemies of his favourite dictator and his favourite brand of nonconformity. In actual fact, of course, he and the other controversialists of the sixteenth and seventeenth centuries did nothing but harm to the cause of true religion, for which, on one side or the other, they fought with an equal learning and ingenuity and with the same foul-mouthed intemperance of language. The successive controversies went on, with occasional lucid intervals, for about two hundred years—Papists arguing with anti-Papists, Protestants with other Protestants, Jesuits with Quietists and Jansenists. When the noise finally died down, Christianity (which, like any other religion, can survive only if it manifests the fruits of the Spirit) was all but dead; the real religion of most educated Europeans was now nationalistic idolatry. During the eighteenth century this change to idolatry seemed (after the atrocities committed in the name of Christianity by Wallenstein and Tilly) to be a change for the better. This was because the ruling classes were determined that the horrors of the wars of religion should not be repeated and therefore deliberately tempered power politics with gentlemanliness. Symptoms of gentlemanliness can still be observed in the Napoleonic and Crimean wars. But the national Molochs were steadily devouring the eighteenth-century ideal. During the first and second World Wars we have witnessed the total elimination of the old checks and self-restraints. The consequences of political idolatry now display themselves without the smallest mitigation either of humanistic honour and etiquette or of transcendental religion. By its internecine quarrels over words, forms of organization, money and power, historic Christianity consummated the work of self-destruction, to which its excessive preoccupation with things in time had from the first so tragically committed it.

> Sell your cleverness and buy bewilderment;
> Cleverness is mere opinion, bewilderment is intuition.
> *Jalal-uddin Rumi*

> Reason is like an officer when the King appears;
> The officer then loses his power and hides himself.
> Reason is the shadow cast by God; God is the sun.
> *Jalal-uddin Rumi*

Non-rational creatures do not look before or after, but live in the animal eternity of a perpetual present; instinct is their animal grace and constant inspiration; and they are never tempted to live otherwise than in accord with their own animal *dharma*, or immanent law. Thanks to his reasoning powers and to the instrument of reason, language, man (in his merely human condition) lives nostalgically, apprehensively and hopefully in the past and future as well as in the present; has no instincts to tell him what to do; must rely on personal cleverness, rather than on inspiration from the divine Nature of Things; finds himself in a condition of chronic civil war between passion and prudence and, on a higher level of awareness and ethical sensibility, between egotism and dawning spirituality. But this "wearisome condition of humanity" is the indispensable prerequisite of enlightenment and deliverance. Man must live in time in order to be able to advance into eternity, no longer on the animal, but on the spiritual level; he must be conscious of himself as a separate ego in order to be able consciously to transcend separate self-hood; he must do battle with the lower self in order that he may become identified with that higher Self within him, which is akin to the divine Not-Self; and finally he must make use of his cleverness in order to pass beyond cleverness to the intellectual vision of Truth, the immediate, unitive knowledge of the divine Ground. Reason and its works "are not and cannot be a proximate means of union with God." The proximate means is "intellect," in the scholastic sense of the word, or spirit. In the last analysis the use and purpose of reason is to create the internal and external conditions favourable to its own transfiguration by and into spirit. It is the lamp by which it finds the way to go beyond itself. We see, then, that as a means to a proximate means to an End, discursive reasoning is of enormous value. But if, in our pride and madness, we treat it as a proximate means to the divine End (as so many religious people have done and still do), or if, denying the existence of an eternal End, we regard it as at once the means to Progress and its ever-receding goal in time, cleverness becomes the enemy, a source of spiritual blindness, moral evil and social disaster. At no period in history has cleverness been so highly valued or, in certain directions, so widely and efficiently trained as at the present time. And at no time have intellectual vision and spirituality been less esteemed, or the End to which they are proximate means less widely and less earnestly sought for. Because technology advances, we fancy that we are making corresponding progress all along the line; because we have considerable power over inanimate nature, we are convinced that we are the self-sufficient masters of our fate and captains of our souls; and because cleverness has given us technology and power, we believe, in spite of all the evidence to the contrary, that we have only to go on being yet cleverer in a yet more systematic way to achieve social order, international peace and personal happiness.

In Wu Ch'êng-ên's extraordinary masterpiece (so admirably translated by Mr. Arthur Waley) there is an episode, at once comical and profound, in which Monkey (who, in the allegory, is the incarnation of human cleverness) gets to heaven and there causes so much trouble that at last Buddha has to be called in to deal with him. It ends in the following passage.

> "I'll have a wager with you," said Buddha. "If you are really so clever, jump off the palm of my right hand. If you succeed, I'll tell the Jade Emperor to come and live with me in the Western Paradise, and you shall have his throne without more ado. But if you fail, you shall go back to earth and do penance there for many a kalpa before you come back to me with your talk."
>
> "This Buddha," Monkey thought to himself, "is a perfect fool. I can jump a hundred and eight thousand leagues, while his palm cannot be as much as eight inches across. How could I fail to jump clear of it?"
>
> "You're sure you're in a position to do this for me?" he asked.

"Of course I am," said Buddha.

He stretched out his right hand, which looked about the size of a lotus leaf. Monkey put his cudgel behind his ear, and leapt with all his might. "That's all right," he said to himself. "I'm right off it now." He was whizzing so fast that he was almost invisible, and Buddha, watching him with the eye of wisdom, saw a mere whirligig shoot along.

Monkey came at last to five pink pillars, sticking up into the air. "This is the end of the World," said Monkey to himself. "All I have got to do is to go back to Buddha and claim my forfeit. The Throne is mine."

"Wait a minute," he said presently, "I'd better just leave a record of some kind, in case I have trouble with Buddha." He plucked a hair and blew on it with magic breath, crying, "Change!" It changed at once into a writing brush charged with heavy ink, and at the base of the central pillar he wrote, "The Great Sage Equal to Heaven reached this place." Then, to mark his disrespect, he relieved nature at the bottom of the first pillar, and somersaulted back to where he had come from. Standing on Buddha's palm, he said, "Well, I've gone and come back. You can go and tell the Jade Emperor to hand over the palaces of Heaven."

"You stinking ape," said Buddha, "you've been on the palm of my hand all the time."

"You're quite mistaken," said Monkey. "I got to the end of the World, where I saw five flesh-coloured pillars sticking up into the sky. I wrote something on one of them. I'll take you there and show you, if you like."

"No need for that," said Buddha. "Just look down."

Monkey peered down with his fiery, steely eyes, and there at the base of the middle finger of Buddha's hand he saw written the words, "The Great Sage Equal to Heaven reached this place," and from the fork between the thumb and first finger came a smell of monkey's urine.

From Monkey

And so, having triumphantly urinated on the proffered hand of Wisdom, the Monkey within us turns back and, full of a bumptious confidence in his own omnipotence, sets out to re-fashion the world of men and things into something nearer to his heart's desire. Sometimes his intentions are good, sometimes consciously bad. But, whatever the intentions may be, the results of action undertaken by even the most brilliant cleverness, when it is unenlightened by the divine Nature of Things, unsubordinated to the Spirit, are generally evil. That this has always been clearly understood by humanity at large is proved by the usages of language. "Cunning" and "canny" are equivalent to "knowing," and all three adjectives pass a more or less unfavourable moral judgment on those to whom they are aplied. "Conceit" is just "concept"; but what a man's mind conceives most clearly is the supreme value of his own ego. "Shrewd," which is the participial form of "shrew," meaning malicious, and is connected with "beshrew," to curse, is now applied, by way of rather dubious compliment, to astute business men and attorneys. Wizards are so called because they are wise—wise, of course, in the sense that, in American slang, a "wise guy" is wise. Conversely, an idiot was once popularly known as an innocent. "This use of innocent," says Richard Trench, "assumes that to hurt and harm is the chief employment, towards which men turn their intellectual powers; that where they are wise, they are oftenest wise to do evil." Meanwhile it goes without saying that cleverness and accumulated knowledge are indispensable, but always as means to proximate means, and never as proximate means or, what is even worse, as ends in themselves. *Quid faceret eruditio sine dilectione?* says St. Bernard. *Inflaret. Quid, absque eruditione dilectio? Erraret.* What would learning do without love? It would puff up. And love without learning? It would go astray.

> Such as men themselves are, such will God Himself seem to them to be.
>
> *John Smith, the Platonist*

> Men's minds perceive second causes,
> But only prophets perceive the action of the First Cause.
> *Jalal-uddin Rumi*

The amount and kind of knowledge we acquire depends first upon the will and, second, upon our psycho-physical constitution and the modifications imposed upon it by environment and our own choice. Thus, Professor Burkitt has pointed out that, where technological discovery is concerned "man's desire has been the important factor. Once something is definitely wanted, again and again it has been produced in an extremely short time. . . . Conversely, nothing will teach the Bushmen of South Africa to plant and herd. They have no desire to do so." The same is true in regard to ethical and spiritual discoveries. "You are as holy as you wish to be," was the motto given by Ruysbroeck to the students who came to visit him. And he might have added, "You can therefore know as much of Reality as you wish to know"—for knowledge is in the knower according to the mode of the knower, and the mode of the knower is, in certain all-important respects, within the knower's control. Liberating knowledge of God comes to the pure in heart and poor in spirit; and though such purity and poverty are enormously difficult of achievement, they are nevertheless possible to all.

> She said, moreover, that if one would attain to purity of mind it was necessary to abstain altogether from any judgment on one's neighbour and from all empty talk about his conduct. In creatures one should always seek only for the will of God. With great force she said: "For no reason whatever should one judge the actions of creatures or their motives. Even when we see that it is an actual sin, we ought not to pass judgment on it, but have holy and sincere compassion and offer it up to God with humble and devout prayer."
>
> *From the Testament of*
> *St. Catherine of Siena, written down by Tommaso di Petra*

This total abstention from judgment upon one's fellows is only one of the conditions of inward purity. The others have already been described in the section on "Mortification."

> Learning consists in adding to one's stock day by day. The practise of Tao consists in subtracting day by day: subtracting and yet again subtracting until one has reached inactivity.
>
> *Lao Tzu*

It is the inactivity of self-will and ego-centered cleverness that makes possible the activity within the emptied and purified soul of the eternal Suchness. And when eternity is known in the heights within, it is also known in the fulness of experience, outside in the world.

> Didst thou ever descry a glorious eternity in a winged moment of time? Didst thou ever see a bright infinite in the narrow point of an object? Then thou knowest what spirit means—the spire-top, whither all things ascend harmoniously, where they meet and sit contented in an unfathomed Depth of Life.
>
> *Peter Sterry*

CHAPTER VIII

Religion and Temperament

IT SEEMS best at this point to turn back for a moment from ethics to psychology, where a very important problem awaits us—a problem to which the exponents of the Perennial Philosophy have given a great deal of attention. What precisely is the relation between individual constitution and temperament on the one hand and the kind and degree of spiritual knowledge on the other? The materials for a comprehensively accurate answer to this question are not available —except, perhaps, in the form of that incommunicable science, based upon intuition and long practice, that exists in the minds of experienced "spiritual directors." But the answer that *can* be given, though incomplete, is highly significant.

All knowledge, as we have seen, is a function of being. Or, to phrase the same idea in scholastic terms, the thing known is in the knower according to the mode of the knower. In the Introduction reference was made to the effect upon knowledge of changes of being along what may be called its vertical axis, in the direction of sanctity or its opposite. But there is also variation in the horizontal plane. Congenitally by psychophysical constitution, each one of us is born into a certain position on this horizontal plane. It is a vast territory, still imperfectly explored, a continent stretching all the way from imbecility to genius, from shrinking weakness to aggressive strength, from cruelty to Pickwickian kindliness, from self-revealing sociability to taciturn misanthropy and love of solitude, from an almost frantic lasciviousness to an almost untempted continence. From any point on this huge expanse of possible human nature an individual can move almost indefinitely up or down, towards union with the divine Ground of his own and all other beings, or towards the last, the infernal extremes of separateness and selfhood. But where horizontal movement is concerned there is far less freedom. It is impossible for one kind of physical constitution to transform itself into another kind; and the particular temperament associated with a given physical constitution can be modified only within narrow limits. With the best will in the world and the best social environment, all that anyone can hope to do is to make the best of his congenital psycho-physical make-up; to change the fundamental patterns of constitution and temperament is beyond his power.

In the course of the last thirty centuries many attempts have been made to work out a classification system in terms of which human differences could be measured and described. For example, there is the ancient Hindu method of classifying people according to the psycho-physico-social categories of caste. There are the primarily medical classifications associated with the name of Hippocrates, classifications in terms of two main "habits"—the phthisic and the apoplectic—or of the four humours (blood, phlegm, black bile and yellow bile) and the four qualities (hot, cold, moist and dry). More recently there have been the various physiognomic systems of the eighteenth and early nineteenth centuries; the crude and merely psychological dichotomy of introversion and extraversion; the more complete, but still inadequate, psycho-physical classifications proposed by Kretschmer, Stockard, Viola and others; and finally the system, more comprehensive, more flexibly adequate to the complex facts than all those which preceded it, worked out by Dr. William Sheldon and his collaborators.

In the present section our concern is with classifications of human differences in relation to the problems of the spiritual life. Traditional systems will be described and illustrated, and the findings of the Perennial Philosophy will be compared with the conclusions reached by the most recent scientific research.

In the West, the traditional Catholic classification of human beings is based upon the Gospel anecdote of Martha and Mary. The way of Martha is the way of salvation through action, the way of Mary is the way through contemplation. Following

Aristotle, who in this as in many other matters was in accord with the Perennial Philosophy, Catholic thinkers have regarded contemplation (the highest term of which is the unitive knowledge of the Godhead) as man's final end, and therefore have always held that Mary's was indeed the better way.

Significantly enough, it is in essentially similar terms that Dr. Radin classifies and (by implication) evaluates primitive human beings in so far as they are philosophers and religious devotees. For him there is no doubt that the higher mono-theistic forms of primitive religion are created (or should one rather say, with Plato, *discovered*?) by people belonging to the first of the two great psycho-physical classes of human beings—the men of thought. To those belonging to the other class, the men of action, is due the creation or discovery of the lower, unphilosophical, polytheistic kinds of religion.

This simple dichotomy is a classification of human differences that is valid so far as it goes. But like all such dichotomies, whether physical (like Hippocrates' division of humanity into those of phthisic and those of apoplectic habit) or psychological (like Jung's classification in terms of introvert and extravert), this grouping of the religious into those who think and those who act, those who follow the way of Martha and those who follow the way of Mary, is inadequate to the facts. And of course no director of souls, no head of a religious organization, is ever, in actual practice, content with this all too simple system. Underlying the best Catholic writing on prayer and the best Catholic practice in the matter of recognizing voca-tions and assigning duties, we sense the existence of an implicit and unformulated classification of human differences more complete and more realistic than the explicit dichotomy of action and contemplation.

In Hindu thought the outlines of this completer and more adequate classification are clearly indicated. The ways leading to the delivering union with God are not two, but three—the way of works, the way of knowledge and the way of devotion. In the Bhagavad Gita Sri Krishna instructs Arjuna in all three paths—liberation through action without attachment; liberation through knowledge of the Self and the Absolute Ground of all being with which it is identical; and liberation through intense devotion to the personal God or the divine incarnation.

Do without attachment the work you have to do; for a man who does his work without attachment attains the Supreme Goal verily. By action alone men like Janaka attained perfection.

But there is also the way of Mary.

Freed from passion, fear and anger, absorbed in Me, taking refuge in Me, and purified by the fires of Knowledge, many have become one with my Being.

And again:

Those who have completely controlled their senses and are of even mind under all conditions and thus contemplate the Imperishable, the Ineffable, the Unmanifest, the Omnipresent, the Incomprehensible, the Eternal—they, devoted to the welfare of all beings, attain Me alone and none else.

But the path of contemplation is not easy.

The task of those whose minds are set on the Unmanifest is the more difficult; for, to those who are in the body, the realization of the Unmanifest is hard. But those who consecrate all their actions to Me (as the personal God, or as the divine Incarnation), who regard Me as the supreme Goal, who worship Me and meditate upon Me with single-minded concentration—for those whose minds are thus absorbed in Me, I become ere long the Saviour from the world's ocean of mortality.

These three ways of deliverance are precisely correlated with the three categories, in terms of which Sheldon has worked out what is, without question, the best and most adequate classification of human differences. Human beings, he has shown, vary continuously between the viable extremes of a tri-polar system; and physical and psychological measurements can be devised, whereby any given individual may be accurately located in relation to the three co-ordinates. Or we can put the matter differently and say that any given individual is a mixture, in varying proportions, of three physical and three closely related psychological components. The strength of each component can be measured according to empirically determined procedures. To the three physical components Sheldon gives the names of endomorphy, mesomorphy and ectomorphy. The individual with a high degree of endomorphy is predominantly soft and rounded and may easily become grossly fat. The high mesomorph is hard, big-boned and strong-muscled. The high ectomorph is slender and has small bones and stringy, weak, unemphatic muscles. The endomorph has a huge gut, a gut that may be more than twice as heavy and twice as long as that of the extreme ectomorph. In a real sense his or her body is built around the digestive tract. The centrally significant fact of mesomorphic physique, on the other hand, is the powerful musculature, while that of the ectomorph is the over-sensitive and (since the ratio of body surface to mass is higher in ectomorphs than in either of the other types) relatively unprotected nervous system.

With endomorphic constitution is closely correlated a temperamental pattern, which Sheldon calls viscerotonia. Significant among the viscerotonic traits are love of food and, characteristically, love of eating in common; love of comfort and luxury; love of ceremoniousness; indiscriminate amiability and love of people as such; fear of solitude and craving for company; uninhibited expression of emotion; love of childhood, in the form of nostalgia towards one's own past and in an intense enjoyment of family life; craving for affection and social support, and need of people when in trouble. The temperament that is related to mesomorphy is called somatotonia. In this the dominating traits are love of muscular activity, aggressiveness and lust for power; indifference to pain; callousness in regard to other people's feelings; a love of combat and competitiveness; a high degree of physical courage; a nostalgic feeling, not for childhood, but for youth, the period of maximum muscular power; a need for activity when in trouble.

From the foregoing descriptions it will be seen how inadequate is the Jungian conception of extraversion, as a simple antithesis to introversion. Extraversion is not simple; it is of two radically different kinds. There is the emotional, sociable extraversion of the viscerotonic endomorph—the person who is always seeking company and telling everybody just what he feels. And there is the extraversion of the big-muscled somatotonic—the person who looks outward on the world as a place where he can exercise power, where he can bend people to his will and shape things to his heart's desire. One is the genial extraversion of the salesman, the Rotarian good mixer, the liberal Protestant clergyman. The other is the extraversion of the engineer who works off his lust for power on things, of the sportsman and the professional blood-and-iron soldier, of the ambitious business executive and politician, of the dictator, whether in the home or at the head of a state.

With cerebrotonia, the temperament that is correlated with ectomorphic physique, we leave the genial world of Pickwick, the strenuously competitive world of Hotspur, and pass into an entirely different and somewhat disquieting kind of universe—that of Hamlet and Ivan Karamazov. The extreme cerebrotonic is the over-alert, over-sensitive introvert, who is more concerned with what goes on behind his eyes—with the constructions of thought and imagination, with the variations of feeling and consciousness—than with that external world, to which, in their different ways, the viscerotonic and the somatotonic pay their primary attention and allegiance. Cerebrotonics have little or no desire to dominate, nor do they feel the viscerotonic's indiscriminate liking for people as people; on the contrary they want to live and let live, and their passion for privacy is intense. Solitary confinement, the most terrible punishment that can be inflicted on the soft, round, genial person, is, for the cerebrotonic, no punishment at all. For him the ultimate horror is the boarding school and the barracks. In company cerebrotonics are nervous and shy, tensely inhibited and unpredictably moody. (It is a significant fact that no extreme cerebrotonic has ever been a good actor or actress.) Cerebrotonics hate to slam doors or raise their voices, and suffer acutely from the unrestrained bellowing and trampling of the somatotonic. Their manner is restrained, and when it comes to expressing their feelings they are extremely reserved. The emotional gush of the viscerotonic strikes them as offensively shallow and even insincere, nor have they any patience with viscerotonic ceremoniousness and love of luxury and magnificence. They do not easily form habits and find it hard to adapt their lives to the routines, which come so naturally to somatotonics. Owing to their over-sensitiveness, cerebrotonics are often extremely, almost insanely sexual; but they are hardly ever tempted to take to drink—for alcohol, which heightens the natural aggressiveness of the somatotonic and increases the relaxed amiability of the viscerotonic, merely makes them feel ill and depressed. Each in his own way, the viscerotonic and the somatotonic are well adapted to the world they live in; but the introverted cerebrotonic is in some sort incommensurable with the things and people and institutions that surround him. Consequently a remarkably high proportion of extreme cerebrotonics fail to make good as normal citizens and average pillars of society. But if many fail, many also become abnormal on the higher side of the average. In universities, monasteries and research laboratories —wherever sheltered conditions are provided for those whose small guts and feeble muscles do not permit them to eat or fight their way through the ordinary rough and tumble—the percentage of outstandingly gifted and accomplished cerebrotonics will almost always be very high. Realizing the importance of this extreme, over-evolved and scarcely viable type of human being, all civilizations have provided in one way or another for its protection.

In the light of these descriptions we can understand more clearly the Bhagavad Gita's classification of paths to salvation. The path of devotion is the path naturally followed by the person in whom the viscerotonic component is high. His inborn tendency to externalize the emotions he spontaneously feels in regard to persons can be disciplined and canalized, so that a merely animal gregariousness and a merely human kindliness become transformed into charity—devotion to the personal God and universal good will and compassion towards all sentient beings.

The path of works is for those whose extraversion is of the somatotonic kind, those who in all circumstances feel the need to "do something." In the unregenerate somatotonic this craving for action is always associated with aggressiveness, self-assertion and the lust for power. For the born *Kshatriya*, or warrior-ruler, the task, as Krishna explains to Arjuna, is to get rid of those fatal accompaniments to the love of action and to work without regard to the fruits of work, in a state of complete non-attachment to self. Which is, of course, like everything else, a good deal easier said than done.

Finally, there is the way of knowledge, through the modification of consciousness, until it ceases to be ego-centred and becomes centred in and united with the divine Ground. This is the way to which the extreme cerebrotonic is naturally drawn. His special discipline consists in the mortification of his innate tendency towards introversion for its own sake, towards thought and imagination and self-analysis as ends in themselves rather than as means towards the ultimate transcendence of phantasy and discursive reasoning in the timeless act of pure intellectual intuition.

Within the general population, as we have seen, variation is continuous, and in most people the three components are fairly evenly mixed. Those exhibiting extreme predominance of any one component are relatively rare. And yet, in spite of their rarity, it is by the thought-patterns characteristic of these extreme individuals that theology and ethics, at any rate on the theoretical side, have been mainly dominated. The reason for this is simple. Any extreme position is more uncompromisingly clear and therefore more easily recognized and understood than the intermediate positions, which are the natural thought-pattern of the person in whom the constituent components of personality are evenly balanced. These intermediate positions, it should be noted, do not in any sense contain or reconcile the extreme positions; they are merely other thought-patterns added to the list of possible systems. The construction of an all-embracing system of metaphysics, ethics and psychology is a task that can never be accomplished by any single individual, for the sufficient reason that he *is* an individual with one particular kind of constitution and temperament and therefore capable of knowing only according to the mode of his own being. Hence the advantages inherent in what may be called the anthological approach to truth.

The Sanskrit *dharma*—one of the key words in Indian formulations of the Perennial Philosophy—has two principal meanings. The *dharma* of an individual is, first of all, his essential nature, the intrinsic law of his being and development. But *dharma* also signifies the law of righteousness and piety. The implications of this double meaning are clear: a man's duty, how he ought to live, what he ought to believe and what he ought to do about his beliefs—these things are conditioned by his essential nature, his constitution and temperament. Going a good deal further than do the Catholics, with their doctrine of vocations, the Indians admit the right of individuals with different *dharmas* to worship different aspects or conceptions of the divine. Hence the almost total absence, among Hindus and Buddhists, of bloody persecutions, religious wars and proselytizing imperialism.

It should, however, be remarked that, within its own ecclesiastical fold, Catholicism has been almost as tolerant as Hinduism and Mahayana Buddhism. Nominally one, each of these religions consists, in fact, of a number of very different religions, covering the whole gamut of thought and behaviour from fetishism, through polytheism, through legalistic monotheism, through devotion to the sacred humanity of the Avatar, to the profession of the Perennial Philosophy and the practice of a purely spiritual religion that seeks the unitive knowledge of the Absolute Godhead. These tolerated religions-within-a-religion are not, of course, regarded as equally valuable or equally true. To worship polytheistically may be one's *dharma*; nevertheless the fact remains that man's final end is the unitive knowledge of the Godhead, and all the historical formulations of the Perennial Philosophy are agreed that every human being ought, and perhaps in some way or other actually will, achieve that end. "All souls," writes Father Garrigou-Lagrange, "receive a general remote call to the mystical life; and if all were faithful in avoiding, as they should, not merely mortal but venial sin, if they were, each according to his condition, docile to the Holy Ghost, and if they lived long enough, a day would come when they would receive the proximate and efficacious vocation to a high perfection and to the mystical life properly so called." With this statement Hindu and Buddhist theologians would probably agree; but they would add that every soul will in fact eventually attain this "high perfection." All are called, but in any given generation few are chosen, because few choose themselves. But the series of conscious existences, corporeal or incorporeal, is indefinitely long; there is therefore time and opportunity for everyone to learn the necessary lessons. Moreover, there will always be helpers. For periodically there are "descents" of the Godhead into physical form; and at all times there are future Buddhas ready, on the threshold of reunion with the Intelligible Light, to renounce the bliss of immediate liberation in order to return as saviours and teachers again and again into the world of suffering and time and evil, until at last every sentient being shall have been delivered into eternity.

The practical consequences of this doctrine are clear enough. The lower forms of religion, whether emotional, active or intellectual, are never to be accepted as final. True, each of them comes naturally to persons of a certain kind of constitution and temperament; but the *dharma* or duty of any given individual is not to remain complacently fixed in the imperfect religion that happens to suit him; it is rather to transcend it, not by impossibly denying the modes of thought, behaviour and feeling that are natural to him, but by making use of them, so that by means of nature he may pass beyond nature. Thus the introvert uses "discrimination" (in the Indian phrase), and so learns to distinguish the mental activities of the ego from the principial consciousness of the Self, which is akin to, or identical with, the divine Ground. The emotional extravert learns to "hate his father and mother" (in other words to give up his selfish attachment to the pleasures of indiscriminately loving and being loved), concentrates his devotion on the personal or incarnate aspect of God, and comes at last to love the Absolute Godhead by an act, no longer of feeling, but of will illuminated by knowledge. And finally there is that other kind of extravert, whose concern is not with the pleasures of giving or receiving affection, but with the satisfaction of his lust for power over things, events and persons. Using his own nature to transcend his own nature, he must follow the path laid down in the Bhagavad Gita for the bewildered Arjuna—the path of work without attachment to the fruits of work, the path of what St. François de Sales calls "holy indifference," the path that leads through the forgetting of self to the discovery of the Self.

In the course of history it has often happened that one or other of the imperfect religions has been taken too seriously and regarded as good and true in itself, instead of as a means to the ultimate end of all religion. The effects of such mistakes are often disastrous. For example, many Protestant sects have insisted on the necessity, or at least the extreme desirability, of a violent conversion. But violent conversion, as Sheldon has pointed out, is a phenomenon confined almost exclusively to persons with a high degree of somatotonia. These persons are so intensely extraverted as to be quite unaware of what is happening in the lower levels of their minds. If for any reason their attention comes to be turned inwards, the resulting self-knowledge, because of its novelty and strangeness, presents itself with the force and quality of a revelation and their *metanoia*, or change of mind, is sudden and thrilling. This change may be to religion, or it may be to something else—for example, to psycho-analysis. To insist upon the necessity of violent conversion as the only means to salvation is about as sensible as it would be to insist upon the necessity of having a large face, heavy bones and powerful muscles. To those naturally subject to this kind of emotional upheaval, the doctrine that makes salvation dependent on conversion gives a complacency that is quite fatal to spiritual growth, while those who are incapable of it are filled with a no less fatal despair. Other examples of inadequate theologies based upon psychological ignorance could easily be cited. One remembers, for instance, the sad case of Calvin, the cerebrotonic who took his own intellectual constructions so seriously that he lost all sense of reality, both human and spiritual. And then there is our liberal Protestantism, that predominantly viscerotonic heresy, which seems to have forgotten the very existence of the Father, Spirit and Logos and equates Christianity with an emotional attachment to Christ's humanity or, (to use the currently popular phrase) "the personality of Jesus," worshipped idolatrously as though there were no other God. Even within all-comprehensive Catholicism we constantly hear complaints of the ignorant and self-centred directors, who impose upon the souls under their charge a religious *dharma* wholly unsuited to their nature—with results which writers such as St. John of the Cross describe as wholly pernicious. We see, then, that it is natural for us to think of God as possessed of the qualities which our temperament tends to make us perceive in Him; but unless nature finds a way of transcending itself by means of itself, we are lost. In the last analysis Philo is quite right in saying that those who do not conceive God purely and simply as the One injure, not God of course, but themselves and, along with themselves, their fellows.

The way of knowledge comes most naturally to persons whose temperament is predominantly cerebrotonic. By this I do not mean that the following of this way is easy for the cerebrotonic. His specially besetting sins are just as difficult to overcome as are the sins which beset the power-loving somatotonic and the extreme viscerotonic with his gluttony for food and comfort and social approval. Rather I mean that the idea that such a way exists and can be followed (either by discrimination, or through non-attached work and one-pointed devotion) is one which spontaneously occurs to the cerebrotonic. At all levels of culture he is the natural monotheist; and this natural monotheist, as Dr. Radin's examples of primitive theology clearly show, is often a monotheist of the *tat tvam asi*, inner-light school. Persons committed by their temperament to one or other of the two kinds of extraversion are natural polytheists. But natural polytheists can, without much difficulty, be convinced of the theoretical superiority of monotheism. The nature of human reason is such that there is an intrinsic plausibility about any hypothesis which seeks to explain the manifold in terms of unity, to reduce apparent multiplicity to essential identity. And from this theoretical monotheism the half-converted polytheist can, if he chooses, go on (through practices suitable to his own particular temperament) to the actual realization of the divine Ground of his own and all other beings. He *can*, I repeat, and sometimes he actually does. But very often he does not. There are many theoretical monotheists whose whole life and every action prove that in reality they are still what their temperament inclines them to be—polytheists, worshippers not of the one God they sometimes talk about, but of the many gods, nationalistic and technological, financial and familial, to whom in practice they pay all their allegiance.

In Christian art the Saviour has almost invariably been represented as slender, small-boned, unemphatically muscled. Large, powerful Christs are a rather shocking exception to a very ancient rule. Of Rubens' crucifixions William Blake contemptuously wrote:

> I understood Christ was a carpenter
> And not a brewer's servant, my good sir.

In a word, the traditional Jesus is thought of as a man of predominantly ectomorphic physique and therefore, by implication, of predominantly cerebrotonic temperament. The central core of primitive Christian doctrine confirms the essential correctness of the iconographic tradition. The religion of the Gospels is what we should expect from a cerebrotonic—not, of course, from any cerebrotonic, but from one who had used the psycho-physical peculiarities of his own nature to transcend nature, who had followed his particular *dharma* to its spiritual goal. The insistence that the Kingdom of Heaven is within; the ignoring of ritual; the slightly contemptuous attitude towards legalism, towards the ceremonial routines of organized religion, towards hallowed days and places; the general other-worldliness; the emphasis laid upon restraint, not merely of overt action, but even of desire and unexpressed intention; the indifference to the splendours of material civilization and the love of poverty as one of the greatest of goods; the doctrine that non-attachment must be carried even into the sphere of family relationships and that even devotion to the highest goals of merely human ideals, even the righteousness of the Scribes and Pharisees, may be idolatrous distractions from the love of God—all these are characteristically cerebrotonic ideas, such as would never have occurred spontaneously to the extraverted power lover or the equally extraverted viscerotonic.

Primitive Buddhism is no less predominantly cerebrotonic than primitive Christianity, and so is Vedanta, the metaphysical discipline which lies at the heart of Hinduism. Confucianism, on the contrary, is a mainly viscerotonic system—familial, ceremonious and thoroughly this-worldly. And in Mohammedanism we find a system which incorporates strongly somatotonic elements. Hence Islam's black record of holy wars and persecutions—a record comparable to that of later Christianity, after that religion had so far compromised with unregenerate somatotonia as to call its ecclesiastical organization "the Church Militant."

So far as the achievement of man's final end is concerned, it is as much of a handicap to be an extreme cerebrotonic or an extreme viscerotonic as it is to be an extreme somatotonic. But whereas the cerebrotonic and the viscerotonic cannot do much harm except to themselves and those in immediate contact with them, the extreme somatotonic, with his native aggressiveness, plays havoc with whole societies. From one point of view civilization may be defined as a complex of religious, legal and educational devices for preventing extreme somatotonics from doing too much mischief, and for directing their irrepressible energies into socially desirable channels. Confucianism and Chinese culture have sought to achieve this end by inculcating filial piety, good manners and an amiably viscerotonic epicureanism—the whole reinforced somewhat incongruously by the cerebrotonic spirituality and restraints of Buddhism and classical Taoism. In India the caste system represents an attempt to subordinate military, political and financial power to spiritual authority; and the education given to all classes still insists so strongly upon the fact that man's final end is unitive knowledge of God that even at the present time, even after nearly two hundred years of gradually accelerating Europeanization, successful somatotonics will, in middle life, give up wealth, position and power to end their days as humble seekers after enlightenment. In Catholic Europe, as in India, there was an effort to subordinate temporal power to spiritual authority; but since the Church itself exercised temporal power through the agency of political prelates and mitred business men, the effort was never more than partially successful. After the Reformation even the pious wish to limit temporal power by means of spiritual authority was completely abandoned. Henry VIII made himself, in Stubbs's words, "the Pope, the whole Pope, and something more than the Pope," and his example has been followed by most heads of states ever since. Power has been limited only by other powers, not by an appeal to first principles as interpreted by those who are morally and spiritually qualified to know what they are talking about. Meanwhile, the interest in religion has everywhere declined and even among believing Christians the Perennial Philosophy has been to a great extent replaced by a metaphysic of inevitable progress and an evolving God, by a passionate concern, not with eternity, but with future time. And almost suddenly, within the last quarter of a century, there has been consummated what Sheldon calls a "somatotonic revolution," directed against all that is characteristically cerebrotonic in the theory and practice of traditional Christian culture. Here are a few symptoms of this somatotonic revolution.

In traditional Christianity, as in all the great religious formulations of the Perennial Philosophy, it was axiomatic that contemplation is the end and purpose of action. Today the great majority even of professed Christians regard action (directed towards material and social progress) as the end, and analytic thought (there is no question any longer of integral thought, or contemplation) as the means to that end.

In traditional Christianity, as in the other formulations of the Perennial Philosophy, the secret of happiness and the way to salvation were to be sought, not in the external environment, but in the individual's state of mind with regard to the environment. Today the all-important thing is not the state of the mind, but the state of the environment. Happiness and moral progress depend, it is thought, on bigger and better gadgets and a higher standard of living.

In traditional Christian education the stress was all on restraint; with the recent rise of the "progressive school" it is all on activity and "self-expression."

Traditionally Christian good manners outlawed all expressions of pleasure in the satisfaction of physical appetites. "You may love a screeching owl, but you must not love a roasted fowl"—such was the rhyme on which children were brought up in the nurseries of only fifty years ago. Today the young unceasingly proclaim how much they "love" and "adore" different kinds of food and drink; adolescents and adults talk about the "thrills" they derive from the stimulation of their sexuality. The popular philosophy of life has ceased to be based on the classics of devotion and the rules of aristocratic good breeding, and is now moulded by the writers of advertising copy, whose one idea is to persuade everybody to be as extraverted and uninhibitedly greedy as possible, since of course it is only the possessive, the restless, the distracted, who spend money on the things that advertisers want to sell. Technological progress is in part the product of the somatotonic revolution, in part the producer and sustainer of that revolution. The extraverted attention results in technological discoveries. (Significantly enough, a high degree of material civilization has always been associated with the large-scale and officially sanctioned practice of polytheism.) In their turn, technological discoveries have resulted in mass production; and mass production, it is obvious, cannot be kept going at full blast except by persuading the whole population to accept the somatotonic *Weltanschauung* and act accordingly.

Like technological progress, with which it is so closely associated in so many ways, modern war is at once a cause and a result of the somatotonic revolution. Nazi education, which was specifically education for war, had two principal aims: to encourage the manifestation of somatotonia in those most richly endowed with that component of personality, and to make the rest of the population feel ashamed of its relaxed amiability or its inward-looking sensitiveness and tendency towards self-restraint and tender-mindedness. During the war the enemies of Nazism have been compelled, of course, to borrow from the Nazis' educational philosophy. All over the world millions of young men and even of young women are being systematically educated to be "tough" and to value "toughness" beyond every other moral quality. With this system of somatotonic ethics is associated the idolatrous and polytheistic theology of nationalism—a pseudo-religion far stronger at the present time for evil and division than is Christianity, or any other monotheistic religion, for unification and good. In the past most societies tried systematically to discourage somatotonia. This was a measure of self-defense; they did not want to be physically destroyed by the power-loving aggressiveness of their most active minority, and they did not want to be spiritually blinded by an excess of extra-version. During the last few years all this has been changed. What, we may apprehensively wonder, will be the result of the current world-wide reversal of an immemorial social policy? Time alone will show.

CHAPTER IX

Self-Knowledge

> In other living creatures ignorance of self is nature; in man it is vice.
>
> *Boethius*

VICE may be defined as a course of behaviour consented to by the will and having results which are bad, primarily because they are God-eclipsing and, secondarily, because they are physically or psychologically harmful to the agent or his fellows. Ignorance of self is something that answers to this description. In its origins it is voluntary; for by introspection and by listening to other people's judgments of our character we can all, if we so desire, come to a very shrewd understanding of our flaws and weaknesses and the real, as opposed to the avowed and advertised, motives of our actions. If most of us remain ignorant of ourselves, it is because self-knowledge is painful and we prefer the pleasures of illusion. As for the consequences of such ignorance, these are bad by every criterion, from the utilitarian to the transcendental. Bad because self-ignorance leads to unrealistic behaviour and so causes every kind of trouble for everyone concerned; and bad because, without self-knowledge, there can be no true humility, therefore no effective self-naughting, therefore no unitive knowledge of the divine Ground underlying the self and ordinarily eclipsed by it.

The importance, the indispensable necessity, of self-knowledge has been stressed by the saints and doctors of every one of the great religious traditions. To us in the West, the most familiar voice is that of Socrates. More systematically than Socrates the Indian exponents of the Perennial Philosophy harped on the same theme. There is, for example, the Buddha, whose discourse on "The Setting-Up of Mindfulness" expounds (with that positively inexorable exhaustiveness characteristic of the Pali scriptures) the whole art of self-knowledge in all its branches—knowledge of one's body, one's senses, one's feelings, one's thoughts. This art of self-knowledge is practised with two aims in view. The proximate aim is that "a brother, as to the body, continues so to look upon the body, that he remains ardent, self-possessed and mindful, having overcome both the hankering and dejection common in the world. And in the same way as to feelings, thoughts and ideas, he so looks upon each that he remains ardent, self-possessed and mindful, without hankering or dejection." Beyond and through this desirable psychological condition lies the final end of man, knowledge of that which underlies the individualized self. In their own vocabulary, Christian writers express the same ideas.

A man has many skins in himself, covering the depths of his heart. Man knows so many things; he does not know himself. Why, thirty or forty skins or hides, just like an ox's or a bear's, so thick and hard, cover the soul. Go into your own ground and learn to know yourself there.

Eckhart

Fools regard themselves as awake now—so personal is their knowledge. It may be as a prince or it may be as a herdsman, but so cock-sure of themselves!

Chuang Tzu

This metaphor of waking from dreams recurs again and again in the various expositions of the Perennial Philosophy. In this context liberation might be defined as the process of waking up out of the nonsense, nightmares and illusory pleasures of what is ordinarily called real life into the awareness of eternity. The "sober certainty of waking bliss"—that wonderful phrase in which Milton described the experience of the noblest kind of music—comes, I suppose, about as near as words can get to enlightenment and deliverance.

> Thou (the human being) art that which is not. I am that I am. If thou perceivest this truth in thy soul, never shall the enemy deceive thee; thou shalt escape all his snares.
>
> *St. Catherine of Siena*

> Knowledge of ourselves teaches us whence we come, where we are and whither we are going. We come from God and we are in exile; and it is because our potency of affection tends towards God that we are aware of this state of exile.
>
> *Ruysbroeck*

Spiritual progress is through the growing knowledge of the self as nothing and of the Godhead as all-embracing Reality. (Such knowledge, of course, is worthless if it is merely theoretical; to be effective, it must be realized as an immediate, intuitive experience and appropriately acted upon.) Of one great master of the spiritual life Professor Étienne Gilson writes: "The displacement of fear by Charity by way of the practice of humility—in that consists the whole of St. Bernard's ascesis, its beginning, its development and its term." Fear, worry, anxiety—these form the central core of individualized selfhood. Fear cannot be got rid of by personal effort, but only by the ego's absorption in a cause greater than its own interests. Absorption in any cause will rid the mind of some of its fears; but only absorption in the loving and knowing of the divine Ground can rid it of *all* fear. For when the cause is less than the highest, the sense of fear and anxiety is transferred from the self to the cause—as when heroic self-sacrifice for a loved individual or institution is accompanied by anxiety in regard to that for which the sacrifice is made. Whereas if the sacrifice is made for God, and for others for

God's sake, there can be no fear or abiding anxiety, since nothing can be a menace to the divine Ground and even failure and disaster are to be accepted as being in accord with the divine will. In few men and women is the love of God intense enough to cast out this projected fear and anxiety for cherished persons and institutions. The reason is to be sought in the fact that few men and women are humble enough to be capable of loving as they should. And they lack the necessary humility because they are without the fully realized knowledge of their own personal nothingness.

Humility does not consist in hiding our talents and virtues, in thinking ourselves worse and more ordinary than we are, but in possessing a clear knowledge of all that is lacking in us and in not exalting ourselves for that which we have, seeing that God has freely given it us and that, with all His gifts, we are still of infinitely little importance.

Lacordaire

As the light grows, we see ourselves to be worse than we thought. We are amazed at our former blindness as we see issuing from our heart a whole swarm of shameful feelings, like filthy reptiles crawling from a hidden cave. But we must be neither amazed nor disturbed. We are not worse than we were; on the contrary, we are better. But while our faults diminish, the light we see them by waxes brighter, and we are filled with horror. So long as there is no sign of cure, we are unaware of the depth of our disease; we are in a state of blind presumption and hardness, the prey of self-delusion. While we go with the stream, we are unconscious of its rapid course; but when we begin to stem it ever so little, it makes itself felt.

Fénelon

My daughter, build yourself two cells. First a real cell, so that you do not run about much and talk, unless it is needful, or you can do it out of love for your neighbour. Next build yourself a spiritual cell, which you can always take with you, and that is the cell of true self-knowledge; you will find there the knowledge of God's goodness to you. Here there are really two cells in one, and if you

live in one you must also live in the other; otherwise the
soul will either despair or be presumptuous. If you dwelt
in self-knowledge alone, you would despair; if you dwelt
in the knowledge of God alone, you would be tempted to
presumption. One must go with the other, and thus you
will reach perfection.

St. Catherine of Siena

CHAPTER X

Grace and Free Will

DELIVERANCE is out of time into eternity, and is achieved by
obedience and docility to the eternal Nature of Things. We
have been given free will, in order that we may will our self-
will out of existence and so come to live continuously in a
"state of grace." All our actions must be directed, in the last
analysis, to making ourselves passive in relation to the activity
and the being of divine Reality. We are, as it were, aeolian
harps, endowed with the power either to expose themselves
to the wind of the Spirit or to shut themselves away from it.

The Valley Spirit never dies.
It is called the Mysterious Female.
And the doorway of the Mysterious Female
Is the base from which Heaven and Earth spring.
It is there within us all the time.
Draw upon it as you will, it never runs dry.

Lao Tzu

In every exposition of the Perennial Philosophy the human
soul is regarded as feminine in relation to the Godhead, the
personal God and even the Order of Nature. *Hubris*, which is
the original sin, consists in regarding the personal ego as
self-sufficiently masculine in relation to the Spirit within and
to Nature without, and in behaving accordingly.

St. Paul drew a very useful and illuminating distinction
between the *psyche* and the *pneuma*. But the latter word never
achieved any degree of popularity, and the hopelessly am·
biguous term, *psyche*, came to be used indifferently for either

the personal consciousness or the spirit. And why, in the Western church, did devotional writers choose to speak of man's *anima* (which for the Romans signified the lower, animal soul) instead of using the word traditionally reserved for the rational soul, namely *animus?* The answer, I suspect, is that they were anxious to stress by every means in their power the essential femininity of the human spirit in its relations with God. *Pneuma*, being grammatically neuter, and *animus*, being masculine, were felt to be less suitable than *anima* and *psyche*. Consider this concrete example; given the structure of Greek and Latin, it would have been very difficult for the speakers of these languages to identify anything but a grammatically feminine soul with the heroine of the Song of Songs—an allegorical figure who, for long centuries, played the same part in Christian thought and sentiment as the Gopi Maidens played in the theology and devotion of the Hindus.

> Take note of this fundamental truth. Everything that works in nature and creature, except sin, is the working of God in nature and creature. The creature has nothing else in its power but the free use of its will, and its free will hath no other power but that of concurring with, or resisting, the working of God in nature. The creature with its free will can bring nothing into being, nor make any alteration in the working of nature; it can only change its own state or place in the working of nature, and so feel or find something in its state that it did not feel or find before.
>
> *William Law*

Defined in psychological terms, grace is something other than our self-conscious personal self, by which we are helped. We have experience of three kinds of such helps—animal grace, human grace and spiritual grace. Animal grace comes when we are living in full accord with our own nature on the biological level—not abusing our bodies by excess, not interfering with the workings of our indwelling animal intelligence by conscious cravings and aversions, but living wholesomely and laying ourselves open to the "virtue of the sun and the spirit of the air." The reward of being thus in harmony with Tao or the Logos in its physical and physiological aspects is a sense of well-being, an awareness of life as good, not for any reason, but just because it is life. There is no question, when we are in a condition of animal grace, of *propter vitam vivendi perdere causas*; for in this state there is no distinction between the reasons for living and life itself. Life, like virtue, is then its own reward. But, of course, the fulness of animal grace is reserved for animals. Man's nature is such that he must live a self-conscious life in time, not in a blissful sub-rational eternity on the hither side of good and evil. Consequently animal grace is something that he knows only spasmodically in an occasional holiday from self-consciousness, or as an accompaniment to other states, in which life is not its own reward but has to be lived for a reason outside itself.

Human grace comes to us either from persons, or from social groups, or from our own wishes, hopes and imaginings projected outside ourselves and persisting somehow in the psychic medium in a state of what may be called second-hand objectivity. We have all had experience of the different types of human grace. There is, for example, the grace which, during childhood, comes from mother, father, nurse or beloved teacher. At a later stage we experience the grace of friends; the grace of men and women morally better and wiser than ourselves; the grace of the *guru*, or spiritual director. Then there is the grace which comes to us because of our attachment to country, party, church or other social organization— a grace which has helped even the feeblest and most timid individuals to achieve what, without it, would have been the impossible. And finally there is the grace which we derive from our ideals, whether low or high, whether conceived of in abstract terms or bodied forth in imaginary personifications. To this last type, it would seem, belong many of the graces experienced by the pious adherents of the various religions. The help received by those who devotedly adore or pray to some personal saint, deity or Avatar is often, we may guess, not a genuinely spiritual grace, but a human grace, coming back to the worshipper from the vortex of psychic power set up by repeated acts (his own and other people's) of faith, yearning and imagination.

Spiritual grace cannot be received continuously or in its fulness, except by those who have willed away their self-will to the point of being able truthfully to say, "Not I, but God in me." There are, however, few people so irremediably self-condemned to imprisonment within their own personality as to be wholly incapable of receiving the graces which are from instant to instant being offered to every soul. By fits and starts most of us contrive to forget, if only partially, our preoccupation with "I," "me," "mine," and so become capable of receiving, if only partially, the graces which, in that moment, are being offered us.

Spiritual grace originates from the divine Ground of all being, and it is given for the purpose of helping man to achieve his final end, which is to return out of time and self-hood to that Ground. It resembles animal grace in being derived from a source wholly other than our self-conscious, human selves; indeed, it is the same thing as animal grace, but manifesting itself on a higher level of the ascending spiral that leads from matter to the Godhead. In any given instance, human grace may be wholly good, inasmuch as it helps the recipient in the task of achieving the unitive knowledge of God; but because of its source in the individualized self, it is always a little suspect and, in many cases, of course, the help it gives is help towards the achievement of ends very different from the true end of our existence.

> All our goodness is a loan; God is the owner. God works and his work is God.
>
> *St. John of the Cross*

> Perpetual inspiration is as necessary to the life of goodness, holiness and happiness as perpetual respiration is necessary to animal life.
>
> *William Law*

Conversely, of course, the life of goodness, holiness and beatitude is a necessary condition of perpetual inspiration. The relations between action and contemplation, ethics and spirituality, are circular and reciprocal. Each is at once cause and effect.

> It was when the Great Way declined that human kindness and morality arose.
>
> *Lao Tzu*

Chinese verbs are tenseless. This statement as to a hypothetical event in history refers at the same time to the present and the future. It means simply this: that with the rise of self-consciousness, animal grace is no longer sufficient for the conduct of life, and must be supplemented by conscious and deliberate choices between right and wrong—choices which have to be made in the light of a clearly formulated ethical code. But, as the Taoist sages are never tired of repeating, codes of ethics and deliberate choices made by the surface will are only a second best. The individualized will and the superficial intelligence are to be used for the purpose of recapturing the old animal relation to Tao, but on a higher, spiritual level. The goal is perpetual inspiration from sources beyond the personal self; and the means are "human kindness and morality," leading to the charity, which is unitive knowledge of Tao, as at once the Ground and Logos.

> Lord, Thou has given me my being of such a nature that it can continually make itself more able to receive thy grace and goodness. And this power, which I have of Thee, wherein I have a living image of thine almighty power, is free will. By this I can either enlarge or restrict my capacity for Thy grace.
>
> *Nicholas of Cusa*

> Shun asked Ch'eng, saying, "Can one get Tao so as to have it for oneself?"
>
> "Your very body," replied Ch'eng, "is not your own. How should Tao be?"
>
> "If my body," said Shun, "is not my own, pray whose is it?"
>
> "It is the delegated image of God," replied Ch'eng. "Your life is not your own. It is the delegated harmony of God. Your individuality is not your own. It is the delegated adaptability of God. Your posterity is not your own. It is the delegated exuviae of God. You move, but know not how. You are at rest, but know not why. You taste, but know not the cause. These are the operations of God's laws. How then should you get Tao so as to have it for your own?"
>
> *Chuang Tzu*

It is within my power either to serve God, or not to serve Him. Serving Him I add to my own good and the good of the whole world. Not serving Him, I forfeit my own good and deprive the world of that good, which was in my power to create.

Leo Tolstoy

God did not deprive thee of the operation of his love, but thou didst deprive Him of thy cooperation. God would never have rejected thee, if thou hadst not rejected his love. O all-good God, thou dost not forsake unless forsaken, thou never takest away thy gifts until we take away our hearts.

St. François de Sales

Ch'ing, the chief carpenter, was carving wood into a stand for musical instruments. When finished, the work appeared to those who saw it as though of supernatural execution; and the Prince of Lu asked him, saying, "What mystery is there in your art?"

"No mystery, Your Highness," replied Ch'ing. "And yet there is something. When I am about to make such a stand, I guard against any diminution of my vital power. I first reduce my mind to absolute quiescence. Three days in this condition, and I become oblivious of any reward to be gained. Five days, and I become oblivious of any fame to be acquired. Seven days, and I become unconscious of my four limbs and my physical frame. Then, with no thought of the Court present in my mind, my skill becomes concentrated, and all disturbing elements from without are gone. I enter some mountain forest, I search for a suitable tree. It contains the form required, which is afterwards elaborated. I see the stand in my mind's eye, and then set to work. Beyond that there is nothing. I bring my own native capacity into relation with that of the wood. What was suspected to be of supernatural execution in my work was due solely to this."

Chuang Tzu

The artist's inspiration may be either a human or a spiritual grace, or a mixture of both. High artistic achievement is impossible without at least those forms of intellectual, emotional and physical mortification appropriate to the kind of art which is being practised. Over and above this course of what may be called professional mortification, some artists have practised the kind of self-naughting which is the indispensable pre-condition of the unitive knowledge of the divine Ground. Fra Angelico, for example, prepared himself for his work by means of prayer and meditation; and from the foregoing extract from Chuang Tzu we see how essentially religious (and not merely professional) was the Taoist craftsman's approach to his art.

Here we may remark in passing that mechanization is incompatible with inspiration. The artisan could do and often did do a thoroughly bad job. But if, like Ch'ing, the chief carpenter, he cared for his art and were ready to do what was necessary to make himself docile to inspiration, he could and sometimes did do a job so good that it seemed "as though of supernatural execution." Among the many and enormous advantages of efficient automatic machinery is this: it is completely fool-proof. But every gain has to be paid for. The automatic machine is fool-proof; but just because it is fool-proof it is also grace-proof. The man who tends such a machine is impervious to every form of aesthetic inspiration, whether of human or of genuinely spiritual origin. "Industry without art is brutality." But actually Ruskin maligns the brutes. The industrious bird or insect is inspired, when it works, by the infallible animal grace of instinct—by Tao as it manifests itself on the level immediately above the physiological. The industrial worker at his fool-proof and grace-proof machine does his job in a man-made universe of punctual automata—a universe that lies entirely beyond the pale of Tao on any level, brutal, human or spiritual.

In this context we may mention those sudden theophanies which are sometimes vouchsafed to children and sometimes to adults, who may be poets or Philistines, learned or unsophisticated, but who have this in common, that they have done nothing at all to prepare for what has happened to them. These gratuitous graces, which have inspired much literary and pictorial art, some splendid and some (where inspiration was not seconded by native talent) pathetically inadequate, seem generally to belong to one or other of two main classes—sudden and profoundly impressive perception of ultimate

Reality as Love, Light and Bliss, and a no less impressive perception of it as dark, awe-inspiring and inscrutable Power.
In memorable forms, Wordsworth has recorded his own experience of both these aspects of the divine Ground.

> There was a time when meadow, grove and stream,
> The earth and every common sight,
>   To me did seem
>   Apparelled in celestial light.

And so on. But that was not the only vision.

>   Lustily
> I dipped my oars into the silent lake,
> And, as I rose upon the stroke, my boat
> Went heaving through the water like a swan;
> When, from behind that craggy steep, till then
> The horizon's bound, a huge peak, black and huge,
> As if with voluntary power instinct,
> Upreared its head. I struck and struck again,
> And growing still in stature, the grim shape
> Towered up between me and the stars. . . .
>   But after I had seen
> That spectacle, for many days my brain
> Worked with a dim and undetermined sense
> Of unknown modes of being; o'er my thoughts
> There hung a darkness, call it solitude,
> Or blank desertion.

Significantly enough, it is to this second aspect of Reality
that primitive minds seem to have been most receptive. The
formidable God, to whom Job at last submits, is an "unknown
mode of Being," whose most characteristic creations are
Behemoth and Leviathan. He is the sort of God who calls,
in Kierkegaard's phrase, for "teleological suspensions of
morality," chiefly in the form of blood sacrifices, even human
sacrifices. The Hindu goddess, Kali, in her more frightful
aspects, is another manifestation of the same unknown mode
of Being. And by many contemporary savages the underlying
Ground is apprehended and theologically rationalized as
sheer, unmitigated Power, which has to be propitiatively wor-

shipped and, if possible, turned to profitable use by means
of a compulsive magic.

To think of God as mere Power, and not also, at the same
time as Power, Love and Wisdom, comes quite naturally to
the ordinary, unregenerate human mind. Only the totally selfless are in a position to know experimentally that, in spite
of everything, "all will be well" and, in some way, already *is*
well. "The philosopher who denies divine providence," says
Rumi, "is a stranger to the perception of the saints." Only
those who have the perception of the saints can know all the
time and by immediate experience that divine Reality manifests itself as a Power that is loving, compassionate and wise.
The rest of us are not yet in a spiritual position to do more
than accept their findings on faith. If it were not for the records they have left behind, we should be more inclined to
agree with Job and the primitives.

> Inspirations prevent us, and even before they are thought
> of make themselves felt; but after we have felt them it is
> ours either to consent to them, so as to second and follow
> their attractions, or else to dissent and repulse them.
> They make themselves felt without us, but they do not
> make us consent without us.
>
> *St. François de Sales*

> Our free will can hinder the course of inspiration, and
> when the favourable gale of God's grace swells the sails
> of our soul, it is in our power to refuse consent and
> thereby hinder the effect of the wind's favour; but when
> our spirit sails along and makes its voyage prosperously,
> it is not we who make the gale of inspiration blow for
> us, nor we who make our sails swell with it, nor we who
> give motion to the ship of our heart; but we simply
> receive the gale, consent to its motion and let our ship
> sail under it, not hindering it by our resistance.
>
> *St. François de Sales*

> Grace is necessary to salvation, free will equally so—but
> grace in order to give salvation, free will in order to re-
> ceive it. Therefore we should not attribute part of the
> good work to grace and part to free will; it is performed
> in its entirety by the common and inseparable action of

both; entirely by grace, entirely by free will, but spring-
ing from the first in the second.

St. Bernard

St. Bernard distinguishes between *voluntas communis* and
voluntas propria. Voluntas communis is common in two senses;
it is the will to share, and it is the will common to man and
God. For practical purposes it is equivalent to charity. *Voluntas propria* is the will to get and hold for oneself, and is
the root of all sin. In its cognitive aspect, *voluntas propria* is
the same as *sensum proprium,* which is one's own opinion,
cherished because it is one's own and therefore always morally
wrong, even though it may be theoretically correct.

Two students from the University of Paris came to visit
Ruysbroeck and asked him to furnish them with a short
phrase or motto, which might serve them as a rule of life.
    Vos estis tam sancti sicut vultis, Ruysbroeck answered.
"You are as holy as you will to be."

God is bound to act, to pour Himself into thee as soon as
He shall find thee ready.

Eckhart

The will is that which has all power; it makes heaven
and it makes hell; for there is no hell but where the will
of the creature is turned from God, nor any heaven but
where the will of the creature worketh with God.

William Law

O man, consider thyself! Here thou standest in the earnest
perpetual strife of good and evil; all nature is continually
at work to bring forth the great redemption; the whole
creation is travailing in pain and laborious working to
be delivered from the vanity of time; and wilt thou be
asleep? Everything thou hearest or seest says nothing,
shows nothing to thee but what either eternal light or
eternal darkness has brought forth; for as day and night
divide the whole of our time, so heaven and hell divide
all our thoughts, words and actions. Stir which way thou
wilt, do or design what thou wilt, thou must be an agent
with the one or the other. Thou canst not stand still,
because thou livest in the perpetual workings of tem-

poral and eternal nature; if thou workest not with the good, the evil that is in nature carries thee along with it. Thou hast the height and depth of eternity in thee and therefore, be doing what thou wilt, either in the closet, the field, the shop or the church, thou art sowing that which grows and must be reaped in eternity.

William Law

God expects but one thing of you, and that is that you should come out of yourself in so far as you are a created being and let God be God in you.

Eckhart

For those who take pleasure in theological speculations based upon scriptural texts and dogmatic postulates, there are the thousands of pages of Catholic and Protestant controversy upon grace, works, faith and justification. And for students of comparative religion there are scholarly commentaries on the Bhagavad Gita, on the works of Ramanuja and those later Vaishnavites, whose doctrine of grace bears a striking resemblance to that of Luther; there are histories of Buddhism which duly trace the development of that religion from the Hinayanist doctrine that salvation is the fruit of strenuous self-help to the Mahayanist doctrine that it cannot be achieved without the grace of the Primordial Buddha, whose inner consciousness and "great compassionate heart" constitute the eternal Suchness of things. For the rest of us, the foregoing quotations from writers within the Christian and early Taoist tradition provide, it seems to me, an adequate account of the observable facts of grace and inspiration and their relation to the observable facts of free will.

CHAPTER XI

Good and Evil

DESIRE is the first datum of our consciousness; we are born into sympathy and antipathy, wishing and willing. Unconsciously at first, then consciously, we evaluate: "This is good, that is bad." And a little later we discover obligation. "This, being good, ought to be done; that, being bad, ought not to be done."

All evaluations are not equally valid. We are called upon to pass judgment on what our desires and dislikes affirm to be good or bad. Very often we discover that the verdict of the higher court is at variance with the decision reached so quickly and light-heartedly in the court of first instance. In the light of what we know about ourselves, our fellow beings and the world at large, we discover that what at first seemed good may, in the long run or in the larger context, be bad; and that what at first seemed bad may be a good which we feel ourselves under obligation to accomplish.

When we say that a man is possessed of penetrating moral insight we mean that his judgment of value-claims is sound; that he knows enough to be able to say what is good in the longest run and the largest context. When we say that a man has a strong moral character, we mean that he is ready to act upon the findings of his insight, even when these findings are unpleasantly or even excruciatingly at variance with his first, spontaneous valuations.

In actual practice moral insight is never a strictly personal matter. The judge administers a system of law and is guided by precedent. In other words, every individual is the member of a community, which has a moral code based upon past findings of what in fact is good in the longer run and the wider context. In most circumstances most of the members of any given society permit themselves to be guided by the generally accepted code of morals; a few reject the code, either in its entirety or in part; and a few choose to live by another, higher and more exacting code. In Christian phraseology, there are the few who stubbornly persist in living in a state of mortal sin and antisocial lawlessness; there are the many who obey the laws, make the Precepts of Morality their guide, repent of mortal sins when they commit them, but do not make much effort to avoid venial sins; and finally there are the few whose righteousness "exceeds the righteousness of the scribes and Pharisees," who are guided by the Counsels of Perfection and have the insight to perceive and the character to avoid venial sins and even imperfections.

Philosophers and theologians have sought to establish a theoretical basis for the existing moral codes, by whose aid individual men and women pass judgment on their spontaneous evaluations. From Moses to Bentham, from Epicurus to Calvin, from the Christian and Buddhist philosophies of universal love to the lunatic doctrines of nationalism and racial superiority—the list is long and the span of thought enormously wide. But fortunately there is no need for us to consider these various theories. Our concern is only with the Perennial Philosophy and with the system of ethical principles which those who believe in that philosophy have used, when passing judgment on their own and other people's evaluations. The questions that we have to ask in this section are simple enough, and simple too are the answers. As always, the difficulties begin only when we pass from theory to practice, from ethical principle to particular application.

Granted that the ground of the individual soul is akin to, or identical with, the divine Ground of all existence, and granted that this divine Ground is an ineffable Godhead that manifests itself as personal God or even as the incarnate Logos, what is the ultimate nature of good and evil, and what the true purpose and last end of human life?

The answers to these questions will be given to a great extent in the words of that most surprising product of the English eighteenth century, William Law. (How very odd our educational system is! Students of English literature are forced to read the graceful journalism of Steele and Addison, are expected to know all about the minor novels of Defoe and the tiny elegances of Matthew Prior. But they can pass all their examinations *summa cum laude* without having so much as looked into the writings of a man who was not only a master of English prose, but also one of the most interesting thinkers of his period and one of the most endearingly saintly figures in the whole history of Anglicanism.) Our current neglect of Law is yet another of the many indications that twentieth-century educators have ceased to be concerned with questions of ultimate truth or meaning and (apart from mere vocational training) are interested solely in the dissemination of a rootless and irrelevant culture, and the fostering of the solemn foolery of scholarship for scholarship's sake.

Nothing burns in hell but the self.

Theologia Germanica

The mind is on fire, thoughts are on fire. Mind-consciousness and the impressions received by the mind, and the sensations that arise from the impressions that the mind receives—these too are on fire.

And with what are they on fire? With the fire of greed, with the fire of resentment, with the fire of infatuation; with birth, old age and death, with sorrow and lamentation, with misery and grief and despair they are on fire.

From the Buddha's Fire Sermon

If thou has not seen the devil, look at thine own self.

Jalal-uddin Rumi

Your own self is your own Cain that murders your own Abel. For every action and motion of self has the spirit of Anti-Christ and murders the divine life within you.

William Law

The city of God is made by the love of God pushed to the contempt of self; the earthly city, by the love of self pushed to the contempt of God.

St. Augustine

The difference between a good and a bad man does not lie in this, that the one wills that which is good and the other does not, but solely in this, that the one concurs with the living inspiring spirit of God within him, and the other resists it, and can be chargeable with evil only because he resists it.

William Law

People should think less about what they ought to do and more about what they ought to be. If only their being were good, their works would shine forth brightly. Do not imagine that you can ground your salvation upon actions; it must rest on what you *are*. The ground upon which good character rests is the very same ground from which man's work derives its value, namely a mind wholly turned to God. Verily, if you were so minded, you might tread on a stone and it would be a more pious work than if you, simply for your own profit, were to receive the Body of the Lord and were wanting in spiritual detachment.

Eckhart

Man is made by his belief. As he believes, so he is.

Bhagavad Gita

It is mind which gives to things their quality, their foundation and their being. Whoever speaks or acts with impure mind, him sorrow follows, as the wheel follows the steps of the ox that draws the cart.

Dhammapada

The nature of a man's being determines the nature of his actions; and the nature of his being comes to manifestation first of all in the mind. What he craves and thinks, what he believes and feels—this is, so to speak, the Logos, by whose agency an individual's fundamental character performs its creative acts. These acts will be beautiful and morally good if the being is God-centred, bad and ugly if it is centred in the personal self. "The stone," says Eckhart, "performs its work without ceasing, day and night." For even when it is not actually falling the stone has weight. A man's being is his potential energy directed towards or away from God; and it is by this potential energy that he will be judged as good or evil—for it is possible, in the language of the Gospel, to commit adultery and murder in the heart, even while remaining blameless in action.

Covetousness, envy, pride and wrath are the four elements of self, or nature, or hell, all of them inseparable from it. And the reason why it must be thus, and cannot be otherwise, is because the natural life of the creature is brought forth for the participation of some high supernatural good in the Creator. But it could have no fitness, no possible capacity to receive such good, unless it was in itself both an extremity of want and an extremity of desire for some high good. When therefore this natural life is deprived of or fallen from God, it can be nothing else in itself but an extremity of want continually desiring, and an extremity of desire continually wanting. And because it is that, its whole life can be nothing else but a plague and torment of covetousness, envy, pride and wrath, all which is precisely nature, self, or hell. Now covetousness, pride and envy are not three different things, but only three different names for the restless workings of one and the same will or desire. Wrath, which is a fourth birth from these three, can have no existence till one or all of these three are contradicted, or have something done to them that is contrary to their will. These four properties generate their own torment. They have no outward cause, nor any inward power of altering themselves. And therefore all self or nature must be in this state until some supernatural good comes into it, or gets a birth in it. Whilst man indeed lives among the vanities of time, his covetousness, envy, pride and wrath may be in a tolerable state, may hold him to a mixture of peace and trouble; they may have at times their gratifications as well as their torments. But when death has put an end to the vanity of all earthly cheats, the soul that is not born again of the supernatural Word and Spirit of God, must find itself unavoidably devoured or shut up in its own insatiable, unchangeable, self-tormenting covetousness, envy, pride and wrath.

William Law

It is true that you cannot properly express the degree of your sinfulness; but that is because it is impossible, in this life, to represent sins in all their true ugliness; nor shall we ever know them as they really are except in the light of God. God gives to some souls an impression of the enormity of sin, by which He makes them feel that sin is incomparably greater than it seems. Such souls must conceive their sins as faith represents them (that is, as they are in themselves), but must be content to describe them in such human words as their mouth is able to utter.

Charles de Condren

Lucifer, when he stood in his natural nobility, as God had created him, was a pure noble creature. But when he kept to self, when he possessed himself and his natural nobility as a property, he fell and became, instead of an angel, a devil. So it is with man. If he remains in himself and possesses himself of his natural nobility as a property, he falls and becomes, instead of a man, a devil.

The Following of Christ

If a delicious fragrant fruit had a power of separating
itself from the rich spirit, fine taste, smell and colour,
which it receives from the virtue of the air and the
spirit of the sun, or if it could, in the beginning of its
growth, turn away from the sun and receive no virtue
from it, then it would stand in its own first birth of
wrath, sourness, bitterness, astringency, just as the devils
do, who have turned back into their own dark root and
have rejected the Light and Spirit of God. So that the
hellish nature of a devil is nothing but its own first
forms of life withdrawn or separated from the heavenly
Light and Love; just as the sourness, bitterness and
astringency of a fruit are nothing else but the first form
of its vegetable life, before it has reached the virtue of
the sun and the spirit of the air. And as a fruit, if it had
a sensibility of itself, would be full of torment as soon
as it was shut up in the first forms of its life, in its own
astringency, sourness and stinging bitterness, so the angels,
when they had turned back into these very same first
forms of their own life, and broke off from the heavenly
Light and Love of God, became their own hell. No hell
was made for them, no new qualities came into them,
no vengeance or pains from the Lord of Love fell on
them; they only stood in that state of division and separation from the Son and Holy Spirit of God, which by
their own motion they had made for themselves. They had
nothing in them but what they had from God, the first
forms of a heavenly life; but they had them in a state
of self-torment, because they had separated them from
birth of Love and Light.

William Law

In all the possibility of things there is and can be but
one happiness and one misery. The one misery is nature
and creature left to itself, the one happiness is the Life,
the Light, the Spirit of God, manifested in nature and
creature. This is the true meaning of the words of Our
Lord: There is but one that is good, and that is God.

William Law

Men are not in hell because God is angry with them;
they are in wrath and darkness because they have done to

the light, which infinitely flows forth from God, as that man does to the light of the sun, who puts out his own eyes.

William Law

Though the light and comfort of the outward world keeps even the worst of men from any constant strong sensibility of that wrathful, fiery, dark and self-tormenting nature that is the very essence of every fallen unregenerate soul, yet every man in the world has more or less frequent and strong intimations given him that so it is with him in the inmost ground of his soul. How many inventions are some people forced to have recourse to in order to keep off a certain inward uneasiness, which they are afraid of and know not whence it comes? Alas, it is because there is a fallen spirit, a dark aching fire within them, which has never had its proper relief and is trying to discover itself and calling out for help at every cessation of worldly joy.

William Law

In the Hebrew-Christian tradition the Fall is subsequent to creation and is due exclusively to the egocentric use of a free will, which ought to have remained centred in the divine Ground and not in the separate selfhood. The myth of Genesis embodies a very important psychological truth, but falls short of being an entirely satisfactory symbol, because it fails to mention, much less to account for, the fact of evil and suffering in the non-human world. To be adequate to our experience the myth would have to be modified in two ways. In the first place, it would have to make clear that creation, the incomprehensible passage from the unmanifested One into the manifest multiplicity of nature, from eternity into time, is not merely the prelude and necessary condition of the Fall; to some extent it *is* the Fall. And in the second place, it would have to indicate that something analogous to free will may exist below the human level.

That the passage from the unity of spiritual to the manifoldness of temporal being is an essential part of the Fall is clearly stated in the Buddhist and Hindu renderings of the Perennial Philosophy. Pain and evil are inseparable from individual existence in a world of time; and, for human beings,

there is an intensification of this inevitable pain and evil
when the desire is turned towards the self and the many,
rather than towards the divine Ground. To this we might
speculatively add the opinion that perhaps even subhuman
existences may be endowed (both individually and collectively,
as kinds and species) with something resembling the power
of choice. There is the extraordinary fact that "man stands
alone"—that, so far as we can judge, every other species is a
species of living fossils, capable only of degeneration and extinction, not of further evolutionary advance. In the phraseology of Scholastic Aristotelianism, matter possesses an appetite for form—not necessarily for the best form, but for
form as such. Looking about us in the world of living things,
we observe (with a delighted wonder, touched occasionally,
it must be admitted, with a certain questioning dismay) the
innumerable forms, always beautiful, often extravagantly odd
and sometimes even sinister, in which the insatiable appetite
of matter has found its satisfaction. Of all this living matter
only that which is organized as human beings has succeeded
in finding a form capable, at any rate on the mental side, of
further development. All the rest is now locked up in forms
that can only remain what they are or, if they change, only
change for the worse. It looks as though, in the cosmic intelligence test, all living matter, except the human, had succumbed, at one time or another during its biological career,
to the temptation of assuming, not the ultimately best, but
the immediately most profitable form. By an act of something
analogous to free will every species, except the human, has
chosen the quick returns of specialization, the present rapture
of being perfect, but perfect on a low level of being. The result is that they all stand at the end of evolutionary blind
alleys. To the initial cosmic Fall of creation, of multitudinous
manifestation in time, they have added the obscurely biological equivalent of man's voluntary Fall. As species, they have
chosen the immediate satisfaction of the self rather than the
capacity for reunion with the divine Ground. For this wrong
choice, the non-human forms of life are punished negatively,
by being debarred from realizing the supreme good, to which
only the unspecialized and therefore freer, more highly conscious human form is capable. But it must be remembered,
of course, that the capacity for supreme good is achieved only
at the price of becoming also capable of extreme evil. Animals

do not suffer in so many ways, nor, we may feel pretty certain, to the same extent as do men and women. Further, they are quite innocent of that literally diabolic wickedness which, together with sanctity, is one of the distinguishing marks of the human species.

We see then that, for the Perennial Philosophy, good is the separate self's conformity to, and finally annihilation in, the divine Ground which gives it being; evil, the intensification of separateness, the refusal to know that the Ground exists. This doctrine is, of course, perfectly compatible with the formulation of ethical principles as a series of negative and positive divine commandments, or even in terms of social utility. The crimes which are everywhere forbidden proceed from states of mind which are everywhere condemned as wrong; and these wrong states of mind are, as a matter of empirical fact, absolutely incompatible with that unitive knowledge of the divine Ground, which, according to the Perennial Philosophy, is the supreme good.

CHAPTER XII

Time and Eternity

THE universe is an everlasting succession of events; but its ground, according to the Perennial Philosophy, is the timeless now of the divine Spirit. A classical statement of the relationship between time and eternity may be found in the later chapters of the "Consolations of Philosophy," where Boethius summarizes the conceptions of his predecessors, notably of Plotinus.

It is one thing to be carried through an endless life, another thing to embrace the whole presence of an endless life together, which is manifestly proper to the divine Mind.

The temporal world seems to emulate in part that which it cannot fully obtain or express, tying itself to whatever presence there is in this exiguous and fleeting moment—a presence which, since it carries a certain image of that abiding Presence, gives to whatever may partake of it the quality of seeming to have being. But because it could not stay, it undertook an infinite journey of time; and so it came to pass that, by going, it continued that life, whose plenitude it could not comprehend by staying.

Boethius

Since God hath always an eternal and present state, His knowledge, surpassing time's notions, remaineth in the simplicity of His presence and, comprehending the infinite of what is past and to come, considereth all things as though they were in the act of being accomplished.

Boethius

Knowledge of what is happening now does not determine the event. What is ordinarily called God's foreknowledge is in reality a timeless now-knowledge, which is compatible with the freedom of the human creature's will in time.

The manifest world and whatever is moved in any sort take their causes, order and forms from the stability of the divine Mind. This hath determined manifold ways for doing things; which ways being considered in the purity of God's understanding are named Providence; but being referred to those things which he moveth and disposeth are called Fate. . . . Providence is the very divine Reason itself, which disposeth all things. But Fate is a disposition inherent in changeable things, by which Providence connecteth all things in their due order. For Providence equally embraceth all things together, though diverse, though infinite; but Fate puts into motion all things, distributed by places, forms and times; so that the unfolding of the temporal order, being united in the foresight of the divine Mind is Providence, and the same uniting, being digested and unfolded in time, is called Fate. . . . As a workman conceiving the form of anything in his mind, taketh his work in hand and executeth by order of time that which he had simply and in a moment foreseen, so God by his Providence disposeth whatever is to be done with simplicity and stability, and by Fate effecteth by manifold ways and in the order of time those

very things which he disposeth. . . . All that is under
Fate is also subject to Providence. But some things which
are under Providence are above the course of Fate. For
they are those things which, being stably fixed in virtue
of their nearness to the first divinity, exceed the order of
Fate's mobility.

Boethius

The concept of a clock enfolds all succession in time. In
the concept the sixth hour is not earlier than the seventh
or eighth, although the clock never strikes the hour, save
when the concept biddeth.

Nicholas of Cusa

From Hobbes onwards, the enemies of the Perennial Philosophy have denied the existence of an eternal now. According
to these thinkers, time and change are fundamental; there is
no other reality. Moreover, future events are completely inde-
terminate, and even God can have no knowledge of them.
Consequently God cannot be described as Alpha and Omega—
merely as Alpha and Lambda, or whatever other intermediate
letter of the temporal alphabet is now in process of being
spelled out. But the anecdotal evidence collected by the Society
for Psychical Research and the statistical evidence accumulated
during many thousands of laboratory tests for extra-sensory
perception point inescapably to the conclusion that even human
minds are capable of foreknowledge. And if a finite consciousness can know what card is going to be turned up three
seconds from now, or what shipwreck is going to take place
next week, then there is nothing impossible or even intrinsically improbable in the idea of an infinite consciousness that
can know now events indefinitely remote in what, for us, is
future time. The "specious present" in which human beings
live may be, and perhaps always is, something more than a
brief section of transition from known past to unknown future,
regarded, because of the vividness of memory, as the instant
we call "now"; it may and perhaps always does contain a
portion of the immediate and even of the relatively distant
future. For the Godhead, the specious present may be precisely that *interminabilis vitae tota simul et perpetua pos-
sessio,* of which Boethius speaks.

The existence of the eternal now is sometimes denied on the

ground that a temporal order cannot co-exist with another order which is non-temporal; and that it is impossible for a changing substance to be united with a changeless substance. This objection, it is obvious, would be valid if the non-temporal order were of a mechanical nature, or if the changeless substance were possessed of spatial and material qualities. But according to the Perennial Philosophy, the eternal now is a consciousness; the divine Ground is spirit; the being of Brahman is *chit*, or knowledge. That a temporal world should be known and, in being known, sustained and perpetually created by an eternal consciousness is an idea which contains nothing self-contradictory.

Finally we come to the arguments directed against those who have asserted that the eternal Ground can be unitively known by human minds. This claim is regarded as absurd because it involves the assertion, "At one time I am eternal, at another time I am in time." But this statement is absurd only if man is a being of a twofold nature, capable of living on only one level. But if, as the exponents of the Perennial Philosophy have always maintained, man is not only a body and a psyche, but also a spirit, and if he can at will live either on the merely human plane or else in harmony and even in union with the divine Ground of his being, then the statement makes perfectly good sense. The body is always in time, the spirit is always timeless and the psyche is an amphibious creature compelled by the laws of man's being to associate itself to some extent with its body, but capable, if it so desires, of experiencing and being identified with its spirit and, through its spirit, with the divine Ground. The spirit remains always what it eternally is; but man is so constituted that his psyche cannot always remain identified with the spirit. In the statement, "At one time I am eternal, at another time I am in time," the word "I" stands for the psyche, which passes from time to eternity when it is identified with the spirit and passes again from eternity to time, either voluntarily or by involuntary necessity, when it chooses or is compelled to identify itself with the body.

"The Sufi," says Jalal-uddin Rumi, "is the son of time present." Spiritual progress is a spiral advance. We start as infants in the animal eternity of life in the moment, without anxiety for the future or regret for the past; we grow up into the specifically human condition of those who look before and after, who live to a great extent, not in the present but in memory and anticipation, not spontaneously but by rule and with prudence, in repentance and fear and hope; and we can continue, if we so desire, up and on in a returning sweep towards a point corresponding to our starting place in animality, but incommensurably above it. Once more life is lived in the moment—the life now, not of a sub-human creature, but of a being in whom charity has cast out fear, vision has taken the place of hope, selflessness has put a stop to the positive egotism of complacent reminiscence and the negative egotism of remorse. The present moment is the only aperture through which the soul can pass out of time into eternity, through which grace can pass out of eternity into the soul, and through which charity can pass from one soul in time to another soul in time. That is why the Sufi and, along with him, every other practising exponent of the Perennial Philosophy is, or tries to be, a son of time present

> Past and future veil God from our sight;
> Burn up both of them with fire. How long
> Wilt thou be partitioned by these segments, like a reed?
> So long as a reed is partitioned, it is not privy to secrets,
> Nor is it vocal in response to lip and breathing.
>
> *Jalal-uddin Rumi*

> This emptying of the memory, though the advantages of it are not so great as those of the state of union, yet merely because it delivers souls from much sorrow, grief and sadness, besides imperfections and sins, is in reality a great good.
>
> *St. John of the Cross*

In the idealistic cosmology of Mahayana Buddhism memory plays the part of a rather maleficent demiurge. "When the triple world is surveyed by the Bodhisattva, he perceives that its existence is due to memory that has been accumulated since the beginningless past, but wrongly interpreted." (Lankavatara Sutra), The word here translated as "memory," means literally "perfuming." The mind-body carried with it the ineradicable smell of all that has been thought and done, desired and felt, throughout its racial and personal past. The Chinese translate the Sanskrit term by two symbols, signifying "habit-energy." The world is what (in our eyes) it is, because of all the consciously or unconsciously and physiologically remembered habits formed by our ancestors or by ourselves, either in our present life or in previous existences. These remembered bad habits cause us to believe that multiplicity is the sole reality and that the idea of "I," "me," "mine" represents the ultimate truth. *Nirvana* consists in "seeing into the abode of reality as it is," and not reality *quoad nos*, as it seems to us. Obviously, this cannot be achieved so long as there is an "us," to which reality can be relative. Hence the need, stressed by every exponent of the Perennial Philosophy, for mortification, for dying to self. And this must be a mortification not only of the appetites, the feelings and the will, but also of the reasoning powers, of consciousness itself and of that which makes our consciousness what it is— our personal memory and our inherited habit-energies. To achieve complete deliverance, conversion from sin is not enough; there must also be a conversion of the mind, a *paravritti*, as the Mahayanists call it, or revulsion in the very depths of consciousness. As the result of this revulsion, the habit-energies of accumulated memory are destroyed and, along with them, the sense of being a separate ego. Reality is no longer perceived *quoad nos* (for the good reason that there is no longer a *nos* to perceive it), but as it is in itself. In Blake's words, "If the doors of perception were cleansed, everything would be seen as it is, infinite." By those who are pure in heart and poor in spirit, Samsara and Nirvana, appearance and reality, time and eternity are experienced as one and the same.

> Time is what keeps the light from reaching us. There is no greater obstacle to God than time. And not only time but temporalities, not only temporal things but temporal affections; not only temporal affections but the very taint and smell of time.
>
> *Eckhart*

Rejoice in God all the time, says St Paul. He rejoices all the time who rejoices above time and free from time. Three things prevent a man from knowing God. The first is time, the second is corporeality, the third is multiplicity. That God may come in, these things must go

out—except thou have them in a higher, better way:
multitude summed up to one in thee.

Eckhart

Whenever God is thought of as being wholly in time, there
is a tendency to regard Him as a "numinous" rather than a
moral being, a God of mere unmitigated Power rather than
a God of Power, Wisdom and Love, an inscrutable and dangerous potentate to be propitiated by sacrifices, not a Spirit to be
worshipped in spirit. All this is only natural; for time is a
perpetual perishing and a God who is wholly in time is a
God who destroys as fast as He creates. Nature is as incompre-
hensibly appalling as it is lovely and bountiful. If the Divine
does not transcend the temporal order in which it is immanent,
and if the human spirit does not transcend its time-bound soul,
then there is no possibility of "justifying the ways of God to
man." God as manifested in the universe is the irresistible
Being who speaks to Job out of the whirlwind, and whose
emblems are Behemoth and Leviathan, the war horse and
the eagle. It is this same Being who is described in the Apocalyptic eleventh chapter of the Bhagavad Gita. "O Supreme
Spirit," says Arjuna, addressing himself to the Krishna whom
he now knows to be the incarnation of the Godhead, "I long
to see your Isvara-form"—that is to say, his form as God of
the world, Nature, the temporal order. Krishna answers, "You
shall behold the whole universe, with all things animate and
inanimate, within this body of mine." Arjuna's reaction to the
revelation is one of amazement and fear.

Ah, my God, I see all gods within your body;
Each in his degree, the multitude of creatures;
See Lord Brahma seated upon his lotus,
See all the sages and the holy serpents.

Universal Form, I see you without limit,
Infinite of eyes, arms, mouths and bellies—
See, and find no end, midst or beginning.

There follows a long passage, enlarging on the omnipotence
and all-comprehensiveness of God in his Isvara-form. Then the
quality of the vision changes, and Arjuna realizes, with fear

and trembling, that the God of the universe is a God of destruction as well as of creation.

> Now with frightful tusks your mouths are gnashing,
> Flaring like the fires of Doomsday morning—
> North, south, east and west seem all confounded—
> Lord of devas, world's abode, have mercy! . . . .

> Swift as many rivers streaming to the ocean,
> Rush the heroes to your fiery gullets,
> Moth-like to meet the flame of their destruction.
> Headlong these plunge into you and perish. . . .

> Tell me who you are, and were from the beginning,
> You of aspect grim. O God of gods, be gracious.
> Take my homage, Lord. From me your ways are hidden.

"Tell me who you are." The answer is clear and unequivocal.

> I am come as Time, the waster of the peoples,
> Ready for the hour that ripens to their ruin.

But the God who comes so terribly as Time also exists timelessly as the Godhead, as Brahman, whose essence is *Sat, Chit, Ananda*, Being, Awareness, Bliss; and within and beyond man's time-tortured psyche is his spirit, "uncreated and uncreatable," as Eckhart says, the Atman which is akin to or even identical with Brahman. The Gita, like all other formulations of the Perennial Philosophy, justifies God's ways to man by affirming —and the affirmation is based upon observation and immediate experience—that man can, if he so desires, die to his separate temporal selfness and so come to union with timeless Spirit. It affirms, too, that the Avatar becomes incarnate in order to assist human beings to achieve this union. This he does in three ways—by teaching the true doctrine in a world blinded by voluntary ignorance; by inviting souls to a "carnal love" of his humanity, not indeed as an end in itself, but as the means to spiritual love-knowledge of Spirit; and finally by serving as a channel of grace.

God who is Spirit can only be worshipped in spirit and for his own sake; but God in time is normally worshipped by material means with a view to achieving temporal ends. God in time is manifestly the destroyer as well as the creator; and because this is so, it has seemed proper to worship him by methods which are as terrible as the destructions he himself inflicts. Hence, in India, the blood sacrifices to Kali, in her aspect as Nature-the-Destroyer; hence those offerings of children to "the Molochs," denounced by the Hebrew prophets; hence the human sacrifices practised, for example, by the Phoenicians, the Carthaginians, the Druids, the Aztecs. In all such cases the divinity addressed was a god in time, or a personification of Nature, which is nothing else but Time itself, the devourer of its own offspring; and in all cases the purpose of the rite was to obtain a future benefit or to avoid one of the enormous evils which Time and Nature for ever hold in store. For this it was thought to be worth while to pay a high price in that currency of suffering, which the Destroyer so evidently valued. The importance of the temporal end justified the use of means that were intrinsically terrible, because intrinsically time-like. Sublimated traces of these ancient patterns of thought and behaviour are still to be found in certain theories of the Atonement, and in the conception of the Mass as a perpetually repeated sacrifice of the God-Man.

In the modern world the gods to whom human sacrifice is offered are personifications, not of Nature, but of man's own, home-made political ideals. These, of course, all refer to events in time—actual events in the past or the present, fancied events in the future. And here it should be noted that the philosophy which affirms the existence and the immediate realizableness of eternity is related to one kind of political theory and practice; the philosophy which affirms that what goes on in time is the only reality, results in a different kind of theory and justifies quite another kind of political practice. This has been clearly recognized by Marxist writers,* who point out that when Christianity is mainly preoccupied with events in time, it is a "revolutionary religion," and that when, under mystical influences, it stresses the Eternal Gospel, of which the historical or pseudo-historical facts recorded in Scripture are but symbols, it becomes politically "static" and "reactionary."

This Marxian account of the matter is somewhat oversimplified. It is not quite true to say that all theologies and philosophies whose primary concern is with time, rather than eternity,

* See, for example, Professor J. B. S. Haldane's *The Marxist Philosophy and the Sciences*.

are necessarily revolutionary. The aim of all revolutions is to make the future radically different from and better than the past. But some time-obsessed philosophies are primarily concerned with the past, not the future, and their politics are entirely a matter of preserving or restoring the *status quo* and getting back to the good old days. But the retrospective time-worshippers have one thing in common with the revolutionary devotees of the bigger and better future; they are prepared to use unlimited violence to achieve their ends. It is here that we discover the essential difference between the politics of eternity-philosophers and the politics of time-philosophers. For the latter, the ultimate good is to be found in the temporal world—in a future, where everyone will be happy because all are doing and thinking something either entirely new and unprecedented or, alternatively, something old, traditional and hallowed. And because the ultimate good lies in time, they feel justified in making use of any temporal means for achieving it. The Inquisition burns and tortures in order to perpetuate a creed, a ritual and an ecclesiastico-politico-financial organization regarded as necessary to men's eternal salvation. Bible-worshipping Protestants fight long and savage wars, in order to make the world safe for what they fondly imagine to be the genuinely antique Christianity of apostolic times. Jacobins and Bolsheviks are ready to sacrifice millions of human lives for the sake of a political and economic future gorgeously unlike the present. And now all Europe and most of Asia has had to be sacrificed to a crystal-gazer's vision of perpetual Co-Prosperity and the Thousand-Year Reich. From the records of history it seems to be abundantly clear that most of the religions and philosophies which take time too seriously are correlated with political theories that inculcate and justify the use of large-scale violence. The only exceptions are those simple Epicurean faiths, in which the reaction to an all too real time is "Eat, drink and be merry, for tomorrow we die." This is not a very noble, nor even a very realistic kind of morality. But it seems to make a good deal more sense than the revolutionary ethic: "Die (and kill), for tomorrow someone else will eat, drink and be merry." In practice, of course, the prospect even of somebody else's future merriment is extremely precarious. For the process of wholesale dying and killing creates material, social and psychological conditions that practically guarantee the revolution against the achievement of its beneficent ends.

For those whose philosophy does not compel them to take time with an excessive seriousness the ultimate good is to be sought neither in the revolutionary's progressive social apocalypse, nor in the reactionary's revived and perpetuated past, but in an eternal divine now which those who sufficiently desire this good can realize as a fact of immediate experience. The mere act of dying is not in itself a passport to eternity; nor can wholesale killing do anything to bring deliverance either to the slayers or the slain or their posterity. The peace that passes all understanding is the fruit of liberation into eternity; but in its ordinary everyday form peace is also the root of liberation. For where there are violent passions and compelling distractions, this ultimate good can never be realized. That is one of the reasons why the policy correlated with eternity-philosophies is tolerant and non-violent. The other reason is that the eternity, whose realization is the ultimate good, is a kingdom of heaven within. Thou art That; and though That is immortal and impassible, the killing and torturing of individual "thous" is a matter of cosmic significance, inasmuch as it interferes with the normal and natural relationship between individual souls and the divine eternal Ground of all being. Every violence is, over and above everything else, a sacrilegious rebellion against the divine order.

Passing now from theory to historical fact, we find that the religions, whose theology has been least preoccupied with events in time and most concerned with eternity, have been consistently the least violent and the most humane in political practice. Unlike early Judaism, Christianity and Mohammedanism (all of them obsessed with time), Hinduism and Buddhism have never been persecuting faiths, have preached almost no holy wars and have refrained from that proselytizing religious imperialism, which has gone hand in hand with the political and economic oppression of the coloured peoples. For four hundred years, from the beginning of the sixteenth century to the beginning of the twentieth, most of the Christian nations of Europe have spent a good part of their time and energy in attacking, conquering and exploiting their non-Christian neighbours in other continents. In the course of these centuries many individual churchmen did their best to mitigate the consequences of such iniquities; but none of the major

Christian churches officially condemned them. The first collective protest against the slave system, introduced by the English and the Spaniards into the New World, was made in 1688 by the Quaker Meeting of Germantown. This fact is highly significant. Of all Christian sects in the seventeenth century, the Quakers were the least obsessed with history, the least addicted to the idolatry of things in time. They believed that the inner light was in all human beings and that salvation came to those who lived in conformity with that light and was not dependent on the profession of belief in historical or pseudo-historical events, nor on the performance of certain rites, nor on the support of a particular ecclesiastical organization. Moreover their eternity-philosophy preserved them from the materialistic apocalypticism of that progress-worship which in recent times has justified every kind of iniquity from war and revolution to sweated labour, slavery and the exploitation of savages and children—has justified them on the ground that the supreme good is in future time and that any temporal means, however intrinsically horrible, may be used to achieve that good. Because Quaker theology was a form of eternity-philosophy, Quaker political theory rejected war and persecution as means to ideal ends, denounced slavery and proclaimed racial equality. Members of other denominations had done good work for the African victims of the white man's rapacity. One thinks, for example, of St. Peter Claver at Cartagena. But this heroically charitable "slave of the slaves" never raised his voice against the institution of slavery or the criminal trade by which it was sustained; nor, so far as the extant documents reveal, did he ever, like John Woolman, attempt to persuade the slave-owners to free their human chattels. The reason, presumably, was that Claver was a Jesuit, vowed to perfect obedience and constrained by his theology to regard a certain political and ecclesiastical organization as being the mystical body of Christ. The heads of this organization had not pronounced against slavery or the slave trade. Who was he, Pedro Claver, to express a thought not officially approved by his superiors?

Another practical corollary of the great historical eternity-philosophies, such as Hinduism and Buddhism, is a morality inculcating kindness to animals. Judaism and orthodox Christianity taught that animals might be used as things, for the realization of man's temporal ends. Even St. Francis' attitude towards the brute creation was not entirely unequivocal. True, he converted a wolf and preached sermons to birds; but when Brother Juniper hacked the feet off a living pig in order to satisfy a sick man's craving for fried trotters, the saint merely blamed his disciple's intemperate zeal in damaging a valuable piece of private property. It was not until the nineteenth century, when orthodox Christianity had lost much of its power over European minds, that the idea that it might be a good thing to behave humanely towards animals began to make headway. This new morality was correlated with the new interest in Nature, which had been stimulated by the romantic poets and the men of science. Because it was not founded upon an eternity-philosophy, a doctrine of divinity dwelling in all living creatures, the modern movement in favour of kindness to animals was and is perfectly compatible with intolerance, persecution and systematic cruelty towards human beings. Young Nazis are taught to be gentle with dogs and cats, ruthless with Jews. That is because Nazism is a typical time-philosophy, which regards the ultimate good as existing, not in eternity, but in the future. Jews are, *ex hypothesi*, obstacles in the way of the realization of the supreme good; dogs and cats are not. The rest follows logically.

Selfishness and partiality are very inhuman and base qualities even in the things of this world; but in the doctrines of religion they are of a baser nature. Now, this is the greatest evil that the division of the church has brought forth; it raises in every communion a selfish, partial orthodoxy, which consists in courageously defending all that it has, and condemning all that it has not. And thus every champion is trained up in defense of their own truth, their own learning and their own church, and he has the most merit, the most honour, who likes everything, defends everything, among themselves, and leaves nothing uncensored in those that are of a different communion. Now, how can truth and goodness and union and religion be more struck at than by such defenders of it? If you ask why the great Bishop of Meaux wrote so many learned books against all parts of the Reformation, it is because he was born in France and bred up in the bosom of Mother Church. Had he been born in England, had Oxford or Cambridge been his *Alma Mater*, he might have rivalled our great Bishop Stillingfleet, and would have wrote as many learned folios against the Church of Rome as he has done. And yet I will venture to say that if each Church could produce but one man apiece that had the piety of an apostle and the impartial love of the first Christians in the first Church at Jerusalem, that a Protestant and a Papist of this stamp would not want half a sheet of paper to hold their articles of union, nor be half an hour before they were of one religion. If, therefore, it should be said that churches are divided, estranged and made unfriendly to one another by a learning, a logic, a history, a criticism in the hands of partiality, it would be saying that which each particular church too much proves to be true. Ask why even the best amongst the Catholics are very shy of owning the validity of the orders of our Church; it is because they are afraid of removing any odium from the Reformation. Ask why no Protestants anywhere touch upon the benefit or necessity of celibacy in those who are separated from worldly business to preach the gospel; it is because that would be seeming to lessen the Roman error of not suffering marriage in her clergy. Ask why even the most worthy and pious among the clergy of the Established Church are afraid to assert the sufficiency of the Divine Light, the necessity of seeking only the guidance and inspiration of the Holy Spirit; it is because the Quakers, who have broke off from the church, have made this doctrine their corner-stone. If we loved truth as such, if we sought for it for its own sake, if we loved our neighbour as ourselves, if we desired nothing by our religion but to be acceptable to God, if we equally desired the salvation of all men, if we were afraid of error only because of its harmful nature to us and our fellow-creatures, then nothing of this spirit could have any place in us.

There is therefore a catholic spirit, a communion of saints in the love of God and all goodness, which no one can learn from that which is called orthodoxy in particular churches, but is only to be had by a total dying to all worldly views, by a pure love of God, and by such an unction from above as delivers the mind from all selfishness and makes it love truth and goodness with an equality of affection in every man, whether he is Christian, Jew or Gentile. He that would obtain this divine and catholic spirit in this disordered, divided state of things, and live in a divided part of the church without partaking of its division, must have these three truths deeply fixed in his mind. First, that universal love, which gives the whole strength of the heart to God, and makes us love every man as we love ourselves, is the noblest, the most divine, the Godlike state of the soul, and is the utmost perfection to which the most perfect religion can raise us; and that no religion does any man any good but so far as it brings this perfection of love into him. This truth will show us that true orthodoxy can nowhere be found but in a pure disinterested love of God and our neighbour. Second, that in this present divided state of the church, truth itself is torn and divided asunder; and that, therefore, he can be the only true catholic who has more of truth and less of error than is hedged in by any divided part. This truth will enable us to live in a divided part unhurt by its division, and keep us in a true liberty and fitness to be edified and assisted by all the good that we hear or see in any other part of the church. . . . Thirdly, he must always have in mind this great truth, that it is the glory of the Divine Justice to have no respect of parties or persons, but to stand equally disposed to that which is right and wrong as well in the Jew as in the Gentile. He therefore that would like as God likes, and condemn as God condemns, must have neither the eyes of the Papist nor the Protestant; he must like no truth the less because Ignatius Loyola or John Bunyan were very zealous for it, nor have the less aversion to any error, because Dr. Trapp or George Fox had brought it forth.

William Law

Dr. Trapp was the author of a religious tract entitled "On the Nature, Folly, Sin and Danger of Being Righteous Overmuch." One of Law's controversial pieces was an answer to this work.

Benares is to the East, Mecca to the West; but explore your own heart, for there are both Rama and Allah.

Kabir

Like the bee gathering honey from different flowers, the wise man accepts the essence of different Scriptures and sees only the good in all religions.

From the Srimad Bhagavatam

His Sacred Majesty the King does reverence to men of all sects, whether ascetics or householders, by gifts and various forms of reverence. His Sacred Majesty, however, cares not so much for gifts or external reverence as that there should be a growth in the essence of the matter in all sects. The growth of the essence of the matter assumes various forms, but the root of it is restraint of speech, to wit, a man must not do reverence to his own sect or disparage that of another without reason. Depreciation should be for specific reasons only; for the sects of other people all deserve reverence for one reason or another. . . . He who does reverence to his own sect, while disparaging the sects of others wholly from attachment to his own, with intent to enhance the glory of his own sect, in reality by such conduct inflicts the severest injury on his own sect. Concord therefore is meritorious, to wit, hearkening and hearkening willingly to the Law of Piety, as accepted by other people.

Edict of Asoka

It would be difficult, alas, to find any edict of a Christian king to match Asoka's. In the West the good old rule, the simple plan, was glorification of one's own sect, disparagement and even persecution of all others. Recently, however, governments have changed their policy. Proselytizing and persecuting zeal is reserved for the political pseudo-religions, such as Communism, Fascism and nationalism; and unless they are thought to stand in the way of advance towards the temporal ends professed by such pseudo-religions, the various manifestations of the Perennial Philosophy are treated with a contemptuously tolerant indifference.

The children of God are very dear but very queer, very nice but very narrow.

Sadhu Sundar Singh

Such was the conclusion to which the most celebrated of Indian converts was forced after some years of association with his fellow Christians. There are many honourable exceptions, of course; but the rule even among learned Protestants and Catholics is a certain blandly bumptious provincialism which, if it did not constitute such a grave offence against charity and truth, would be just uproariously funny. A hundred years ago, hardly anything was known of Sanskrit, Pali or Chinese. The ignorance of European scholars was sufficient reason for their provincialism. Today, when more or less adequate translations are available in plenty, there is not only no reason for it, there is no excuse. And yet most European and American authors of books about religion and metaphysics write as though nobody had ever thought about these subjects, except the Jews, the Greeks and the Christians of the Mediterranean basin and western Europe. This display of what, in the twentieth century, is an entirely voluntary and deliberate ignorance is not only absurd and discreditable; it is also socially dangerous. Like any other form of imperialism, theological imperialism is a menace to permanent world peace. The reign of violence will never come to an end until, first, most human beings accept the same, true philosophy of life; until, second, this Perennial Philosophy is recognized as the highest factor common to all the world religions; until, third, the adherents of every religion renounce the idolatrous time-philosophies, with which, in their own particular faith, the Perennial Philosophy of eternity has been overlaid; until, fourth, there is a world-wide rejection of all the political pseudo-religions, which place man's supreme good in future time and therefore justify and commend the commission of every sort of present iniquity as a means to that end. If these conditions are not fulfilled, no amount of political planning, no economic blue-prints however ingeniously drawn, can prevent the recrudescence of war and revolution.

CHAPTER XIII

Salvation, Deliverance, Enlightenment

SALVATION—but from what? Deliverance—out of which particular situation into what other situation? Men have given many answers to these questions, and because human temperaments are of such profoundly different kinds, because social situations are so various and fashions of thought and feeling so compelling while they last, the answers are many and mutually incompatible.

There is first of all material salvationism. In its simplest form this is merely the will to live expressing itself in a formulated desire to escape from circumstances that menace life. In practice, the effective fulfilment of such a wish depends on two things: the application of intelligence to particular economic and political problems, and the creation and maintenance of an atmosphere of good will, in which intelligence can do its work to the best advantage. But men are not content to be merely kind and clever within the limits of a concrete situation. They aspire to relate their actions, and the thoughts and feelings accompanying those actions, to general principles and a philosophy on the cosmic scale. When this directing and explanatory philosophy is not the Perennial Philosophy or one of the historical theologies more or less closely connected with the Perennial Philosophy, it takes the form of a pseudo-religion, a system of organized idolatry. Thus, the simple wish not to starve, the well-founded conviction that it is very difficult to be good or wise or happy when one is desperately hungry, comes to be elaborated, under the influence of the metaphysic of Inevitable Progress, into prophetic Utopianism; the desire to escape from oppression and exploitation comes to be explained and guided by a belief in apocalyptic revolutionism, combined, not always in theory, but invariably in practice, with the Moloch-worship of the nation as the highest of all goods. In all these cases salvation is regarded as a deliverance, by means of a variety of political and economic devices, out of the miseries and evils associated with bad material conditions into another set of future material conditions so much better than the present that, somehow or other, they will cause everybody to be perfectly happy, wise and virtuous. Officially promulgated in all the totalitarian countries, whether of the right or the left, this confession of faith is still only semi-official in the nominally Christian world of capitalistic democracy, where it is drummed into the popular mind, not by the representatives of state or church, but by those most influential of popular moralists and philosophers, the writers of advertising copy (the only authors in all the history of literature whose works are read every day by every member of the population).

In the theologies of the various religions, salvation is also regarded as a deliverance out of folly, evil and misery into happiness, goodness and wisdom. But political and economic means are held to be subsidiary to the cultivation of personal holiness, to the acquiring of personal merit and to the maintenance of personal faith in some divine principle or person having power, in one way or another, to forgive and sanctify the individual soul. Moreover the end to be achieved is not regarded as existing in some Utopian future period, beginning, say, in the twenty-second century or perhaps even a little earlier, if our favourite politicians remain in power and make the right laws; the end exists "in heaven." This last phrase has two very different meanings. For what is probably the majority of those who profess the great historical religions, it signifies and has always signified a happy posthumous condition of indefinite personal survival, conceived of as a reward for good behaviour and correct belief and a compensation for the miseries inseparable from life in a body. But for those who, within the various religious traditions, have accepted the Perennial Philosophy as a theory and have done their best to live it out in practice, "heaven" is something else. They aspire to be delivered out of separate selfhood in time and into eternity as realized in the unitive knowledge of the divine Ground. Since the Ground can and ought to be unitively known in the present life (whose ultimate end and purpose is nothing but this knowledge), "heaven" is not an exclusively posthumous condition. He only is completely "saved" who is delivered here and now. As to the means to salvation, these are simultaneously ethical, intellectual and spiritual and have been summed up with admirable clarity and economy in the Buddha's Eightfold Path. Complete deliverance is conditional on the following: first, Right Belief in the all too obvious truth that the cause of pain and evil is craving for separative, ego-centred existence, with its corollary that there can be no deliverance from evil, whether personal or collective, except by getting rid of such craving and the obsession of "I," "me," "mine"; second, Right Will, the will to deliver oneself and others; third, Right Speech, directed by compassion and charity towards all sentient beings; fourth, Right Action, with the aim of creating and maintaining peace and good will; fifth, Right Means of Livelihood, or the choice only of such professions as are not harmful, in their exercise, to any human being or, if possible, any living creature; sixth, Right Effort towards Self-control; seventh, Right Attention or Recollectedness, to be practised in all the circumstances of life, so that we may never do evil by mere thoughtlessness, because "we know not what we do"; and, eighth, Right Contemplation, the unitive knowledge of the Ground, to which recollectedness and the ethical self-naughting prescribed in the first six branches of the Path give access. Such then are the means which it is within the power of the human being to employ in order to achieve man's final end and be "saved." Of the means which are employed by the divine Ground for helping human beings to reach their goal, the Buddha of the Pali scriptures (a teacher whose dislike of "footless questions" is no less intense than that of the severest experimental physicist of the twentieth century) declines to speak. All he is prepared to talk about is "sorrow and the ending of sorrow"—the huge brute fact of pain and evil and the other, no less empirical fact that there is a method, by which the individual can free himself from evil and do something to diminish the sum of evil in the world around him. It is only in Mahayana Buddhism that the mysteries of grace are discussed with anything like the fulness of treatment accorded to the subject in the speculations of Hindu and especially Christian theology. The primitive, Hinayana teaching on deliverance is simply an elaboration of the Buddha's last recorded words: "Decay is inherent in all component things. Work out your own salvation with diligence." As in the well-known passage quoted below, all the stress is upon personal effort.

> Therefore, Ananda, be ye lamps unto yourselves, be ye a refuge to yourselves. Betake yourselves to no external refuge. Hold fast to the Truth as a lamp; hold fast to the Truth as a refuge. Look not for a refuge in anyone beside yourselves. And those, Ananda, who either now or after I am dead shall be a lamp unto themselves, shall betake themselves to no external refuge, but holding fast to the Truth as their lamp, and holding fast to the Truth as their refuge, shall not look for refuge to anyone beside themselves—it is they who shall reach the very topmost Height. But they must be anxious to learn.

What follows is a passage freely translated from the Chandogya Upanishad. The truth which this little myth is meant to illustrate is that there are as many conceptions of salvation as there are degrees of spiritual knowledge and that the kind of liberation (or enslavement) actually achieved by any individual soul depends upon the extent to which that soul chooses to dissipate its essentially voluntary ignorance.

That Self who is free from impurities, from old age and death, from grief and thirst and hunger, whose desire is true and whose desires come true—that Self is to be sought after and enquired about, that Self is to be realized.

The Devas (gods or angels) and the Asuras (demons or titans) both heard of this Truth. They thought: "Let us seek after and realize this Self, so that we can obtain all worlds and the fulfilment of all desires."

Thereupon Indra from the Devas and Virochana from the Asuras approached Prajapati, the famous teacher. They lived with him as pupils for thirty-two years. Then Prajapati asked them: "For what reason have you both lived here all this time?"

They replied: "We have heard that one who realizes the Self obtains all the worlds and all his desires. We have lived here because we want to be taught the Self."

Prajapati said to them: "The person who is seen in the eye—that is the Self. That is immortal, that is fearless and that is Brahman."

"Sir," enquired the disciples, "who is seen reflected in water or in a mirror?"

"He, the Atman," was the reply. "He indeed is seen in all these." Then Prajapati added: "Look at yourselves in the water, and whatever you do not understand, come and tell me."

Indra and Virochana pored over their reflections in the water, and when they were asked what they had seen of the Self, they replied: "Sir, we see the Self; we see even the hair and nails."

Then Prajapati ordered them to put on their finest clothes and look again at their "selves" in the water. This they did and when asked again what they had seen, they answered: "We see the Self, exactly like ourselves, well adorned and in our finest clothes."

Then said Prajapati: "The Self is indeed seen in these. That Self is immortal and fearless, and that is Brahman." And the pupils went away, pleased at heart.

But looking after them, Prajapati lamented thus: "Both of them departed without analysing or discriminating, and without comprehending the true Self. Whoever follows this false doctrine of the Self must perish."

Satisfied that he had found the Self, Virochana returned to the Asuras and began to teach them that the bodily self alone is to be worshipped, that the body alone is to be served, and that he who worships the ego and serves the body gains both worlds, this and the next. And this in effect is the doctrine of the Asuras.

But Indra, on his way back to the Devas, realized the uselessness of this knowledge. "As this Self," he reflected, "seems to be well adorned when the body is well adorned, well dressed when the body is well dressed, so too will it be blind if the body is blind, lame if the body is lame, deformed if the body is deformed. Nay more, this same Self will die, when the body dies. I see no good in such knowledge." So Indra returned to Prajapati for further instruction. Prajapati compelled him to live with him for another span of thirty-two years; after which he began to instruct him, step by step, as it were.

Prajapati said: "He who moves about in dreams, enjoying and glorified—he is the Self. That is immortal and fearless, and that is Brahman."

Pleased at heart, Indra again departed. But before he had rejoined the other angelic beings, he realized the uselessness of that knowledge also. "True it is," he thought within himself, "that this new Self is not blind if the body is blind, not lame, nor hurt, if the body is lame or hurt. But even in dreams the Self is conscious of many sufferings. So I see no good in this teaching."

Accordingly he went back to Prajapati for more instruction, and Prajapati made him live with him for thirty-two years more. At the end of that time Prajapati taught him thus: "When a person is asleep, resting in perfect tranquility, dreaming no dreams, then he realizes the Self. That is immortal and fearless, and that is Brahman."

Satisfied, Indra went away. But even before he had

reached home, he felt the uselessness of this knowledge also. "When one is asleep," he thought, "one does not know oneself as 'This is I.' One is not in fact conscious of any existence. That state is almost annihilation. I see no good in this knowledge either."

So Indra went back once again to be taught. Prajapati bade him stay with him for five years more. At the end of that time Prajapati taught him the highest truth of the Self.

"This body," he said, "is mortal, forever in the clutch of death. But within it resides the Self, immortal, and without form. This Self, when associated in consciousness with the body, is subject to pleasure and pain; and so long as this association continues, no man can find freedom from pains and pleasures. But when the association comes to an end, there is an end also of pain and pleasure. Rising above physical consciousness, knowing the Self as distinct from the sense-organs and the mind, knowing Him in his true light, one rejoices and one is free."

From the Chandogya Upanishad

Having realized his own self as the Self, a man becomes selfless; and in virtue of selflessness he is to be conceived as unconditioned. This is the highest mystery, betokening emancipation; through selflessness he has no part in pleasure or pain, but attains absoluteness.

Maitrayana Upanishad

We should mark and know of a very truth that all manner of virtue and goodness, and even that Eternal Good, which is God Himself, can never make a man virtuous, good or happy so long as it is outside the soul, that is, so long as the man is holding converse with outward things through his senses and reason, and doth not withdraw into himself and learn to understand his own life, who and what he is.

Theologia Germanica

Indeed, the saving truth has never been preached by the Buddha, seeing that one has to realize it within oneself.

Sutralamkara

In what does salvation consist? Not in any historic faith
or knowledge of anything absent or distant, not in any
variety of restraints, rules and methods of practising
virtue, not in any formality of opinion about faith and
works, repentance, forgiveness of sins, or justification and
sanctification, not in any truth or righteousness that you
can have from yourself, from the best of men and books,
but solely and wholly from the life of God, or Christ of
God, quickened and born again in you, in other words in
the restoration and perfect union of the first twofold life
in humanity.

William Law

Law is using here the phraseology of Boehme and those other
"Spiritual Reformers," whom the orthodox Protestants, Lu-
theran, Calvinistic and Anglican, agreed (it was one of the
very few points they were able to agree on) either to ignore or
to persecute. But it is clear that what he and they call the new
birth of God within the soul is essentially the same fact of
experience as that which the Hindus, two thousand and more
years before, described as the realization of the Self as within
and yet transcendentally other than the individual ego.

Not by the slothful, nor the fool, the undiscerning, is that
Nirvana to be reached, which is the untying of all knots.

Iti-vuttaka

This seems sufficiently self-evident. But most of us take
pleasure in being lazy, cannot be bothered to be constantly
recollected and yet passionately desire to be saved from the
results of sloth and unawareness. Consequently there has been
a widespread wish for and belief in Saviours who will step
into our lives, above all at the hour of their termination, and,
like Alexander, cut the Gordian knots which we have been
too lazy to untie. But God is not mocked. The nature of things
is such that the unitive knowledge of the Ground which is
contingent upon the achievement of a total selflessness cannot
possibly be realized, even with outside help, by those who are
not yet selfless. The salvation obtained by belief in the saving
power of Amida, say, or Jesus is not the total deliverance described in the Upanishads, the Buddhist scriptures and the

writings of the Christian mystics. It is something different, not merely in degree, but in kind.

> Talk as much philosophy as you please, worship as many gods as you like, observe all ceremonies, sing devoted praises to any number of divine beings—liberation never comes, even at the end of a hundred aeons, without the realization of the Oneness of Self.
>
> *Shankara*

> This Self is not realizable by study nor even by intelligence and learning. The Self reveals its essence only to him who applies himself to the Self. He who has not given up the ways of vice, who cannot control himself, who is not at peace within, whose mind is distracted, can never realize the Self, though full of all the learning in the world.
>
> *Katha Upanishad*

> Nirvana is where there is no birth, no extinction; it is seeing into the state of Suchness, absolutely transcending all the categories constructed by mind; for it is the Tatha-gata's inner consciousness.
>
> *Lankavatara Sutra*

The false or at best imperfect salvations described in the Chandogya Upanishad are of three kinds. There is first the pseudo-salvation associated with the belief that matter is the ultimate Reality. Virochana, the demonic being who is the apotheosis of. power-loving, extraverted somatotonia, finds it perfectly natural to identify himself with his body, and he goes back to the other Titans to seek a purely material salvation. Incarnated in the present century, Virochana would have been an ardent Communist, Fascist or nationalist. Indra sees through material salvationism and is then offered dream-salvation, deliverance out of bodily existence into the intermediate world between matter and spirit—that fascinatingly odd and exciting psychic universe, out of which miracles and foreknowledge, "spirit communications" and extra-sensory perceptions make their startling irruptions into ordinary life. But this freer kind of individualized existence is still all too personal and ego-centric to satisfy a soul conscious of its own incompleteness and eager to be made whole. Indra accordingly goes

further and is tempted to accept the undifferentiated consciousness of deep sleep, of false *samadhi* and quietistic trance, as
the final deliverance. But he refuses, in Brahmananda's words,
to mistake *tamas* for *sattvas*, sloth and sub-consciousness for
poise and super-consciousness. And so, by discrimination, he
comes to the realization of the Self, which is the enlightenment
of the darkness that is ignorance and the deliverance from the
mortal consequences of that ignorance.

The illusory salvations, against which we are warned in the
other extracts, are of a different kind. The emphasis here is
upon idolatry and superstition—above all the idolatrous worship of the analytical reason and its notions, and the superstitious belief in rites, dogmas and confessions of faith as being
somehow magically efficacious in themselves. Many Christians,
as Law implies, have been guilty of these idolatries and super-
stitions. For them, complete deliverance into union with the
divine Ground is impossible, either in this world or post-
humously. The best they can hope for is a meritorious but still
egocentric life in the body and some sort of happy posthumous
"longevity," as the Chinese call it, some form of survival,
paradisal perhaps, but still involved in time, separateness and
multiplicity.

The beatitude into which the enlightened soul is delivered
is something quite different from pleasure. What, then, is its
nature? The quotations which follow provide at least a partial
answer. Blessedness depends on non-attachment and selflessness, therefore can be enjoyed without satiety and without
revulsion; is a participation in eternity, and therefore remains
itself without diminution or fluctuation.

> Henceforth in the real Brahman, he (the liberated spirit)
> becomes perfected and another. His fruit is the untying
> of bonds. Without desires, he attains to bliss eternal and
> immeasurable, and therein abides.
>
> *Maitrayana Upanishad*

> God is to be enjoyed, creatures only used as means to
> That which is to be enjoyed.
>
> *St. Augustine*

> There is this difference between spiritual and corporal
> pleasures, that corporal ones beget a desire before we have

obtained them and, after we have obtained them, a disgust; but spiritual pleasures, on the contrary, are not cared for when we have them not, but are desired when we have them.

St. Gregory the Great

When a man is in one of these two states (beatitude or dark night of the soul) all is right with him, and he is as safe in hell as in heaven. And so long as a man is on earth, it is possible for him to pass often-times from the one to the other—nay, even within the space of a day and night, and all without his own doing. But when a man is in neither of these two states, he holds converse with the creatures, and wavereth hither and thither and knoweth not what manner of man he is.

Theologia . Germanica

Much of the literature of Sufism is poetical. Sometimes this poetry is rather strained and extravagant, sometimes beautiful with a luminous simplicity, sometimes darkly and almost disquietingly enigmatic. To this last class belong the utterances of that Moslem saint of the tenth century, Niffari the Egyptian. This is what he wrote on the subject of salvation.

God made me behold the sea, and I saw the ships sinking and the planks floating; then the planks too were submerged. And God said to me, "Those who voyage are not saved." And He said to me, "Those who, instead of voyaging, cast themselves into the sea, take a risk." And He said to me, "Those who voyage and take no risk shall perish." And He said to me, "The surface of the sea is a gleam that cannot be reached. And the bottom is a darkness impenetrable. And between the two are great fishes, which are to be feared."

The allegory is fairly clear. The ships that bear the individual voyagers across the sea of life are sects and churches, collections of dogmas and religious organizations. The planks which also sink at last are all good works falling short of total self-surrender and all faith less absolute than the unitive knowledge of God. Liberation into eternity is the result of "throwing oneself into the sea"; in the language of the Gospels, one must lose one's life in order to save it. But throwing oneself into the sea is a risky business—not so risky, of course, as travelling in a vast *Queen Mary*, fitted up with the very latest in dogmatic conveniences and liturgical decorations, and bound either for Davy Jones's locker or at best, the wrong port, but still quite dangerous enough. For the surface of the sea—the divine Ground as it is manifested in the world of time and multiplicity—gleams with a reflected radiance that can no more be seized than the image of beauty in a mirror; while the bottom, the Ground as it is eternally in itself seems merely darkness to the analytic mind, as it peers down into the depths; and when the analytic mind decides to join the will in the final necessary plunge into self-naughting it must run the gantlet, as it sinks down, of those devouring pseudo-salvations described in the Chandogya Upanishad—dream-salvation into that fascinating psychic world, where the ego still survives, but with a happier and more untrammelled kind of life, or else the sleep-salvation of false *samadhi*, of unity in sub-consciousness instead of unity in super-consciousness.

Niffari's estimate of any individual's chances of achieving man's final end does not err on the side of excessive optimism. But then no saint or founder of a religion, no exponent of the Perennial Philosophy, has ever been optimistic. "Many are called, but few are chosen." Those who do not choose to be chosen cannot hope for anything better than some form of partial salvation under conditions that will permit them to advance towards complete deliverance.

CHAPTER XIV

Immortality and Survival

IMMORTALITY is participation in the eternal now of the divine Ground; survival is persistence in one of the forms of time. Immortality is the result of total deliverance. Survival is the lot of those who are partially delivered into some heaven, or who are not delivered at all, but find themselves, by the law of their own untranscended nature, compelled to choose some purgatorial or embodied servitude even more painful than the one they have just left.

> Goodness and virtue make men know and love, believe and delight in their immortality. When the soul is purged and enlightened by true sanctity, it is more capable of those divine irradiations, whereby it feels itself in conjunction with God. It knows that almighty Love, by which it lives, is stronger than death. It knows that God will never forsake His own life, which He has quickened in the soul. Those breathings and gaspings after an eternal participation of Him are but the energy of His own breath within us.
>
> *John Smith, the Platonist*

> I have maintained ere this and I still maintain that I already possess all that is granted to me in eternity. For God in the fulness of his Godhead dwells eternally in his image —the soul.
>
> *Eckhart*

> Troubled or still, water is always water. What difference can embodiment or disembodiment make to the Liberated? Whether calm or in tempest, the sameness of the Ocean suffers no change.
>
> *Yogavasistha*

> To the question "Where does the soul go, when the body dies?" Jacob Boehme answered: "There is no necessity for it to go anywhere."

> The word Tathagata (one of the names of the Buddha) signifies one who does not go to anywhere and does not come from anywhere; and therefore is he called Tathagata (Thus-gone), holy and fully enlightened.
>
> *Diamond Sutra*

> Seeing Him alone, one transcends death; there is no other way.
>
> *Svetasvatara Upanishad*

> God, in knowledge of whom standeth our eternal life. . . .
>
> *Book of Common Prayer*

I died a mineral, and became a plant.
I died a plant and rose an animal.
I died an animal and I was man.
Why should I fear? When was I less by dying?
Yet once more I shall die as man, to soar
With the blessed angels; but even from angelhood
I must pass on. All except God perishes.
When I have sacrificed my angel soul,
I shall become that which no mind ever conceived.
O, let me not exist! for Non-Existence proclaims,
"To Him we shall return."

Jalal-uddin Rumi

There is a general agreement, East and West, that life in a body provides uniquely good opportunities for achieving salvation or deliverance. Catholic and Mahayana Buddhist doctrine is alike in insisting that the soul in its disembodied state after death cannot acquire merit, but merely suffers in purgatory the consequences of its past acts. But whereas Catholic orthodoxy declares that there is no possibility of progress in the next world, and that the degree of the soul's beatitude is determined solely by what it has done and thought in its earthly life, the eschatologists of the Orient affirm that there are certain posthumous conditions in which meritorious souls are capable of advancing from a heaven of happy personal survival to genuine immortality in union with the timeless, eternal Godhead. And, of course, there is also the possibility (indeed, for most individuals, the necessity) of returning to some form of embodied life, in which the advance towards complete beatification, or deliverance through enlightenment, can be continued. Meanwhile, the fact that one has been born in a human body is one of the things for which, says Shankara, one should daily give thanks to God.

The spiritual creature which we are has need of a body, without which it could nowise attain that knowledge which it obtains as the only approach to those things, by knowledge of which it is made blessed.

St. Bernard

Having achieved human birth, a rare and blessed incarnation, the wise man, leaving all vanity to those who are

vain, should strive to know God, and Him only, before
life passes into death.

Srimad Bhagavatam

Good men spiritualize their bodies; bad men incarnate
their souls.

Benjamin Whichcote

More precisely, good men spiritualize their mind-bodies; bad
men incarnate and mentalize their spirits. The completely
spiritualized mind-body is a Tathagata, who doesn't go anywhere when he dies, for the good reason that he is already,
actually and consciously, where everyone has always potentially
been without knowing. The person who has not, in this life,
gone into Thusness, into the eternal principle of all states of
being, goes at death into some particular state, either purgatorial or paradisal. In the Hindu scriptures and their commentaries several different kinds of posthumous salvation are
distinguished. The "thus-gone" soul is completely delivered
into complete union with the divine Ground; but it is also
possible to achieve other kinds of *mukti*, or liberation, even
while retaining a form of purified I-consciousness. The nature
of any individual's deliverance after death depends upon three
factors: the degree of holiness achieved by him while in the
body, the particular aspect of the divine Reality to which he
gave his primary allegiance, and the particular path he chose
to follow. Similarly, in the *Divine Comedy*, Paradise has its
various circles; but whereas in the oriental eschatologies the
saved soul can go out of even sublimated individuality, out of
survival even in some kind of celestial time, to a complete
deliverance into the eternal, Dante's souls remain for ever
where (after passing through the unmeritorious sufferings of
purgatory) they find themselves as the result of their single
incarnation in a body. Orthodox Christian doctrine does not
admit the possibility, either in the posthumous state or in
some other embodiment, of any further growth towards the
ultimate perfection of a total union with the Godhead. But in
the Hindu and Buddhist versions of the Perennial Philosophy
the divine mercy is matched by the divine patience: both are
infinite. For oriental theologians there is no eternal damnation; there are only purgatories and then an indefinite series
of second chances to go forward towards not only man's, but

the whole creation's final end—total reunion with the Ground of all being.

Preoccupation with posthumous deliverance is not one of the means to such deliverance, and may easily, indeed, become an obstacle in the way of advance towards it. There is not the slightest reason to suppose that ardent spiritualists are more likely to be saved than those who have never attended a séance or familiarized themselves with the literature, speculative or evidential. My intention here is not to add to that literature, but rather to give the baldest summary of what has been written about the subject of survival within the various religious traditions.

In oriental discussions of the subject, that which survives death is not the personality. Buddhism accepts the doctrine of reincarnation; but it is not a soul that passes on (Buddhism denies the existence of a soul); it is the character. What we choose to make of our mental and physical constitution in the course of our life on earth affects the psychic medium within which individual minds lead a part at least of their amphibious existence, and this modification of the medium results, after the body's death, in the initiation of a new existence either in a heaven, or a purgatory, or another body.

In the Vedanta cosmology there is, over and above the Atman or spiritual Self, identical with the divine Ground, something in the nature of a soul that reincarnates in a gross or subtle body, or manifests itself in some incorporeal state. This soul is not the personality of the defunct, but rather the particularized I-consciousness out of which a personality arises.

Either one of these conceptions of survival is logically self-consistent and can be made to "save the appearances"—in other words, to fit the odd and obscure facts of psychical research. The only personalities with which we have any direct acquaintance are incarnate beings, compounds of a body and some unknown x. But if x plus a body equals a personality, then, obviously, it is impossible for x minus a body to equal the same thing. The apparently personal entities which psychical research sometimes seems to discover can only be regarded as temporary pseudo-personalities compounded of x and the medium's body.

These two conceptions are not mutually exclusive, and survival may be the joint product of a persistent consciousness and a modification of the psychic medium. If this is so, it is possible for a given human being to survive in more than one posthumous form. His "soul"—the non-personal ground and principle of past and future personalities—may go marching on in one mode of being, while the traces left by his thoughts and volitions in the psychic medium may become the origin of new individualized existences, having quite other modes of being.

CHAPTER XV

Silence

The Father uttered one Word; that Word is His Son, and he utters Him for ever in everlasting silence; and in silence the soul has to hear it.

St. John of the Cross

The spiritual life is nothing else but the working of the Spirit of God within us, and therefore our own silence must be a great part of our preparation for it, and much speaking or delight in it will be often no small hindrance of that good which we can only have from hearing what the Spirit and voice of God speaketh within us. . . . Rhetoric and fine language about the things of the spirit is a vainer babble than in other matters; and he that thinks to grow in true goodness by hearing or speaking flaming words or striking expressions, as is now much the way of the world, may have a great deal of talk, but will have little of his conversation in heaven.

William Law

He who knows does not speak;
He who speaks does not know.

Lao Tzu

UNRESTRAINED and indiscriminate talk is morally evil and spiritually dangerous. "But I say unto you, That every idle word that men shall speak, they shall give account thereof in the day of judgment." This may seem a very hard saying. And yet if we pass in review the words we have given vent to in the

course of the average day, we shall find that the greater number of them may be classified under three main heads: words
inspired by malice and uncharitableness towards our neighbours; words inspired by greed, sensuality and self-love; words
inspired by pure imbecility and uttered without rhyme or
reason, but merely for the sake of making a distracting noise.
These are idle words; and we shall find, if we look into the
matter, that they tend to outnumber the words that are dictated by reason, charity or necessity. And if the unspoken
words of our mind's endless, idiot monologue are counted, the
majority for idleness becomes, for most of us, overwhelmingly
large.

All these idle words, the silly no less than the self-regarding
and the uncharitable, are impediments in the way of the unitive knowledge of the divine Ground, a dance of dust and flies
obscuring the inward and the outward Light. The guard of the
tongue (which is also, of course, a guard of the mind) is not
only one of the most difficult and searching of all mortifications; it is also the most fruitful.

> When the hen has laid, she must needs cackle. And what
> does she get by it? Straightway comes the chough and robs
> her of her eggs, and devours all that of which she should
> have brought forth her live birds. And just so that wicked
> chough, the devil, beareth away from the cackling an-
> choresses, and swalloweth up all the goods they have
> brought forth, and which ought, as birds, to bear them
> up towards heaven, if it had not been cackled.
>
> *Modernized from the Ancren Riwle*

> You cannot practise too rigid a fast from the charms of
> worldly talk.
>
> *Fénelon*

> What need of so much news from abroad, when all that
> concerns either life or death is all transacting and at work
> within us?
>
> *William Law*

> My dear Mother, heed well the precepts of the saints, who
> have all warned those who would become holy to speak
> little of themselves and their own affairs.
>
> *St. François de Sales*
> *(in a letter to St. Jeanne de Chantal)*

A dog is not considered a good dog because he is a good barker. A man is not considered a good man because he is a good talker.

Chuang Tzu

The dog barks; the Caravan passes.

Arabic Proverb

It was not from want of will that I have refrained from writing to you, for truly do I wish you all good; but because it seemed to me that enough has been said already to effect all that is needful, and that what is wanting (if indeed anything be wanting) is not writing or speaking—whereof ordinarily there is more than enough—but silence and work. For whereas speaking distracts, silence and work collect the thoughts and strengthen the spirit. As soon therefore as a person understands what has been said to him for his good, there is no further need to hear or to discuss; but to set himself in earnest to practise what he has learnt with silence and attention, in humility, charity and contempt of self.

St. John of the Cross

Molinos (and doubtless he was not the first to use this classification) distinguished three degrees of silence—silence of the mouth, silence of the mind and silence of the will. To refrain from idle talk is hard; to quiet the gibbering of memory and imagination is much harder; hardest of all is to still the voices of craving and aversion within the will.

The twentieth century is, among other things, the Age of Noise. Physical noise, mental noise and noise of desire—we hold history's record for all of them. And no wonder; for all the resources of our almost miraculous technology have been thrown into the current assault against silence. That most popular and influential of all recent inventions, the radio, is nothing but a conduit through which pre-fabricated din can flow into our homes. And this din goes far deeper, of course, than the ear-drums. It penetrates the mind, filling it with a babel of distractions—news items, mutually irrelevant bits of information, blasts of corybantic or sentimental music, continually repeated doses of drama that bring no catharsis, but merely create a craving for daily or even hourly emotional enemas. And where, as in most countries, the broadcasting stations support themselves by selling time to advertisers, the noise is carried from the ears, through the realms of phantasy, knowledge and feeling to the ego's central core of wish and desire. Spoken or printed, broadcast over the ether or on wood-pulp, all advertising copy has but one purpose—to prevent the will from ever achieving silence. Desirelessness is the condition of deliverance and illumination. The condition of an expanding and technologically progressive system of mass production is universal craving. Advertising is the organized effort to extend and intensify craving—to extend and intensify, that is to say, the workings of that force, which (as all the saints and teachers of all the higher religions have always taught) is the principal cause of suffering and wrong-doing and the greatest obstacle between the human soul and its divine Ground.

CHAPTER XVI

Prayer

THE word "prayer" is applied to at least four distinct procedures—petition, intercession, adoration, contemplation. Petition is the asking of something for ourselves. Intercession is the asking of something for other people. Adoration is the use of intellect, feeling, will and imagination in making acts of devotion directed towards God in his personal aspect or as incarnated in human form. Contemplation is that condition of alert passivity, in which the soul lays itself open to the divine Ground within and without, the immanent and transcendent Godhead.

Psychologically, it is all but impossible for a human being to practise contemplation without preparing for it by some kind of adoration and without feeling the need to revert at more or less frequent intervals to intercession and some form at least of petition. On the other hand, it is both possible and easy to practise petition apart not only from contemplation, but also from adoration and, in rare cases of extreme and unmitigated egotism, even from intercession. Petitionary and intercessory prayer may be used—and used, what is more, with what would ordinarily be regarded as success—without any but the most perfunctory and superficial reference to God in any of his aspects. To acquire the knack of getting his petitions answered, a man does not have to know or love God, or even to know or love the image of God in his own mind. All that he requires is a burning sense of the importance of his own ego and its desires, coupled with a firm conviction that there exists, out there in the universe, something not himself which can be wheedled or dragooned into satisfying those desires. If I repeat "My will be done," with the necessary degree of faith and persistency, the chances are that, sooner or later and some- how or other, I shall get what I want. Whether my will coin- cides with the will of God, and whether in getting what I want I shall get what is spiritually, morally or even materially good for me are questions which I cannot answer in advance. Only time and eternity will show. Meanwhile we shall be well ad- vised to heed the warnings of folk-lore. Those anonymous realists who wrote the world's fairy stories knew a great deal about wishes and their fulfilment. They knew, first of all, that in certain circumstances petitions actually get themselves an- swered; but they also knew that God is not the only answerer and that if one asks for something in the wrong spirit, it may in effect be given—but given with a vengeance and not by a divine Giver. Getting what one wants by means of self-regard- ing petition is a form of *hubris*, which invites its condign and appropriate nemesis. Thus, the folk-lore of the North Amer- ican Indian is full of stories about people who fast and pray egotistically, in order to get more than a reasonable man ought to have, and who, receiving what they ask for, thereby bring about their own downfall. From the other side of the world come all the tales of the men and women who make use of some kind of magic to get their petitions answered—always with farcical or catastrophic consequence. Hardly ever do the Three Wishes of our traditional fairy lore lead to anything but a bad end for the successful wisher.

Picture God as saying to you, "My son, why is it that day by day you rise and pray, and genuflect, and even strike the ground with your forehead, nay, sometimes even shed tears, while you say to me: 'My Father, my God, give me wealth!' If I were to give it to you, you would think your- self of some importance, you would fancy you had gained

something very great. Because you asked for it, you have
it. But take care to make good use of it. Before you had it
you were humble; now that you have begun to be rich
you despise the poor. What kind of a good is that which
only makes you worse? For worse you are, since you were
bad already. And that it would make you worse you knew
not; hence you asked it of Me. I gave it you and I proved
you; you have found—and you are found out! Ask of
Me better things than these, greater things than these.
Ask of Me spiritual things. Ask of Me Myself."

St. Augustine

O Lord, I, a beggar, ask of Thee more than a thousand
kings may ask of Thee. Each one has something he needs
to ask of Thee; I have come to ask Thee to give me
Thyself.

Ansari of Herat

In the words of Aquinas, it is legitimate for us to pray for
anything which it is legitimate for us to desire. There are some
things that nobody has the right to desire—such as the fruits
of crime or wrong-doing. Other things may be legitimately
desired by people on one level of spiritual development, but
should not be desired (and indeed cease to be desired) by those
on another, higher level. Thus, St. François de Sales had
reached a point where he could say, "I have hardly any desires,
but if I were to be born again I should have none at all. We
should ask nothing and refuse nothing, but leave ourselves in
the arms of divine Providence without wasting time in any
desire, except to will what God wills of us." But meanwhile
the third clause of the Lord's Prayer is repeated daily by millions, who have not the slightest intention of letting any will
be done, except their own.

The savour of wandering in the ocean of deathless life
    has rid me of all my asking;
As the tree is in the seed, so all diseases are in this asking.

Kabir

Lord, I know not what to ask of thee. Thou only knowest
what I need. Thou lovest me better than I know how to

love myself. Father, give to thy child that which he himself knows not how to ask. Smite or heal, depress me or raise me up: I adore all thy purposes without knowing them. I am silent; I offer myself up in a sacrifice; I yield myself to Thee; I would have no other desire than to accomplish thy will. Teach me to pray. Pray Thyself in me.

Fénelon

(A dervish was tempted by the devil to cease calling upon Allah, on the ground that Allah never answered, "Here am I." The Prophet Khadir appeared to him in a vision with a message from God.)
Was it not I who summoned thee to my service?
Was it not I who made thee busy with my name?
Thy calling "Allah!" *was* my "Here am I."

Jalal-uddin Rumi

I pray God the Omnipotent to place us in the ranks of his chosen, among the number of those whom He directs to the path of safety; in whom He inspires fervour lest they forget him; whom He cleanses from all defilement, that nothing may remain in them except Himself; yea, of those whom He indwells completely, that they may adore none beside Him.

Al-Ghazzali

About intercession, as about so many other subjects, it is William Law who writes most clearly, simply and to the point.

By considering yourself as an advocate with God for your neighbours and acquaintances, you would never find it hard to be at peace with them yourself. It would be easy for you to bear with and forgive those, for whom you particularly implored the divine mercy and forgiveness.

William Law

Intercession is the best arbitrator of all differences, the best promoter of true friendship, the best cure and preservative against all unkind tempers, all angry and haughty passions.

William Law

You cannot possibly have any ill-temper, or show any
unkind behaviour to a man for whose welfare you are so
much concerned, as to be his advocate with God in private. For you cannot possibly despise and ridicule that
man whom your private prayers recommend to the love
and favour of God.

William Law

Intercession, then, is at once the means to, and the expression
of, the love of one's neighbour. And in the same way adoration
is the means to, and the expression of, the love of God—a love
that finds its consummation in the unitive knowledge of the
Godhead which is the fruit of contemplation. It is to these
higher forms of communion with God that the authors of the
following extracts refer whenever they use the word "prayer."

The aim and end of prayer is to revere, to recognize and
to adore the sovereign majesty of God, through what He
is in Himself rather than what He is in regard to us, and
rather to love his goodness by the love of that goodness
itself than for what it sends us.

Bourgoing

In prayer he (Charles de Condren) did not stop at the
frontiers of his knowledge and his reasoning. He adored
God and his mysteries as they are in themselves and not
as he understood them.

Amelote

"What God is in Himself," "God and his mysteries as they are
in themselves"—the phrases have a Kantian ring. But if Kant
was right and the Thing in itself is unknowable, Bourgoing,
De Condren and all the other masters of the spiritual life were
engaged in a wild goose chase. But Kant was right only as
regards minds that have not yet come to enlightenment and
deliverance. To such minds Reality, whether material, psychic
or spiritual, presents itself as it is darkened, tinged and re-
fracted by the medium of their own individual natures. But in
those who are pure in heart and poor in spirit there is no distortion of Reality, because there is no separate selfhood to
obscure or refract, no painted lantern slide of intellectual
beliefs and hallowed imagery to give a personal and historical

colouring to the "white radiance of Eternity." For such minds, as Olier says, "even ideas of the saints, of the Blessed Virgin, and the sight of Jesus Christ in his humanity are impediments in the way of the sight of God in his purity." The Thing in itself *can* be perceived—but only by one who, in himself, is no-thing.

By prayer I do not understand petition or supplication which, according to the doctrines of the schools, is exercised principally by the understanding, being a signification of what the person desires to receive from God. But prayer here specially meant is an offering and giving to God whatsoever He may justly require from us.

Now prayer, in its general notion, may be defined to be an elevation of the mind to God, or more largely and expressly thus: prayer is an actuation of an intellective soul towards God, expressing, or at least implying, an entire dependence on Him as the author and fountain of all good, a will and readiness to give Him his due, which is no less than all love, all obedience, adoration, glory and worship, by humbling and annihilating the self and all creatures in His presence; and lastly, a desire and intention to aspire to an union of spirit with Him.

Hence it appears that prayer is the most perfect and most divine action that a rational soul is capable of. It is of all actions and duties the most indispensably necessary.

Augustine Baker

Lord, teach me to seek thee and reveal Thyself to me when I seek thee. For I cannot seek Thee except Thou teach me, nor find Thee except Thou reveal Thyself. Let me seek thee in longing, let me long for thee in seeking: let me find Thee in love and love Thee in finding. Lord, I acknowledge and I thank Thee that Thou hast created me in this thine image, in order that I may be mindful of Thee, may conceive of Thee and love Thee: but that image has been so consumed and wasted away by vices and obscured by the smoke of wrong-doing that it cannot achieve that for which it was made, except Thou renew it and create it anew. Is the eye of the soul darkened by its infirmity, or dazzled by thy glory? Surely, it is both darkened in itself and dazzled by Thee. Lord, this is the unapproachable light in which Thou dwellest. Truly I see it not, because it is too bright for me; and yet whatever I see, I see through it, as the weak eye sees what it sees through the light of the sun, which in the sun itself it cannot look upon. Oh supreme and unapproachable light, oh holy and blessed truth, how far art thou from me who am so near to Thee, how far art Thou removed from my vision, though I am so near to thine! Everywhere Thou art wholly present, and I see Thee not. In Thee I move and in Thee I have my being, and cannot come to Thee, thou are within me and about me, and I feel Thee not.

St. Anselm

Oh Lord, put no trust in me; for I shall surely fail if Thou uphold me not.

St. Philip Neri

To pretend to devotion without great humility and re-nunciation of all worldly tempers is to pretend to impos-sibilities. He that would be devout must first be humble, have a full sense of his own miseries and wants and the vanity of the world, and then his soul will be full of desire after God. A proud, or vain, or worldly-minded man may use a manual of prayers, but he cannot be de-vout, because devotion is the application of an humble heart to God as its only happiness.

William Law

The spirit, in order to work, must have all sensible images, both good and bad, removed. The beginner in a spiritual course commences with the use of good sensible images, and it is impossible to begin in a good spiritual course with the exercises of the spirit. . . . Those souls who have not a propensity to the interior must abide always in the exercises, in which sensible images are used, and these souls will find the sensible exercises very profitable to themselves and to others, and pleasing to God. And this is the way of the active life. But others, who have the propensity to the interior, do not always remain in the exercises of the senses, but after a time these will give place to the exercises of the spirit, which are independent of the senses and the imagination and consist simply in the elevation of the will of the intellective soul to God. . . . The soul elevates her will towards God, apprehended by the understanding as a spirit, and not as an imaginary thing, the human spirit in this way aspiring to a union with the Divine Spirit.

Augustine Baker

You tell me you do nothing in prayer. But what do you want to do in prayer except what you are doing, which is, presenting and representing your nothingness and misery to God? When beggars expose their ulcers and their necessities to our sight, that is the best appeal they can make. But from what you tell me, you sometimes do nothing of this, but lie there like a shadow or a statue. They put statues in palaces simply to please the prince's eyes. Be content to be that in the presence of God: He will bring the statue to life when He pleases.

St. François de Sales

I have come to see that I do not limit my mind enough simply to prayer, that I always want to do something myself in it, wherein I do very wrong. . . . I wish most definitely to cut off and separate my mind from all that, and to hold it with all my strength, as much as I can, to the sole regard and simple unity. By allowing the fear of being ineffectual to enter into the state of prayer, and by wishing to accomplish something myself, I spoilt it all.

St. Jeanne Chantal

So long as you seek Buddhahood, specifically exercising yourself for it, there is no attainment for you.

Yung-chia Ta-shih

"How does a man set himself in harmony with the Tao?" "I am already out of harmony."

Shih-t'ou

How shall I grasp it? Do not grasp it. That which remains when there is no more grasping is the Self.

Panchadasi

I order you to remain simply either in God or close to
God, without trying to do anything there, and without
asking anything of Him, unless He urges it.

St. François de Sales

Adoration is an activity of the loving, but still separate, individuality. Contemplation is the state of union with the divine
Ground of all being. The highest prayer is the most passive.
Inevitably; for the less there is of self, the more there is of God.
That is why the path to passive, or infused contemplation is
so hard and, for many, so painful—a passage through successive or simultaneous Dark Nights, in which the pilgrim
must die to the life of sense as an end in itself, to the life of
private and even of traditionally hallowed thinking and believing, and finally to the deep source of all ignorance and
evil, the life of the separate, individualized will.

CHAPTER XVII

Suffering

THE Godhead is impassible; for where there is perfection and
unity, there can be no suffering. The capacity to suffer arises
where there is imperfection, disunity and separation from an
embracing totality; and the capacity is actualized to the extent
that imperfection, disunity and separateness are accompanied
by an urge towards the intensification of these creaturely
conditions. For the individual who achieves unity within his
own organism and union with the divine Ground, there is an
end of suffering. The goal of creation is the return of all
sentient beings out of separateness and that infatuating urge-
to-separateness which results in suffering, through unitive
knowledge, into the wholeness of eternal Reality.

The elements which make up man produce a capacity for
pain.
The cause of pain is the craving for individual life.
Deliverance from craving does away with pain.
The way of deliverance is the Eightfold Path.

The Four Noble Truths of Buddhism

The urge-to-separateness, or craving for independent and individualized existence, can manifest itself on all the levels of life, from the merely cellular and physiological, through the instinctive, to the fully conscious. It can be the craving of a whole organism for an intensification of its separateness from the environment and the divine Ground. Or it can be the urge of a part within an organism for an intensification of its own partial life as distinct from (and consequently at the expense of) the life of the organism as a whole. In the first case we speak of impulse, passion, desire, self-will, sin; in the second, we describe what is happening as illness, injury, functional or organic disorder. In both cases the craving for separateness results in suffering, not only for the craver, but also for the craver's sentient environment—other organisms in the external world, or other organs within the same organism. In one way suffering is entirely private; in another, fatally contagious. No living creature is able to experience the suffering of another creature. But the craving for separateness which, sooner or later, directly or indirectly, results in some form of private and unshareable suffering for the craver, also results, sooner or later, directly or indirectly, in suffering (equally private and unshareable) for others. Suffering and moral evil have the same source—a craving for the intensification of the separateness which is the primary datum of all creatureliness.

It will be as well to illustrate these generalizations by a few examples. Let us consider first the suffering inflicted by living organisms on themselves and on other living organisms in the mere process of keeping alive. The cause of such suffering is the craving for individual existence, expressing itself specifically in the form of hunger. Hunger is entirely natural—a part of every creature's *dharma*. The suffering it causes alike to the hungry and to those who satisfy their hunger is inseparable from the existence of sentient creatures. The existence of sentient creatures has a goal and purpose which is ultimately the supreme good of every one of them. But meanwhile the suffering of creatures remains a fact and is a necessary part of creatureliness. In so far as this is the case, creation is the beginning of the Fall. The consummation of the Fall takes place when creatures seek to intensify their separateness beyond the limits prescribed by the law of their being. On the biological level the Fall would seem to have been consummated very frequently during the course of evolutionary history.

Every species, except the human, chose immediate, short-range success by means of specialization. But specialization always leads into blind alleys. It is only by remaining precariously generalized that an organism can advance towards that rational intelligence which is its compensation for not having a body and instincts perfectly adapted to one particular kind of life in one particular kind of environment. Rational intelligence makes possible unparalleled worldly success on the one hand and, on the other, a further advance towards spirituality and a return, through unitive knowledge, to the divine Ground.

Because the human species refrained from consummating the Fall on the biological level, human individuals now possess the momentous power of choosing either selflessness and union with God, or the intensification of separate selfhood in ways and to a degree, which are entirely beyond the ken of the lower animals. Their capacity for good is infinite, since they can, if they so desire, make room within themselves for divine Reality. But at the same time their capacity for evil is, not indeed infinite (since evil is always ultimately self-destructive and therefore temporary), but uniquely great. Hell is total separation from God, and the devil is the will to that separation. Being rational and free, human beings are capable of being diabolic. This is a feat which no animal can duplicate, for no animal is sufficiently clever, sufficiently purposeful, sufficiently strong-willed or sufficiently moral to be a devil. (We should note that, to be diabolic on the grand scale, one must, like Milton's Satan, exhibit in a high degree all the moral virtues, except only charity and wisdom.)

Man's capacity to crave more violently than any animal for the intensification of his separateness results not only in moral evil and the sufferings which moral evil inflicts, in one way or another, upon the victims of evil and the perpetrators of it, but also in certain characteristically human derangements of the body. Animals suffer mainly from contagious diseases, which assume epidemic proportions whenever the urge to reproduction combines with exceptionally favourable circumstances to produce overcrowding, and from diseases due to infestation by parasites. (These last are simply a special case of the sufferings that must inevitably arise when many species of creatures co-exist and can only survive at one another's expense.) Civilized man has been fairly successful in protecting himself against these plagues but in their place he has called up a formidable array of degenerative diseases hardly known among the lower animals. Most of these degenerative diseases are due to the fact that civilized human beings do not, on any level of their being, live in harmony with Tao, or the divine Nature of Things. They love to intensify their selfhood through gluttony, therefore eat the wrong food and too much of it; they inflict upon themselves chronic anxiety over money and, because they crave excitement, chronic over-stimulation; they suffer, during their working hours, from the chronic boredom and frustration imposed by the sort of jobs that have to be done in order to satisfy the artificially stimulated demand for the fruits of fully mechanized mass production. Among the consequences of these wrong uses of the psycho-physical organism are degenerative changes in particular organs, such as the heart, kidneys, pancreas, intestines and arteries. Asserting their partial selfhood in a kind of declaration of independence from the organism as a whole, the degenerating organs cause suffering to themselves and their physiological environment. In exactly the same way the human individual asserts his own partial selfhood and his separateness from his neighbours, from Nature and from God—with disastrous consequences to himself, his family, his friends and society in general. And, reciprocally, a disordered society, professional group or family, living by a false philosophy, influences its members to assert their individual selfhood and separateness, just as the wrong-living and wrong-thinking individual influences his own organs to assert, by some excess or defect of function, their partial selfhood at the expense of the total organism.

The effects of suffering may be morally and spiritually bad, neutral or good, according to the way in which the suffering is endured and reacted to. In other words, it may stimulate in the sufferer a conscious or unconscious craving for the intensification of his separateness; or it may leave the craving such as it was before the suffering; or, finally, it may mitigate it and so become a means for advance towards self-abandonment and the love and knowledge of God. Which of these three alternatives shall be realized depends, in the last analysis, upon the sufferer's choice. This seems to be true even on the sub-human level. The higher animals, at any rate, often seem to resign themselves to pain, sickness and death with a kind of serene acceptance of what the divine Nature of Things has decreed for them. But in other cases there is panic fear and struggle, a frenzied resistance to those decrees. To some extent, at least, the embodied animal self appears to be free, in the face of suffering, to choose self-abandonment or self-assertion. For embodied human selves, this freedom of choice is unquestionable. The choice of self-abandonment in suffering makes possible the reception of grace—grace on the spiritual level, in the form of an accession of the love and knowledge of God, and grace on the mental and physiological levels, in the form of a diminution of fear, self-concern and even of pain.

> When we conceive the love of suffering, we lose the sensibility of the senses and dead, dead we will live in that garden.
>
> *St. Catherine of Siena*

> He who suffers for love does not suffer, for all suffering is forgot.
>
> *Eckhart*

> In this life there is not purgatory, but only heaven or hell; for he who bears afflictions with patience has paradise, and he who does not has hell.
>
> *St. Philip Neri*

Many sufferings are the immediate consequence of moral evil, and these cannot have any good effects upon the sufferer, so long as the causes of his distress are not eradicated.

> Each sin begetteth a special spiritual suffering. A suffering of this kind is like unto that of hell, for the more you suffer, the worse you become. This happeneth to sinners; the more they suffer through their sins, the more wicked they become; and they fall continually more and more into their sins in order to get free from their suffering.
>
> *The Following of Christ*

The idea of vicarious suffering has too often been formulated in crudely juridical and commercial terms. A has committed an offence for which the law decrees a certain punishment; B voluntarily undergoes the punishment; justice and the law-giver's honour are satisfied; consequently A may go free. Or else it is all a matter of debts and repayments. A owes C a sum which he cannot pay; B steps in with the cash and so prevents C from foreclosing on the mortgage. Applied to the facts of man's suffering and his relations to the divine Ground, these conceptions are neither enlightening nor edifying. The orthodox doctrine of the Atonement attributes to God characteristics that would be discreditable even to a human potentate, and its model of the universe is not the product of spiritual insight rationalized by philosophic reflection, but rather the projection of a lawyer's phantasy. But in spite of these deplorable crudities in their formulation, the idea of vicarious suffering and the other, closely related idea of the transferability of merit are based upon genuine facts of experience. The selfless and God-filled person can and does act as a channel through which grace is able to pass into the unfortunate being who has made himself impervious to the divine by the habitual craving for intensifications of his own separateness and selfhood. It is because of this that the saints are able to exercise authority, all the greater for being entirely noncompulsive, over their fellow beings. They "transfer merit" to those who are in need of it; but that which converts the victims of self-will and puts them on the path of liberation is not the merit of the saintly individual—a merit that consists in his having made himself capable of eternal Reality, as a pipe, by being cleaned out, is made capable of water; it is rather the divine charge he carries, the eternal Reality for which he has become the conduit. And similarly, in vicarious suffering, it is not the actual pains experienced by the saint which are redemptive—for to believe that God is angry at sin and that His anger cannot be propitiated except by the offer of a certain sum of pain is to blaspheme against the divine Nature. No, what saves is the gift from beyond the temporal order, brought to those imprisoned in selfhood by these selfless and God-filled persons, who have been ready to accept suffering, in order to help their fellows. The Bodhisattva's vow is a promise to forgo the immediate fruits of enlightenment and to accept rebirth and its inevitable concomitants, pain and death, again and again, until such time as, thanks to his labours and the graces of which, being selfless, he is the channel, all sentient beings shall have come to final and complete deliverance.

I saw a mass of matter of a dull gloomy colour between the North and the East, and was informed that this mass was human beings, in as great misery as they could be, and live; and that I was mixed up with them and henceforth I must not consider myself as a distinct or separate being.

John Woolman

Why must the righteous and the innocent endure undeserved suffering? For anyone who conceives of human individuals as Hume conceived of events and things, as "loose and separate," the question admits of no acceptable answer. But, in fact, human individuals are not loose and separate, and the only reason why we think they are is our own wrongly interpreted self-interest. We want to "do what we damned well like," to have "a good time" and no responsibilities. Consequently, we find it convenient to be misled by the inadequacies of language and to believe (not always, of course, but just when it suits us) that things, persons and events are as completely distinct and separate one from another as the words, by means of which we think about them. The truth is, of course, that we are all organically related to God, to Nature and to our fellow men. If every human being were constantly and consciously in a proper relationship with his divine, natural and social environments there would be only so much suffering as Creation makes inevitable. But actually most human beings are chronically in an improper relation to God, Nature and some at least of their fellows. The results of these wrong relationships are manifest on the social level as wars, revolutions, exploitation and disorder; on the natural level, as waste and exhaustion of irreplaceable resources; on the biological level, as degenerative diseases and the deterioration of racial stocks; on the moral level, as an overweening bumptiousness; and on the spiritual level, as blindness to divine Reality and complete ignorance of the reason and purpose of human existence. In such circumstances it would be extraordinary if the innocent and righteous did not suffer—just as it would be extraordinary if the innocent kidneys and the righteous heart were not to suffer for the sins of a licorous palate and overloaded stomach, sins, we may add, imposed upon those organs by the will of the gluttonous individual to whom they belong, as he himself belongs to a society which other individuals, his contemporaries and predecessors, have built up into a vast and enduring incarnation of disorder, inflicting suffering upon its members and infecting them with its own ignorance and wickedness. The righteous man can escape suffering only by accepting it and passing beyond it; and he can accomplish this only by being converted from righteousness to total selflessness and God-centredness, by ceasing to be just a Pharisee, or good citizen, and becoming "perfect as your Father which is in heaven is perfect." The difficulties in the way of such a transfiguration are, obviously, enormous. But of those who "speak with authority," who has ever said that the road to complete deliverance was easy or the gate anything but "strait and narrow"?

CHAPTER XVIII

Faith

THE word "faith" has a variety of meanings, which it is important to distinguish. In some contexts it is used as a synonym for "trust," as when we say that we have faith in Dr. X's diagnostic skill or in lawyer Y's integrity. Analogous to this is our "faith" in authority—the belief that what certain persons say about certain subjects is likely, because of their special qualifications, to be true. On other occasions "faith" stands for belief in propositions which we have not had occasion to verify for ourselves, but which we know that we could verify if we had the inclination, the opportunity and the necessary capacities. In this sense of the word we have "faith," even though we may never have been to Australia, that there is such a creature as a duck-billed platypus; we have "faith" in the atomic theory, even though we may never have performed the experiments on which that theory rests, and be incapable of understanding the mathematics by which it is supported. And finally there is the "faith," which is a belief in propositions which we know we cannot verify, even if we should desire to do so—propositions such as those of the Athanasian Creed or those which constitute the doctrine of the Immaculate Conception. This kind of "faith" is defined by the Scholastics as an act of the intellect moved to assent by the will.

Faith in the first three senses of the word plays a very important part, not only in the activities of everyday life, but even in those of pure and applied science. *Credo ut intelligam* —and also, we should add, *ut agaim* and *ut vivam*. Faith is a pre-condition of all systematic knowing, all purposive doing and all decent living. Societies are held together, not primarily by the fear of the many for the coercive power of the few, but by a widespread faith in the other fellow's decency. Such a faith tends to create its own object, while the widespread mutual mistrust, due, for example, to war or domestic dissension, creates the object of mistrust. Passing now from the moral to the intellectual sphere, we find faith lying at the root of all organized thinking. Science and technology could not exist unless we had faith in the reliability of the universe—unless, in Clerk Maxwell's words, we implicitly believed that the book of Nature is really a book and not a magazine, a coherent work of art and not a hodge-podge of mutually irrelevant snippets. To this general faith in the reasonableness and trustworthiness of the world the searcher after truth must add two kinds of special faith—faith in the authority of qualified experts, sufficient to permit him to take their word for statements which he personally has not verified; and faith in his own working hypotheses, sufficient to induce him to test his provisional beliefs by means of appropriate action. This action may confirm the belief which inspired it. Alternatively it may bring proof that the original working hypothesis was ill founded, in which case it will have to be modified until it becomes conformable to the facts and so passes from the realm of faith to that of knowledge.

The fourth kind of faith is the thing which is commonly called "religious faith." The usage is justifiable, not because the other kinds of faith are not fundamental in religion just as they are in secular affairs, but because this willed assent to propositions which are known to be unverifiable occurs in religion, and only in religion, as a characteristic addition to faith as trust, faith in authority and faith in unverified but verifiable propositions. This is the kind of faith which, according to Christian theologians, justifies and saves. In its extreme and most uncompromising form, such a doctrine can be very dangerous. Here, for example, is a passage from one of Luther's letters. *Esto peccator, et pecca fortiter; sed fortius crede et gaude in Christo, qui victor est peccati, mortis et mundi. Peccandum est quam diu sic sumus; vita haec non est habitatio justitiae.* ("Be a sinner and sin strongly; but yet more strongly believe and rejoice in Christ, who is the conqueror of sin, death and the world. So long as we are as we are, there must be sinning; this life is not the dwelling place of righteousness.") To the danger that faith in the doctrine of justification by faith may serve as an excuse for and even an invitation to sin must be added another danger, namely, that the faith which is supposed to save may be faith in propositions not merely unverifiable, but repugnant to reason and the moral sense, and entirely at variance with the findings of those who have fulfilled the conditions of spiritual insight into the Nature of Things. "This is the acme of faith," says Luther in his *De Servo Arbitrio*, "to believe that God who saves so few and condemns so many, is merciful; that He is just who, at his own pleasure, has made us necessarily doomed to damnation, so that He seems to delight in the torture of the wretched and to be more deserving of hate than of love. If by any effort of reason I could conceive how God, who shows so much anger and harshness, could be merciful and just, there would be no need of faith." Revelation (which, when it is genuine, is simply the record of the immediate experience of those who are pure enough in heart and poor enough in spirit to be able to see God) says nothing at all of these hideous doctrines, to which the will forces the quite naturally and rightly reluctant intellect to give assent. Such notions are the product, not of the insight of saints, but of the busy phantasy of jurists, who were so far from having transcended selfness and the prejudices of education that they had the folly and presumption to interpret the universe in terms of the Jewish and Roman law with which they happened to be familiar. "Woe unto you lawyers," said Christ. The denunciation was prophetic and for all time.

The core and spiritual heart of all the higher religions is the Perennial Philosophy; and the Perennial Philosophy can be assented to and acted upon without resort to the kind of faith, about which Luther was writing in the foregoing passages. There must, of course, be faith as trust—for confidence in one's fellows is the beginning of charity towards men, and confidence not only in the material, but also the moral and spiritual reliability of the universe, is the beginning of charity or love-knowledge in relation to God. There must also be faith in authority—the authority of those whose selflessness has qualified them to know the spiritual Ground of all being by direct acquaintance as well as by report. And finally there must be faith in such propositions about Reality as are enunciated by philosophers in the light of genuine revelation—propositions which the believer knows that he can, if he is prepared to fulfil the necessary conditions, verify for himself. But, so long as the Perennial Philosophy is accepted in its essential simplicity, there is no need of willed assent to propositions known in advance to be unverifiable. Here it is necessary to add that such unverifiable propositions may become verifiable to the extent that intense faith affects the psychic substratum and so creates an existence, whose derived objectivity can actually be discovered "out there." Let us, however, remember that an existence which derives its objectivity from the mental activity of those who intensely believe in it cannot possibly be the spiritual Ground of the world, and that a mind busily engaged in the voluntary and intellectual activity, which is "religious faith" cannot possibly be in the state of selflessness and alert passivity which is the necessary condition of the unitive knowledge of the Ground. That is why the Buddhists affirm that "loving faith leads to heaven; but obedience to the Dharma leads to Nirvana." Faith in the existence and power of any supernatural entity which is less than ultimate spiritual Reality, and in any form of worship that falls short of self-naughting, will certainly, if the object of faith is intrinsically good, result in improvement of character, and probably in posthumous survival of the improved personality under "heavenly" conditions. But this personal survival within what is still the temporal order is not the eternal life of timeless union with the Spirit. This eternal life "stands in the knowledge" of the Godhead, not in faith in anything less than the Godhead.

> The immortality attained through the acquisition of any objective condition (e.g., the condition—merited through good works, which have been inspired by love of, and faith in, something less than the supreme Godhead—of being united in act to what is worshipped) is liable to end; for it is distinctly stated in the Scriptures that karma is never the cause of emancipation.
>
> *Shankara*

Karma is the causal sequence in time, from which we are delivered solely by "dying to" the temporal self and becoming united with the eternal, which is beyond time and cause. For "as to the notion of a First Cause, or a *Causa Sui*" (to quote the words of an eminent theologian and philosopher, Dr. F. R. Tennant), "we have, on the one hand, to bear in mind that we refute ourselves in trying to establish it by extension of the application of the causal category, for causality when universalized contains a contradiction; and, on the other, to remember that the ultimate Ground simply 'is.'" Only when the individual also "simply is," by reason of his union through love-knowledge with the Ground, can there be any question of complete and eternal liberation.

CHAPTER XIX

God Is Not Mocked

Why hast thou said, "I have sinned so much,
And God in His mercy has not punished my sins"?
How many times do I smite thee, and thou knowest not!
Thou art bound in my chains from head to foot.
On thy heart is rust on rust collected
So that thou art blind to divine mysteries.
When a man is stubborn and follows evil practices,
He casts dust in the eyes of his discernment.
Old shame for sin and calling on God quit him;
Dust five layers deep settles on his mirror,
Rust spots begin to gnaw his iron,
The colour of his jewel grows less and less.

Jalal-uddin Rumi

IF THERE is freedom (and even Determinists consistently act as if they were certain of it) and if (as everyone who has qualified himself to talk about the subject has always been convinced) there is a spiritual Reality, which it is the final end and purpose of consciousness to know; then all life is in the nature of an intelligence test, and the higher the level of awareness and the greater the potentialities of the creature, the more searchingly difficult will be the questions asked. For, in Bagehot's words, "we could not be what we ought to be, if we lived in the sort of universe we should expect. . . . A latent Providence, a confused life, an odd material world, an existence broken short in the midst and on a sudden, are not real difficulties, but real helps; for they, or something like them, are essential conditions of a moral life in a subordinate being." Because we are free, it is possible for us to answer life's questions either well or badly. If we answer them badly, we shall bring down upon ourselves self-stultification. Most often this self-stultification will take subtle and not immediately detectable forms, as when our failure to answer properly makes it impossible for us to realize the higher potentialities of our being. Sometimes, on the contrary, the self-stultification is manifest on the physical level, and may involve not only individuals as individuals, but entire societies, which go down in catastrophe or sink more slowly into decay. The giving of correct answers is rewarded primarily by spiritual growth and progressive realization of latent potentialities, and secondarily (when circumstances make it possible) by the adding of all the rest to the realized kingdom of God. *Karma* exists; but its equivalence of act and award is not always obvious and material, as the earlier Buddhist and Hebrew writers ingenuously imagined that it should be. The bad man in prosperity may, all unknown to himself, be darkened and corroded with inward rust, while the good man under afflictions may be in the rewarding process of spiritual growth. No, God is not mocked; but also, let us always remember, He is not understood.

> *Però nella giustizia sempiterna*
>   *la vista che riceve vostro mondo,*
>   *com'occhio per lo mar, dentro s'interna,*
> *chè, benchè dalla proda veggia il fondo,*
>   *in pelago nol vede, e non di meno*
>   *è lì, ma cela lui l'esser profondo.*

("Wherefore, in the eternal justice, such sight as your earth receives is engulfed, like the eye in the sea; for though by the shore it can see the bottom, in the ocean it cannot see it; yet none the less the bottom is there, but the depth hides it.") Love is the plummet as well as the astrolabe of God's mysteries, and the pure in heart can see far down into the depths of the divine justice, to catch a glimpse, not indeed of the details of the cosmic process, but at least of its principle and nature. These insights permit them to say, with Juliana of Norwich, that all shall be well, that, in spite of time, all *is* well, and that the problem of evil has its solution in the eternity, which men can, if they so desire, experience, but can never describe.

> But, you urge, if men sin from the necessity of their nature, they are excusable; you do not explain, however, what you would infer from this fact. Is it perhaps that God will be prevented from growing angry with them? Or is it rather that they have deserved that blessedness which consists in the knowledge and love of God? If you mean the former, I altogether agree that God does not grow angry and that all things happen by his decree. But I deny that, for this reason, all men ought to be happy. Surely men may be excusable and nevertheless miss happiness, and be tormented in many ways. A horse is excusable for being a horse and not a man; but nevertheless he must needs be a horse and not a man. One who goes mad from the bite of a dog is excusable; yet it is right that he should die of suffocation. So, too, he who cannot rule his passions, nor hold them in check out of respect for the law, while he may be excusable on the ground of weakness, is incapable of enjoying conformity of spirit and knowledge and love of God; and he is lost inevitably.
>
> *Spinoza*

Horizontally and vertically, in physical and temperamental kind as well as in degree of inborn ability and native goodness, human beings differ profoundly one from another. Why? To what end and for what past causes? "Master, who did sin, this man or his parents, that he was born blind?" Jesus answered, "Neither hath this man sinned nor his parents, but that the works of God should be made manifest in him." The man of science, on the contrary, would say that the responsibility rested with the parents who had caused the blindness of their child either by having the wrong kind of genes, or by contracting some avoidable disease. Hindu or Buddhist believers in reincarnation according to the laws of *karma* (the destiny which, by their actions, individuals and groups of individuals impose upon themselves, one another and their descendants) would give another answer and say that, owing to what he had done in previous existences, the blind man had predestined himself to choose the sort of parents from whom he would have to inherit blindness.

These three answers are not mutually incompatible. The parents are responsible for making the child what, by heredity and upbringing, he turns out to be. The soul or character incarnated in the child is of such a nature, owing to past behaviour, that it is forced to select those particular parents. And collaborating with the material and efficient causes is the final cause, the teleological pull from in front. This teleological pull is a pull from the divine Ground of things acting upon that part of the timeless now, which a finite mind must regard as the future. Men sin and their parents sin; but the works of God have to be manifested in every sentient being (either by exceptional ways, as in this case of supernormal healing, or in the ordinary course of events)—have to be manifested again and again, with the infinite patience of eternity, until at last the creature makes itself fit for the perfect and consummate manifestation of unitive knowledge, of the state of "not I, but God in me."

> "*Karma*," according to the Hindus, "never dispels igno-rance, being under the same category with it. Knowledge alone dispels ignorance, just as light alone dispels dark-ness."

In other words, the causal process takes place within time and cannot possibly result in deliverance from time. Such a deliver-ance can only be achieved as a consequence of the intervention of eternity in the temporal domain; and eternity cannot inter-vene unless the individual will makes a creative act of self-denial, thus producing, as it were, a vacuum into which eternity can flow. To suppose that the causal process in time can of itself result in deliverance from time is like supposing that water will rise into a space from which the air has not been previously exhausted.

> The right relation between prayer and conduct is not that conduct is supremely important and prayer may help it, but that prayer is supremely important and conduct tests it.
>
> *Archbishop Temple*

The aim and purpose of human life is the unitive knowledge of God. Among the indispensable means to that end is right conduct, and by the degree and kind of virtue achieved, the degree of liberating knowledge may be assessed and its quality evaluated. In a word, the tree is known by its fruits; God is not mocked.

Religious beliefs and practices are certainly not the only factors determining the behaviour of a given society. But, no less certainly, they are among the determining factors. At least to some extent, the collective conduct of a nation is a test of the religion prevailing within it, a criterion by which we may legitimately judge the doctrinal validity of that religion and its practical efficiency in helping individuals to advance towards the goal of human existence.

In the past the nations of Christendom persecuted in the name of their faith, fought religious wars and undertook crusades against infidels and heretics; today they have ceased to be Christian in anything but name, and the only religion they profess is some brand of local idolatry, such as nationalism, state-worship, boss-worship and revolutionism. From these fruits of (among other things) historic Christianity, what inferences can we draw as to the nature of the tree? The answer has already been given in the section on "Time and Eternity." If Christians used to be persecutors and are now no longer Christians, the reason is that the Perennial Philosophy incorporated in their religion was overlaid by wrong beliefs that led inevitably, since God is never mocked, to wrong actions. These wrong beliefs had one element in common—namely, an overvaluation of happenings in time and an undervaluation of the everlasting, timeless fact of eternity. Thus, belief in the supreme importance for salvation of remote historical events resulted in bloody disputes over the interpretation of the not very adequate and often conflicting records. And belief in the sacredness, nay, the actual divinity, of the ecclesiastico-politico-financial organizations, which developed after the fall of the Roman Empire, not only added bitterness to the all too human struggles for their control, but served to rationalize and justify the worst excesses of those who fought for place, wealth and power within and through the Church. But this is not the whole story. The same overvaluation of events in time, which once caused Christians to persecute and fight religious wars, led at last to a wide-spread indifference to a religion that, in spite of everything, was still in part preoccupied with eternity. But nature abhors a vacuum, and into the yawning void of this indifference there flowed the tide of political idolatry. The practical consequences of such idolatry, as we now see, are total war, revolution and tyranny.

Meanwhile, on the credit side of the balance sheet, we find such items as the following: an immense increase in technical and governmental efficiency and an immense increase in scientific knowledge—each of them a result of the general shift of Western man's attention from the eternal to the temporal order, first within the sphere of Christianity and then, inevitably, outside it.

CHAPTER XX

Tantum religio potuit suadere malorum

Would you know whence it is that so many false spirits have appeared in the world, who have deceived themselves and others with false fire and false light, laying claim to information, illumination and openings of the divine Life, particularly to do wonders under extraordinary calls from God? It is this: they have turned to God without turning from themselves; would be alive to God before they are dead to their own nature. Now religion in the hands of self, or corrupt nature, serves only to discover vices of a worse kind than in nature left to itself. Hence are all the disorderly passions of religious men, which burn in a worse flame than passions only employed about worldly matters; pride, self-exaltation, hatred and persecution, under a cloak of religious zeal, will sanctify actions which nature, left to itself, would be ashamed to own.

William Law

"Turning to God without turning from self"—the formula is absurdly simple; and yet, simple as it is, it explains all the follies and iniquities committed in the name of religion. Those who turn to God without turning from themselves are

tempted to evil in several characteristic and easily recognizable
ways. They are tempted, first of all, to practice magical rites,
by means of which they hope to compel God to answer their
petitions and, in general, to serve their private or collective
ends. All the ugly business of sacrifice, incantation and what
Jesus called "vain repetition" is a product of this wish to treat
God as a means to indefinite self-aggrandisement, rather than
as an end to be reached through total self-denial. Next, they
are tempted to use the name of God to justify what they do in
pursuit of place, power and wealth. And because they believe
themselves to have divine justification for their actions, they
proceed, with a good conscience, to perpetrate abominations,
"which nature, left to itself, would be ashamed to own."
Throughout recorded history, an incredible sum of mischief
has been done by ambitious idealists, self-deluded by their
own verbiage and a lust for power, into a conviction that
they were acting for the highest good of their fellow men. In
the past, the justification for such wickedness was "God" or
"the Church," or "the True Faith"; today idealists kill and
torture and exploit in the name of "the Revolution," "the
New Order," "the World of the Common Man," or simply
"the Future." Finally there are the temptations which arise,
when the falsely religious begin to acquire the powers which
are the fruit of their pious and magical practices. For, let there
be no mistake, sacrifice, incantation and "vain repetition"
actually do produce fruits, especially when practised in con-
junction with physical austerities. Men who turn towards God
without turning away from themselves do not, of course, reach
God; but if they devote themselves energetically enough to
their pseudo-religion, they will get results. Some of these
results are doubtless the product of auto-suggestion. (It was
through "vain repetition" that Coué got his patients to cure
themselves of their diseases.) Others are due, apparently, to
that "something not ourselves" in the psychic medium—that
something which makes, not necessarily for righteousness, but
always for power. Whether this something is a piece of second-
hand objectivity, projected into the medium by the individual worshipper and his fellows and predecessors; whether
it is a piece of first-hand objectivity, corresponding, on the
psychic level, to the data of the material universe; or whether
it is a combination of both these things, it is impossible to
determine. All that need be said in this place is that people

who turn towards God without turning from themselves often seem to acquire a knack of getting their petitions answered and sometimes develop considerable supernormal powers, such as those of psychic healing and extra-sensory perception. But, it may be asked: Is it necessarily a good thing to be able to get one's petitions answered in the way one wants them to be? And how far is it spiritually profitable to be possessed of these "miraculous" powers? These are questions which were considered in the section on "Prayer" and will be further discussed in the chapter on "The Miraculous."

> The Grand Augur, in his ceremonial robes, approached the shambles and thus addressed the pigs. "How can you object to die? I shall fatten you for three months. I shall discipline myself for ten days and fast for three. I shall strew fine grass and place you bodily upon a carved sacrificial dish. Does not this satisfy you?"
>
> Then, speaking from the pigs' point of view, he continued: "It is better perhaps after all, to live on bran and escape from the shambles."
>
> "But then," he added, speaking from his own point of view, "to enjoy honour when alive, one would readily die on a war-shield or in the headsman's basket."
>
> So he rejected the pigs' point of view and adopted his own point of view. In what sense, then, was he different from the pigs?
>
> *Chuang Tzu*

Anyone who sacrifices anything but his own person or his own interests is on exactly the same level as Chuang Tzu's pigs. The pigs seek their own advantage inasmuch as they prefer life and bran to honour and the shambles; the sacrificers seek their own advantage inasmuch as they prefer the magical, God-constraining death of pigs to the death of their own passions and self-will. And what applies to sacrifice, applies equally to incantations, rituals and vain repetitions, when these are used (as they all too frequently are, even in the higher religions) as a form of compulsive magic. Rites and vain repetitions have a legitimate place in religion as aids to recollectedness, reminders of truth momentarily forgotten in the turmoil of worldly distractions. When spoken or performed as a kind of magic, their use is either completely pointless;

or else (and this is worse) it may have ego-enhancing results, which do not in any way contribute to the attainment of man's final end.

> The vestments of Isis are variegated to represent the cosmos; that of Osiris is white, symbolizing the Intelligible Light beyond the cosmos.
>
> *Plutarch*

So long as the symbol remains, in the worshipper's mind, firmly attached and instrumental to that which is symbolized, the use of such things as white and variegated vestments can do no harm. But if the symbol breaks loose, as it were, and becomes an end in itself, then we have, at the best, a futile aestheticism and sentimentality, at the worst a form of psychologically effective magic.

> All externals must yield to love; for they are for the sake of love, and not love for them.
>
> *Hans Denk*

> Ceremonies in themselves are not sin; but whoever supposes that he can attain to life either by baptism or by partaking of bread is still in superstition.
>
> *Hans Denk*

> If you be always handling the letter of the Word, always licking the letter, always chewing upon that, what great thing do you? No marvel you are such starvelings.
>
> *John Everard*

While the Right Law still prevailed, innumerable were the converts who fathomed the depths of the Dharma by merely listening to half a stanza or even to a single phrase of the Buddha's teaching. But as we come to the age of similitude and to these latter days of Buddhism, we are indeed far away from the Sage. People find themselves drowning in a sea of letters; they do not know how to get at the one substance which alone is truth. This was what caused the appearance of the Fathers (of Zen Buddhism) who, pointing directly at the human mind, told us to see here the ultimate ground of all things and thereby to attain Buddhahood. This is known as a special transmission outside the scriptural teaching. If one is endowed with superior talents or a special sharpness of mind, a gesture or a word will suffice to give one an immediate knowledge of the truth. Hence, since they were advocates of 'special transmission,' Ummon treated the (historical) Buddha with the utmost irreverence and Yakusan forbade his followers even to read the sutras.

Zen is the name given to this branch of Buddhism, which keeps itself away from the Buddha. It is also called the mystical branch, because it does not adhere to the literal meaning of the sutras. It is for this reason that those who blindly follow the steps of Buddha are sure to deride Zen, while those who have no liking for the letter are naturally inclined towards the mystical approach. The followers of the two schools know how to shake the head at each other, but fail to realize that they are after all complementary. Is not Zen one of the six virtues of perfection? If so, how can it conflict with the teachings of the Buddha? In my view, Zen is the outcome of the Buddha's teaching, and the mystical issues from the letters. There is no reason why a man should shun Zen because of the Buddha's teaching; nor need we disregard the letters on account of the mystical teachings of Zen. . . . Students of scriptural Buddhism run the risk of becoming sticklers for the scriptures, the real meaning of which they fail to understand. By such men ultimate reality is never grasped, and for them Zen would mean salvation. Whereas those who study Zen are too apt to run into the habit of making empty talks and practising sophistry. They fail to understand the significance of letters. To save them, the study of Buddhist scriptures is recommended. It is only when these one-sided views are mutually corrected that there is a perfect appreciation of the Buddha's teaching.

Chiang Chih-chi

It would be hard to find a better summing up of the conclusions, to which any spiritually and psychologically realistic mind must sooner or later come, than the foregoing paragraphs written in the eleventh century by one of the masters of Zen Buddhism.

The extract that follows is a moving protest against the

crimes and follies perpetrated in the name of religion by those sixteenth-century Reformers who had turned to God without turning away from themselves and who were therefore far more keenly interested in the temporal aspects of historic Christianity—the ecclesiastical organization, the logic-chopping, the letter of Scripture—than in the Spirit who must be worshipped in spirit, the eternal Reality in the selfless knowledge of whom stands man's eternal life. Its author was Sebastian Castellio, who was at one time Calvin's favourite disciple, but who parted company with his master when the latter burned Servetus for heresy against his own heresy. Fortunately Castellio was living in Basel when he made his plea for charity and common decency; penned in Geneva, it would have earned him torture and death.

If you, illustrious Prince (the words were addressed to the Duke of Wurtemberg) had informed your subjects that you were coming to visit them at an unnamed time, and had requested them to be prepared in white garments to meet you at your coming, what would you do if on arrival you should find that, instead of robing themselves in white, they had spent their time in violent debate about your person—some insisting that you were in France, others that you were in Spain; some declaring that you would come on horseback, others that you would come by chariot; some holding that you would come with great pomp and others that you would come without any train or following? And what especially would you say if they debated not only with words, but with blows of fist and sword strokes, and if some succeeded in killing and destroying others who differed from them? "He will come on horseback." "No, he will not; it will be by chariot." "You lie." "I do not; *you* are the liar." "Take that"—a blow with the fist. "Take *that*"—a sword-thrust through the body. Prince, what would you think of such citizens? Christ asked us to put on the white robes of a pure and holy life; but what occupies our thoughts? We dispute not only of the way to Christ, but of his relation to God the Father, of the Trinity, of predestination, of free will, of the nature of God, of the angels, of the condition of the soul after death—of a multitude of matters that are not essential to salvation; matters, moreover, which can never be known until our hearts are pure; for they are things which must be spiritually perceived.

Sebastian Castellio

People always get what they ask for; the only trouble is that they never know, until they get it, what it actually is that they have asked for. Thus, Protestants might, if they had so desired, have followed the lead of Castellio and Denk; but they preferred Calvin and Luther—preferred them because the doctrines of justification by faith and of predestination were more exciting than those of the Perennial Philosophy. And not only more exciting, but also less exacting; for if they were true, one could be saved without going through that distasteful process of self-naughting, which is the necessary pre-condition of deliverance into the knowledge of eternal Reality. And not only less exacting, but also more satisfying to the intellectual's appetite for clear-cut formulae and the syllogistic demonstrations of abstract truths. Waiting on God is a bore; but what fun to argue, to score off opponents, to lose one's temper and call it "righteous indignation," and at last to pass from controversy to blows, from words to what St. Augustine so deliciously described as the "benignant asperity" of persecution and punishment!

Choosing Luther and Calvin instead of the spiritual reformers who were their contemporaries, Protestant Europe got the kind of theology it liked. But it also got, along with other unanticipated by-products, the Thirty Years' War, capitalism and the first rudiments of modern Germany. "If we wish," Dean Inge has recently written, "to find a scapegoat on whose shoulders we may lay the miseries which Germany has brought upon the world . . . I am more and more convinced that the worst evil genius of that country is not Hitler or Bismarck or Frederick the Great, but Martin Luther. . . . It (Lutheranism) worships a God who is neither just nor merciful. . . . The Law of Nature, which ought to be the court of appeal against unjust authority, is identified (by Luther) with the existing order of society, to which absolute obedience is due." And so on. Right belief is the first branch of the Eightfold Path leading to deliverance; the root and primal cause of bondage is wrong belief, or ignorance—an ignorance, let us remember, which is never completely invincible, but always, in the last analysis, a matter of will. If we don't know, it is because we find it more convenient not to know. Original ignorance is the same thing as original sin.

CHAPTER XXI

Idolatry

To EDUCATED persons the more primitive kinds of idolatry have ceased to be attractive. They find it easy to resist the temptation to believe that particular natural objects are gods, or that certain symbols and images are the very forms of divine entities and as such must be worshipped and propitiated. True, much fetishistic superstition survives even today. But though it survives, it is not considered respectable. Like drinking and prostitution, the primitive forms of idolatry are tolerated, but not approved. Their place in the accredited hierarchy of values is among the lowest.

How different is the case with the developed and more modern forms of idolatry! These have achieved not merely survival, but the highest degree of respectability. They are recommended by men of science as an up-to-date substitute for genuine religion and by many professional religious teachers are equated with the worship of God. All this may be deplorable; but it is not in the least surprising. Our education disparages the more primitive forms of idolatry; but at the same time it disparages, or at the best it ignores, the Perennial Philosophy and the practice of spirituality. In place of mumbo-jumbo at the bottom and of the immanent and transcendent Godhead at the top, it sets up, as objects of admiration, faith and worship, a pantheon of strictly human ideas and ideals. In academic circles and among those who have been subjected to higher education, there are few fetishists and few devout contemplatives; but the enthusiastic devotees of some form of political or social idolatry are as common as blackberries. Significantly enough, I have observed, when making use of university libraries, that books on spiritual religion were taken out much less frequently than was the case in public libraries, patronized in the main by men and women who had not enjoyed the advantages, or suffered under the handicaps, of prolonged academic instruction.

The many varieties of higher idolatry may be classed under three main heads: technological, political and moral. Technological idolatry is the most ingenuous and primitive of the three; for its devotees, like those of the lower idolatry, believe that their redemption and liberation depend upon material objects—in this case gadgets. Technological idolatry is the religion whose doctrines are promulgated, explicitly or by implication, in the advertisement pages of our newspapers and magazines—the source, we may add parenthetically, from which millions of men, women and children in the capitalistic countries derive their working philosophy of life. In Soviet Russia too, technological idolatry was strenuously preached, becoming, during the years of that country's industrialization, a kind of state religion. So whole-hearted is the modern faith in technological idols that (despite all the lessons of mechanized warfare) it is impossible to discover in the popular thinking of our time any trace of the ancient and profoundly realistic doctrine of *hubris* and inevitable *nemesis*. There is a very general belief that, where gadgets are concerned, we can get something for nothing—can enjoy all the advantages of an elaborate, top-heavy and constantly advancing technology without having to pay for them by any compensating disadvantages.

Only a little less ingenuous are the political idolaters. For the worship of redemptive gadgets these have substituted the worship of redemptive social and economic organizations. Impose the right kind of organizations upon human beings, and all their problems, from sin and unhappiness to nationalism and war, will automatically disappear. Most political idolaters are also technological idolaters—and this in spite of the fact that the two pseudo-religions are finally incompatible, since technological progress at its present rate makes nonsense of any political blue-print, however ingeniously drawn, within a matter, not of generations, but of years and sometimes even of months. Further, the human being is, unfortunately, a creature endowed with free will; and if, for any reason, individuals do not choose to make it work, even the best organization will not produce the results it was intended to produce.

The moral idolaters are realists inasmuch as they see that

gadgets and organizations are not enough to guarantee the triumph of virtue and the increase of happiness, and that the individuals who compose societies and use machines are the arbiters who finally determine whether there shall be decency in personal relationship, order or disorder in society. Material and organizational instruments are indispensable, and a good tool is preferable to a bad one. But in listless or malicious hands the finest instrument is either useless or a means to evil.

The moralists cease to be realistic and commit idolatry inasmuch as they worship, not God, but their own ethical ideals, inasmuch as they treat virtue as an end in itself and not as the necessary condition of the knowledge and love of God—a knowledge and love, without which that virtue will never be made perfect or even socially effective.

What follows is an extract from a very remarkable letter written in 1836 by Thomas Arnold to his old pupil and future biographer, A. P. Stanley. "Fanaticism is idolatry; and it has the moral evil of idolatry in it; that is, a fanatic worships something which is the creation of his own desire, and thus even his self-devotion in support of it is only an apparent self-devotion; for in fact it is making the parts of his nature or his mind, which he least values, offer sacrifice to that which he most values. The moral fault, as it appears to me, is the idolatry—the setting up of some idea which is most kindred to our own minds, and the putting it in the place of Christ, who alone cannot be made an idol and inspire idolatry, because He combines all ideas of perfection and exhibits them in their just harmony and combination. Now in my own mind, by its natural tendency—that is, taking my mind at its best—truth and justice would be the idols I should follow; and they would be idols, for they would not supply *all* the food which the mind wants, and whilst worshipping them, reverence and humility and tenderness might very likely be forgotten. But Christ Himself includes at once truth and justice and all these other qualities too. . . . Narrow-mindedness tends to wickedness, because it does not extend its watchfulness to every part of our moral nature, and the neglect fosters wickedness in the parts so neglected."

As a piece of psychological analysis this is admirable. Its only defect is one of omission; for it neglects to take into account those influxes from the eternal order into the temporal, which are called grace or inspiration. Grace and inspiration are given when, and to the extent to which, a human being gives up self-will and abandons himself, moment by moment, through constant recollectedness and non-attachment, to the will of God. As well as the animal and spiritual graces, whose source is the divine Nature of Things, there are human pseudo-graces—such as, for example, the accessions of strength and virtue that follow self-devotion to some form of political or moral idolatry. To distinguish the true grace from the false is often difficult; but as time and circumstances reveal the full extent of their consequences on the soul, discrimination becomes possible even to observers having no special gifts of insight. Where the grace is genuinely "supernatural," an amelioration in one aspect of the total personality is not paid for by atrophy or deterioration elsewhere. The virtue which is accompanied and perfected by the love and knowledge of God is something quite different from the "righteousness of the scribes and Pharisees" which, for Christ, was among the worst of moral evils. Hardness, fanaticism, uncharitableness and spiritual pride—these are the ordinary by-products of a course of stoical self-improvement by means of personal effort, either unassisted or, if assisted, seconded only by the pseudo-graces which are given when the individual devotes himself to the achievement of an end which is not his true end, when the goal is not God, but merely a magnified projection of his own favourite ideas or moral excellences. The idolatrous worship of ethical values in and for themselves defeats its own object—and defeats it not only because, as Arnold insists, there is a lack of all-round development, but also and above all because even the highest forms of moral idolatry are God-eclipsing and therefore guarantee the idolater against the enlightening and liberating knowledge of Reality.

CHAPTER XXII

Emotionalism

You have spent all your life in the belief that you are wholly devoted to others, and never self-seeking. Nothing so feeds self-conceit as this sort of internal testimony that one is quite free from self-love, and always generously devoted to one's neighbours. But all this devotion that seems to be for others is really for yourself. Your self-love reaches to the point of perpetual self-congratulation that you are free from it; all your sensitiveness is lest you might not be fully satisfied with self; this is at the root of all your scruples. It is the 'I' which makes you so keen and sensitive. You want God as well as man to be always satisfied with you, and you want to be satisfied with yourself in all your dealings with God.

Besides, you are not accustomed to be contented with a simple good will—your self-love wants a lively emotion, a reassuring pleasure, some kind of charm or excitement. You are too much used to be guided by imagination and to suppose that your mind and will are inactive, unless you are conscious of their workings. And thus you are dependent upon a kind of excitement similar to that which the passions arouse, or theatrical representations. By dint of refinement you fall into the opposite extreme— a real coarseness of imagination. Nothing is more opposed, not only to the life of faith, but also to true wisdom. There is no more dangerous illusion than the fancies by which people try to avoid illusion. It is imagination which leads us astray; and the certainty which we seek through imagination, feeling, and taste, is one of the most dangerous sources from which fanaticism springs. This is the gulf of vanity and corruption which God would make you discover in your heart; you must look upon it with the calm and simplicity belonging to true humility. It is mere self-love to be inconsolable at seeing one's own imperfections; but to stand face to face with them, neither flattering nor tolerating them, seeking to correct oneself without becoming pettish—this is to desire what is good for its own sake, and for God's.

Fénelon

A LETTER from the Archbishop of Cambrai—what an event, what a signal honour! And yet it must have been with a certain trepidation that one broke the emblazoned seal. To ask for advice and a frank opinion of oneself from a man, who combines the character of a saint with the talents of a Marcel Proust, is to ask for the severest kind of shock to one's self-esteem. And duly, in the most exquisitely lucid prose, the shock would be administered—and, along with the shock, the spiritual antidote to its excruciating consequences. Fénelon never hesitated to disintegrate a correspondent's complacent ego; but the disintegration was always performed with a view to reintegration on a higher, non-egotistic level.

This particular letter is not only an admirable piece of character analysis; it also contains some very interesting remarks on the subject of emotional excitement in its relation to the life of the spirit.

The phrase, "religion of experience," has two distinct and mutually incompatible meanings. There is the "experience" of which the Perennial Philosophy treats—the direct apprehension of the divine Ground in an act of intuition possible, in its fulness, only to the selflessly pure in heart. And there is the "experience" induced by revivalist sermons, impressive ceremonials, or the deliberate efforts of one's own imagination. This "experience" is a state of emotional excitement—an excitement which may be mild and enduring or brief and epileptically violent, which is sometimes exultant in tone and sometimes despairing, which expresses itself here in song and dance, there in uncontrollable weeping. But emotional excitement, whatever its cause and whatever its nature, is always excitement of that individualized self, which must be died to by anyone who aspires to live to divine Reality. "Experience" as emotion about God (the highest form of this kind of excitement) is incompatible with "experience" as immediate awareness of God by a pure heart which has mortified even its most exalted emotions. That is why Fénelon, in the foregoing extract, insists upon the need for "calm and simplicity," why St. François de Sales is never tired of preaching the serenity which he himself so consistently practised, why all the Buddhist scriptures harp on tranquillity of mind as a necessary condition of deliverance. The peace that passes all understanding is one of the fruits of the spirit. But there is also the peace that does not pass understanding, the humbler peace of emotional self-control and self-denial; this is not a fruit of the spirit, but rather one of its indispensable roots.

The imperfect destroy true devotion, because they seek sensible sweetness in prayer.

St. John of the Cross

The fly that touches honey cannot use its wings; so the soul that clings to spiritual sweetness ruins its freedom and hinders contemplation.

St. John of the Cross

What is true of the sweet emotions is equally true of the bitter. For as some people enjoy bad health, so others enjoy a bad conscience. Repentance is *metanoia*, or "change of mind"; and without it there cannot be even a beginning of the spiritual life—for the life of the spirit is incompatible with the life of that "old man," whose acts, whose thoughts, whose very existence are the obstructing evils which have to be repented. This necessary change of mind is normally accompanied by sorrow and self-loathing. But these emotions are not to be persisted in and must never be allowed to become a settled habit of remorse. In Middle English "remorse" is rendered, with a literalness which to modern readers is at once startling and stimulating, as "again-bite." In this cannibalistic encounter, who bites whom? Observation and self-analysis provide the answer: the creditable aspects of the self bite the discreditable and are themselves bitten, receiving wounds that fester with incurable shame and despair. But, in Fénelon's words, "it is mere self-love to be inconsolable at seeing one's own imperfections." Self-reproach is painful; but the very pain is a reassuring proof that the self is still intact; so long as attention is fixed on the delinquent ego, it cannot be fixed upon God and the ego (which lives upon attention and dies only when that sustenance is withheld) cannot be dissolved in the divine Light.

Eschew as though it were a hell the consideration of yourself and your offences. No one should ever think of these things except to humiliate himself and love Our Lord. It is enough to regard yourself *in general* as a sinner, even as there are many saints in heaven who were such.

Charles de Condren

Faults will turn to good, provided we use them to our own humiliation, without slackening in the effort to correct ourselves. Discouragement serves no possible purpose; it is simply the despair of wounded self-love. The real way of profiting by the humiliation of one's own faults is to face them in their true hideousness, without ceasing to hope in God, while hoping nothing from self.

Fénelon

Came she (Mary Magdalene) down from the height of her desire for God into the depth of her sinful life, and searched in the foul stinking fen and dunghill of her soul? Nay, surely she did not do so. And why? Because God let her know by His grace in her soul that she should never so bring it about. For so might she sooner have raised in herself an ableness to have often sinned than have purchased by that work any plain forgiveness of all her sins.

The Cloud of Unknowing

In the light of what has been said above, we can understand the peculiar spiritual dangers by which every kind of predominantly emotional religion is always menaced. A hell-fire faith that uses the theatrical techniques of revivalism in order to stimulate remorse and induce the crisis of sudden conversion; a saviour cult that is for ever stirring up what St. Bernard calls the *amor carnalis* or fleshly love of the Avatar and personal God; a ritualistic mystery-religion that generates high feelings of awe and reverence and aesthetic ecstasy by means of its sacraments and ceremonials, its music and its incense, its numinous darknesses and sacred lights— in its own special way, each one of these runs the risk of becoming a form of psychological idolatry, in which God is identified with the ego's affective attitude towards God and finally the emotion becomes an end in itself, to be eagerly sought after and worshipped, as the addicts of a drug spend life in the pursuit of their artificial paradise. All this is obvious enough. But it is no less obvious that religions that make no appeal to the emotions have very few adherents. Moreover, when pseudo-religions with a strong emotional appeal make their appearance, they immediately win millions of enthusiastic devotees from among the masses to whom the real religions have ceased to have a meaning or to be a comfort. But whereas no adherent of a pseudo-religion (such as one of our current political idolatries, compounded of nationalism and revolutionism) can possibly go forward into the way of genuine spirituality, such a way always remains open to the adherents of even the most highly emotionalized varieties of genuine religion. Those who have actually followed this way to its end in the unitive knowledge of the divine Ground constitute a very small minority of the total. Many are called; but, since few choose to be chosen, few are chosen. The rest, say the oriental exponents of the Perennial Philosophy, earn themselves another chance, in circumstances more or less propitious according to their deserts, to take the cosmic intelligence test. If they are "saved," their incomplete and undefinitive deliverance is into some paradisal state of freer personal existence, from which (directly or through further incarnations) they may go on to the final release into eternity. If they are "lost," their "hell" is a temporal and temporary condition of thicker darkness and more oppressive bondage to self-will, the root and principle of all evil.

We see, then, that if it is persisted in, the way of emotional religion may lead, indeed, to a great good, but not to the greatest. But the emotional way opens into the way of unitive knowledge, and those who care to go on in this other way are well prepared for their task if they have used the emotional approach without succumbing to the temptations which have beset them on the way. Only the perfectly selfless and enlightened can do good that does not, in some way or other, have to be paid for by actual or potential evils. The religious systems of the world have been built up, in the main, by men and women who were not completely selfless or enlightened. Hence all religions have had their dark and even frightful aspects, while the good they do is rarely gratuitous, but must, in most cases, be paid for, either on the nail or by instalments. The emotion-rousing doctrines and practices, which play so important a part in all the world's organized religions, are no exception to this rule. They do good, but not gratuitously. The price paid varies according to the nature of the individual worshippers. Some of these choose to wallow in emotionalism and, becoming idolaters of feeling, pay for the good of their religion by a spiritual evil that may actually outweigh that good. Others resist the temptation to self-enhancement and go forward to the mortification of self, including the self's emotional side, and to the worship of God rather than of their own feelings and fancies about God. The further they go in this direction, the less they have to pay for the good which emotionalism brought them and which, but for emotionalism, most of them might never have had.

CHAPTER XXIII

The Miraculous

Revelations are the aberration of faith; they are an amusement that spoils simplicity in relation to God, that embarrasses the soul and makes it swerve from its directness in relation to God. They distract the soul and occupy it with other things than God. Special illuminations, auditions, prophecies and the rest are marks of weakness in a soul that cannot support the assaults of temptation or of anxiety about the future and God's judgment upon it. Prophecies are also marks of creaturely curiosity in a soul to whom God is indulgent and to whom, as a father to his importunate child, he gives a few trifling sweetmeats to satisfy its appetite.

J. J. Olier

The slightest degree of sanctifying grace is superior to a miracle, which is supernatural only by reason of its cause, by its mode of production (*quoad modum*), not by its intimate reality; the life restored to a corpse is only the natural life, low indeed in comparison with that of grace.

R. Garrigou-Lagrange

Can you walk on water? You have done no better than a straw. Can you fly in the air? You have done no better than a bluebottle. Conquer your heart; then you may become somebody.

Ansari of Herat

THE abnormal bodily states, by which the immediate awareness of the divine Ground is often accompanied, are not, of course, essential parts of that experience. Many mystics, indeed, deplored such things as being signs, not of divine grace, but of the body's weakness. To levitate, to go into trance, to lose the use of one's senses—in De Condren's words, this is "to receive the effects of God and his holy communications in a very animal and carnal way."

> "One ounce of sanctifying grace," he (St François de Sales) used to say, "is worth more than a hundredweight of those graces which theologians call 'gratuitous,' among which is the gift of miracles. It is possible to receive such gifts and yet to be in mortal sin; nor are they necessary to salvation."
>
> *Jean Pierre Camus*

The Sufis regard miracles as "veils" intervening between the soul and God. The masters of Hindu spirituality urge their disciples to pay no attention to the *siddhis*, or psychic powers, which may come to them unsought, as a by-product of one-pointed contemplation. The cultivation of these powers, they warn, distracts the soul from Reality and sets up insurmountable obstacles in the way of enlightenment and deliverance. A similar attitude is taken by the best Buddhist teachers, and in one of the Pali scriptures there is an ancedote recording the Buddha's own characteristically dry comment on a prodigious feat of levitation performed by one of his disciples. "This," he said, "will not conduce to the conversion of the unconverted, nor to the advantage of the converted." Then he went back to talking about deliverance.

Because they know nothing of spirituality and regard the material world and their hypotheses about it as supremely significant, rationalists are anxious to convince themselves and others that miracles do not and cannot happen. Because they have had experience of the spiritual life and its by-products, the exponents of the Perennial Philosophy are convinced that miracles do happen, but regard them as things of little importance, and that mainly negative and anti-spiritual.

The miracles which at present are in greatest demand, and of which there is the steadiest supply, are those of psychic healing. In what circumstances and to what extent the power of psychic healing should be used has been clearly indicated in the Gospel: "Whether is it easier to say to the sick of the palsy, Thy sins be forgiven thee; or to say, Arise, and take up thy bed and walk?" If one can "forgive sins," one can safely use the gift of healing. But the forgiving of sins is possible, in its fulness, only to those who "speak with authority," in virtue of being selfless channels of the divine Spirit. To these theocentric saints the ordinary, unregenerate human being reacts with a mixture of love and awe—longing to be close to them and yet constrained by their very holiness to say, "Depart from me, for I am a sinful man." Such holiness makes holy to the extent that the sins of those who approach it are forgiven and they are enabled to make a new start, to face the consequences of their past wrong-doings (for of course the consequences remain) in a new spirit that makes it possible for them to neutralize the evil or turn it into positive good. A less perfect kind of forgiveness can be bestowed by those who are not themselves outstandingly holy, but who speak with the delegated authority of an institution which the sinner believes to be in some way a channel of supernatural grace. In this case the contact between unregenerate soul and divine Spirit is not direct, but is mediated through the sinner's imagination.

Those who are holy in virtue of being selfless channels of the Spirit may practise psychic healing with perfect safety; for they will know which of the sick are ready to accept forgiveness along with the mere miracle of a bodily cure. Those who are not holy, but who can forgive sins in virtue of belonging to an institution which is believed to be a channel of grace may also practice healing with a fair confidence that they will not do more harm than good. But unfortunately the knack of psychic healing seems in some persons to be inborn, while others can acquire it without acquiring the smallest degree of holiness. ("It is possible to receive such graces and yet be in mortal sin.") Such persons will use their knack indiscriminately, either to show off or for profit. Often they produce spectacular cures—but lacking the power to forgive sins or even to understand the psychological correlates, conditions or causes of the symptoms they have so miraculously dispelled, they leave a soul empty, swept and garnished against the coming of seven other devils worse than the first.

CHAPTER XXIV

Ritual, Symbol, Sacrament

ASWALA: Yajnavalkya, since everything connected with
the sacrifice is pervaded by death and is subject to death,
by what means can the sacrificer overcome death?

YAJNAVALKYA: By the knowledge of the identity between
the sacrificer, the fire and the ritual word. For the ritual
word is indeed the sacrificer, and the ritual word is the fire,
and the fire, which is one with Brahman, is the sacrificer.
This knowledge leads to liberation. This knowledge leads
one beyond death.

Brihad Aranyaka Upanishad

IN OTHER words, rites, sacraments, and ceremonials are valuable to the extent that they remind those who take part in
them of the true Nature of Things, remind them of what
ought to be and (if only they would be docile to the immanent
and transcendent Spirit) of what actually might be their own
relation to the world and its divine Ground. Theoretically
any ritual or sacrament is as good as any other ritual or sacrament, provided always that the object symbolized be in fact
some aspect of divine Reality and that the relation between
symbol and fact be clearly defined and constant. In the same
way, one language is theoretically as good as another. Human
experience can be thought about as effectively in Chinese as
in English or French. But in practice Chinese is the best
language for those brought up in China, English for those
brought up in England and French for those brought up in
France. It is, of course, much easier to learn the order of a
rite and to understand its doctrinal significance than to master the intricacies of a foreign language. Nevertheless what
has been said of language is true, in large measure, of religious
ritual. For persons who have been brought up to think of God
by means of one set of symbols, it is very hard to think of Him

in terms of other and, in their eyes, unhallowed sets of words, ceremonies and images.

> The Lord Buddha then warned Subhuti, saying, "Sub-huti, do not think that the Tathagata ever considers in his own mind: I ought to enunciate a system of teaching for the elucidation of the Dharma. You should never cherish such a thought. And why? Because if any disciple harboured such a thought he would not only be mis-understanding the Tathagata's teaching, but he would be slandering him as well. Moreover, the expression 'a system of teaching' has no meaning; for Truth (in the sense of Reality) cannot be cut up into pieces and ar-ranged into a system. The words can only be used as a figure of speech."
>
> *Diamond Sutra*

But for all their inadequacy and their radical unlikeness to the facts to which they refer, words remain the most reliable and accurate of our symbols. Whenever we want to have a precise report of facts or ideas, we must resort to words. A ceremony, a carved or painted image, may convey more mean-ings and overtones of meaning in a smaller compass and with greater vividness than can a verbal formula; but it is liable to convey them in a form that is much more vague and in-definite. One often meets, in modern literature, with the notion that mediaeval churches were the architectural, sculp-tural and pictorial equivalents of a theological *summa*, and that mediaeval worshippers who admired the works of art around them were thereby enlightened on the subject of doctrine. This view was evidently not shared by the more earnest churchmen of the Middle Ages. Coulton cites the utterances of preachers who complained that congregations were getting entirely false ideas of Catholicism by looking at the pictures in the churches instead of listening to ser-mons. (Similarly, in our own day the Catholic Indians of Central America have evolved the wildest heresies by brood-ing on the carved and painted symbols with which the Con-quistadors filled their churches.) St. Bernard's objection to the richness of Cluniac architecture, sculpture and ceremonial was motivated by intellectual as well as strictly moral con-siderations. "So great and marvellous a variety of divers forms meets the eye that one is tempted to read in the marbles rather than in the books, to pass the whole day looking at these carvings one after another rather than in meditating on the law of God." It is in imageless contemplation that the soul comes to the unitive knowledge of Reality; consequently, for those who, like St. Bernard and his Cistercians, are really concerned to achieve man's final end, the fewer distracting symbols the better.

Most men worship the gods because they want success in their worldly undertakings. This kind of material success can be gained very quickly (by such worship), here on earth.

Bhagavad Gita

Among those who are purified by their good deeds there are four kinds of men who worship Me: the world-weary, the seeker for knowledge, the seeker for happiness and the man of spiritual discrimination. The man of discrimination is the highest of these. He is continually united with Me. He devotes himself to Me always, and to no other. For I am very dear to that man, and he to Me.

Certainly, all these are noble;
But the man of discrimination
I see as my very Self.
For he alone loves Me
Because I am Myself,
The last and only goal
Of his devoted heart.

Through many a long life
His discrimination ripens;
He makes Me his refuge,
Knows that Brahman is all.
How rare are such great ones!

Men whose discrimination has been blunted by worldly desires, establish this or that ritual or cult and resort to various deities, according to the impulse of their inborn nature. But no matter what deity a devotee chooses to worship, if he has faith, I make his faith unwavering. Endowed with the faith I give him, he worships that deity and gets from it everything he prays for. In reality, I alone am the giver.

But these men of small understanding pray only for what is transient and perishable. The worshippers of the devas will go to the devas. Those who worship Me will come to Me.

Bhagavad Gita

If sacramental rites are constantly repeated in a spirit of faith and devotion, a more or less enduring effect is produced in the psychic medium, in which individual minds bathe and from which they have, so to speak, been crystallized out into personalities more or less fully developed, according to the more or less perfect development of the bodies with which they are associated. (Of this psychic medium an eminent contemporary philosopher, Dr. C. D. Broad, has written, in an essay on telepathy contributed to the *Proceedings of the Society for Psychical Research*, as follows. "We must therefore consider seriously the possibility that a person's experience initiates more or less permanent modifications of structure or process in something which is neither his mind nor his brain. There is no reason to suppose that this substratum would be anything to which possessive adjectives, such as 'mine' and 'yours' and 'his,' could properly be applied, as they can be to minds and animated bodies. . . . Modifications which have been produced in the substratum by certain of M's past experiences are activated by N's present experiences or interests, and they become cause factors in producing or modifying N's later experiences.") Within this psychic medium or non-personal substratum of individual minds, something which we may think of metaphorically as a vortex persists as an independent existence, possessing its own derived and secondary objectivity, so that, wherever the rites are performed, those whose faith and devotion are sufficiently intense actually discover something 'out there,' as distinct from the subjective something in their own imaginations. And so long as this projected psychic entity is nourished by the faith and love of its worshippers, it will possess, not merely objectivity, but power to get people's prayers answered. Ultimately, of course, "I alone am the giver," in the sense that all this happens in accordance with the divine laws governing the universe in its psychic and spiritual, no less than in its material, aspects. Nevertheless, the devas (those imperfect forms under which, because of their own voluntary ignorance, men worship the divine Ground) may be thought of as relatively independent powers. The primitive notion that the gods feed on the sacrifices made to them is simply the crude expression of a profound truth. When their worship falls off, when faith and devotion lose their intensity, the devas sicken and finally die. Europe is full of old shrines, whose saints and Virgins and relics have lost the power and the second-hand psychic objectivity which they once possessed. Thus, when Chaucer lived and wrote, the deva called Thomas Becket was giving to any Canterbury pilgrim, who had sufficient faith, all the boons he could ask for. This once-powerful deity is now stone-dead; but there are still certain churches in the West, certain mosques and temples in the East, where even the most irreligious and un-psychic tourist cannot fail to be aware of some intensely "numinous" presence. It would, of course, be a mistake to imagine that this presence is the presence of that God who is a Spirit and must be worshipped in spirit; it is rather the psychic presence of men's thoughts and feelings about the particular, limited form of God, to which they have resorted "according to the impulse of their inborn nature"—thoughts and feelings projected into objectivity and haunting the sacred place in the same way as thoughts and feeling of another kind, but of equal intensity, haunt the scenes of some past suffering or crime. The presence in these consecrated buildings, the presence evoked by the performance of traditional rites, the presence inherent in a sacramental object, name or formula—all these are real presences, but real presences, not of God or the Avatar, but of something which, though it may reflect the divine Reality, is yet less and other than it.

> Dulcis Jesu memoria
> dans vera cordi gaudia:
> sed super mel et omnia
> ejus dulcis praesentia

"Sweet is the memory of Jesus, giving true joys to the heart; but sweeter beyond honey and all else is his presence." This opening stanza of the famous twelfth-century hymn summarizes in fifteen words the relations subsisting between ritual

and real presence and the character of the worshipper's reaction to each. Systematically cultivated *memoria* (a thing in
itself full of sweetness) first contributes to the evocation, then
results, for certain souls, in the immediate apprehension of
praesentia, which brings with it joys of a totally different
and higher kind. This presence (whose projected objectivity
is occasionally so complete as to be apprehensible not merely
by the devout worshipper, but by more or less indifferent
outsiders) is always that of the divine being who has been
previously remembered, Jesus here, Krishna or Amitabha
Buddha there.

> The value of this practice (repetition of the name of
> Amitabha Buddha) is this. So long as one person prac-
> tises his method (of spirituality) and another practises
> a different method, they counterbalance one another and
> their meeting is just the same as their not meeting.
> Whereas if two persons practise the same method, their
> mindfulness tends to become deeper and deeper, and
> they tend to remember each other and to develop affini-
> ties for each other, life after life. Moreover, whoever
> recites the name of Amitabha Buddha, whether in the
> present time or in future time, will surely see the Buddha
> Amitabha and never become separated from him. By rea-
> son of that association, just as one associating with a
> maker of perfumes becomes permeated with the same
> perfumes, so he will become perfumed by Amitabha's
> compassion, and will become enlightened without resort
> to any other expedient means.
>
> *Surangama Sutra*

We see then that intense faith and devotion, coupled with
perseverance by many persons in the same forms of worship
or spiritual exercise, have a tendency to objectify the idea
or memory which is their content and so to create, in some
sort, a numinous real presence, which worshippers actually
find "out there" no less, and in quite another way, than
"in here." Insofar as this is the case, the ritualist is perfectly correct in attributing to his hallowed acts and words
a power which, in another context, would be called magical.
The *mantram* works, the sacrifice really does something, the
sacrament confers grace *ex opere operato*: these are, or rather

may be, matters of direct experience, facts which anyone who chooses to fulfill the necessary conditions can verify empirically for himself. But the grace conferred *ex opere operato* is not always spiritual grace and the hallowed acts and formulas have a power which is not necessarily from God. Worshippers can, and very often do, get grace and power from one another and from the faith and devotion of their predecessors, projected into independent psychic existences that are hauntingly associated with certain places, words and acts. A great deal of ritualistic religion is not spirituality, but occultism, a refined and well-meaning kind of white magic. Now, just as there is no harm in art, say, or science, but a great deal of good, provided always that these activities are not regarded as ends, but simply as means to the final end of all life, so too there is no harm in white magic, but the possibilities of much good, so long as it is treated, not as true religion, but as one of the roads to true religion—an effective way of reminding people with a certain kind of psycho-physical make-up that there is a God, "in knowledge of whom standeth their eternal life." If ritualistic white magic is regarded as being in itself true religion; if the real presences it evokes are taken to be God in Himself and not the projections of human thoughts and feelings about God or even about something less than God; and if the sacramental rites are performed and attended for the sake of the "spiritual sweetness" experienced and the powers and advantages conferred—then there is idolatry. This idolatry is, at its best, a very lofty and, in many ways, beneficent kind of religion. But the consequences of worshipping God as anything but Spirit and in any way except in spirit and in truth are necessarily undesirable in this sense—that they lead only to a partial salvation and delay the soul's ultimate reunion with the eternal Ground.

That very large numbers of men and women have an ineradicable desire for rites and ceremonies is clearly demonstrated by the history of religion. Almost all the Hebrew prophets were opposed to ritualism. "Rend your hearts and not your garments." "I desire mercy and not sacrifice." "I hate, I despise your feasts; I take no delight in your solemn assemblies." And yet, in spite of the fact that what the prophets wrote was regarded as divinely inspired, the Temple at Jerusalem continued to be, for hundreds of years after their time, the centre of a religion of rites, ceremonials and blood sacrifice. (It may be remarked in passing that the shedding of blood, one's own or that of animals or other human beings, seems to be a peculiarly efficacious way of constraining the "occult" or psychic world to answer petitions and confer supernormal powers. If this is a fact, as from the anthropological and antiquarian evidence it appears to be, it would supply yet another cogent reason for avoiding animal sacrifices, savage bodily austerities and even, since thought is a form of action, that imaginative gloating over spilled blood, which is so common in certain Christian circles.) What the Jews did in spite of their prophets, Christians have done in spite of Christ. The Christ of the Gospels is a preacher and not a dispenser of sacraments or performer of rites; he speaks against vain repetitions; he insists on the supreme importance of private worship; he has no use for sacrifices and not much use for the Temple. But this did not prevent historic Christianity from going its own, all too human, way. A precisely similar development took place in Buddhism. For the Buddha of the Pali scriptures, ritual was one of the fetters holding back the soul from enlightenment and liberation. Nevertheless, the religion he founded has made full use of ceremonies, vain repetitions and sacramental rites.

There would seem to be two main reasons for the observed developments of the historical religions. First, most people do not want spirituality or deliverance, but rather a religion that gives them emotional satisfactions, answers to prayer, supernormal powers and partial salvation in some sort of posthumous heaven. Second, some of those few who do desire spirituality and deliverance find that, for them, the most effective means to those ends are ceremonies, "vain repetitions" and sacramental rites. It is by participating in these acts and uttering these formulas that they are most powerfully reminded of the eternal Ground of all being; it is by immersing themselves in the symbols that they can most easily come through to that which is symbolized. Every thing, event or thought is a point of intersection between creature and Creator, between a more or less distant manifestation of God and a ray, so to speak, of the unmanifest Godhead; every thing, event or thought can therefore be made the doorway through which a soul may pass out of time into eternity. That is why ritualistic and sacramental religion can lead to deliverance. But at the same time every human being loves power and self-enhancement, and every hallowed ceremony, form of words or sacramental rite is a channel through which power can flow out of the fascinating psychic universe into the universe of embodied selves. That is why ritualistic and sacramental religion can also lead away from deliverance.

There is another disadvantage inherent in any system of organized sacramentalism, and that is that it gives to the priestly caste a power which it is all too natural for them to abuse. In a society which has been taught that salvation is exclusively or mainly through certain sacraments, and that these sacraments can be administered effectively only by a professional priesthood, that professional priesthood will possess an enormous coercive power. The possession of such power is a standing temptation to use it for individual satisfaction and corporate aggrandizement. To a temptation of this kind, if repeated often enough, most human beings who are not saints almost inevitably succumb. That is why Christ taught his disciples to pray that they should not be led into temptation. This is, or should be, the guiding principle of all social reform—to organize the economic, political and social relationships between human beings in such a way that there shall be, for any given individual or group within the society, a minimum of temptations to covetousness, pride, cruelty and lust for power. Men and women being what they are, it is only by reducing the number and intensity of temptations that human societies can be, in some measure at least, delivered from evil. Now, the sort of temptations, to which a priestly caste is exposed in a society that accepts a predominantly sacramental religion, are such that none but the most saintly persons can be expected consistently to resist them. What happens when ministers of religion are led into these temptations is clearly illustrated by the history of the Roman church. Because Catholic Christianity taught a version of the Perennial Philosophy, it produced a succession of great saints. But because the Perennial Philosophy was overlaid with an excessive amount of sacramentalism and with an idolatrous preoccupation with things in time, the less saintly members of its hierarchy were exposed to enormous and quite unnecessary temptations and, duly succumbing to them, launched out into persecution, simony, power politics, secret diplomacy, high finance and collaboration with despots.

I very much doubt whether, since the Lord by his grace brought me into the faith of his dear Son, I have ever broken bread or drunk wine, even in the ordinary course of life, without remembrance of, and some devout feeling regarding, the broken body and the blood-shedding of my dear Lord and Saviour.

Stephen Grellet

We have seen that, when they are promoted to be the central core of organized religious worship, ritualism and sacramentalism are by no means unmixed blessings. But that the whole of a man's workaday life should be transformed by him into a kind of continuous ritual, that every object in the world around him should be regarded as a symbol of the world's eternal Ground, that all his actions should be performed sacramentally—this would seem to be wholly desirable. All the masters of the spiritual life, from the authors of the Upanishads to Socrates, from Buddha to St. Bernard are agreed that, without self-knowledge there cannot be adequate knowledge of God, that without a constant recollectedness there can be no complete deliverance. The man who has learnt to regard things as symbols, persons as temples of the Holy Spirit and actions as sacraments, is a man who has learned constantly to remind himself who he is, where he stands in relation to the universe and its Ground, how he should behave towards his fellows and what he must do to come to his final end.

"Because of this indwelling of the Logos," writes Mr. Kenneth Saunders in his valuable study of the Fourth Gospel, the Gita and the Lotus Sutra, "all things have a reality. They are sacraments, not illusions like the phenomenal word of the Vedanta." That the Logos is in things, lives and conscious minds, and they in the Logos, was taught much more emphatically and explicitly by the Vedantists than by the author of the Fourth Gospel; and the same idea is, of course, basic in the theology of Taoism. But though all things in fact exist at the intersection between a divine manifestation and a ray of the unmanifest Godhead, it by no means follows that everyone always knows that this is so. On the contrary, the vast majority of human beings believe that their own selfness and the objects around them possess a reality in themselves, wholly independent of the Logos. This belief leads them to identify their being with their sensations, cravings and private notions, and in its turn this self-identification with what they are not effectively walls them off from divine influence and the very possibility of deliverance. To most of us on most occasions things are not symbols and actions are not sacramental; and we have to teach ourselves, consciously and deliberately, to remember that they are.

> The world is imprisoned in its own activity, except when actions are performed as worship of God. Therefore you must perform every action sacramentally (as if it were *yajna*, the sacrifice that, in its divine Logos-essence, is identical with the Godhead to whom it is offered), and be free from all attachment to results.
>
> *Bhagavad Gita*

Precisely similar teachings are found in Christian writers, who recommend that persons and even things should be regarded as temples of the Holy Ghost and that everything done or suffered should be constantly "offered to God."

It is hardly necessary to add that this process of conscious sacramentalization can be applied only to such actions as are not intrinsically evil. Somewhat unfortunately, the Gita was not originally published as an independent work, but as a theological digression within an epic poem; and since, like most epics, the Mahabharata is largely concerned with the exploits of warriors, it is primarily in relation to warfare that the Gita's advice to act with non-attachment and for God's sake only is given. Now, war is accompanied and followed, among other things, by a widespread dissemination of anger and hatred, pride, cruelty and fear. But, it may be asked, is it possible (the Nature of Things being what it is) to sacramentalize actions, whose psychological by-products are so completely God-eclipsing as are these passions? The Buddha of the Pali scriptures would certainly have answered this question in the negative. So would the Lao Tzu of the Tao Teh King. So would the Christ of the Synoptic Gospels. The Krishna of the Gita (who is also, by a kind of literary accident, the Krishna of the Mahabharata) gives an affirmative answer. But this affirmative answer, it should be remembered, is hedged around with limiting conditions. Non-attached slaughter is recommended only to those, who are warriors by caste, and to whom warfare is a duty and vocation. But what is duty or *dharma* for the Kshatriya is *adharma* and forbidden to the Brahman; nor is it any part of the normal vocation or caste duty of the mercantile and labouring classes. Any confusion of castes, any assumption by one man of another man's vocation and duties of state, is always, say the Hindus, a moral evil and a menace to social stability. Thus, it is the business of the Brahmans to fit themselves to be seers, so that they may be able to explain to their fellow men the nature of the universe, of man's last end and of the way to liberation. When soldiers or administrators, or usurers, or manufacturers or workers usurp the functions of the Brahmans and formulate a philosophy of life in accordance with their variously distorted notions of the universe, then society is thrown into confusion. Similarly, confusion reigns when the Brahman, the man of non-coercive spiritual authority, assumes the coercive power of the Kshatriya, or when the Kshatriya's job of ruling is usurped by bankers and stock jobbers, or finally when the warrior caste's *dharma* of fighting is imposed, by conscription, on Brahman, Vaisya and Sudra alike. The history of Europe during the later Middle Ages and Renaissance is largely a history of the social confusions that arises when large numbers of those who should be seers abandon spiritual authority in favour of money and political power. And contemporary history is the hideous record of what happens when political bosses, businessmen or class-conscious proletarians assume the Brahman's function of formulating a philosophy of life; when usurers dictate policy and debate the issues of war and peace; and when the warrior's caste duty is imposed on all and sundry, regardless of psycho-physical make-up and vocation.

CHAPTER XXV

Spiritual Exercises

RITES, sacraments, ceremonies, liturgies—all these belong to public worship. They are devices, by means of which the individual members of a congregation are reminded of the true Nature of Things and of their proper relations to one another, the universe and God. What ritual is to public worship, spiritual exercises are to private devotion. They are devices to be used by the solitary individual when he enters into his closet, shuts the door and prays to his Father which is in secret. Like all other devices, from psalm singing to Swedish exercises and from logic to internal combustion engines, spiritual exercises can be used either well or badly. Some of those who use spiritual exercises make progress in the life of the spirit; others, using the same exercises, make no progress. To believe that their use either constitutes enlightenment, or guarantees it, is mere idolatry and superstition. To neglect them altogether, to refuse to find out whether and in what way they can help in the achievement of our final end, is nothing but self-opinionatedness and stubborn obscurantism.

> St François de Sales used to say, "I hear of nothing but perfection on every side, so far as talk goes; but I see very few people who really practice it. Everybody has his own notion of perfection. One man thinks it lies in the cut of his clothes, another in fasting, a third in almsgiving, or in frequenting the Sacraments, in meditation, in some special gift of contemplation, or in extraordinary gifts or graces—but they are all mistaken, as it seems to me, because they confuse the means, or the results, with the end and cause.
>
> "For my part, the only perfection I know of is a hearty love of God, and to love one's neighbour as oneself. Charity is the only virtue which rightly unites us to God and man. Such union is our final aim and end, and all the rest is mere delusion."
>
> *Jean Pierre Camus*

St. François himself recommended the use of spiritual exercises as a means to the love of God and one's neighbours, and affirmed that such exercises deserved to be greatly cherished; but this affection for the set forms and hours of mental prayer must never, he warned, be allowed to become excessive. To neglect any urgent call to charity or obedience for the sake of practising one's spiritual exercises would be to neglect the end and the proximate means for the sake of means which are not proximate, but at several removes from the ultimate goal.

Spiritual exercises constitute a special class of ascetic practices, whose purpose is, primarily, to prepare the intellect and emotions for those higher forms of prayer in which the soul is essentially passive in relation to divine Reality, and secondarily, by means of this self-exposure to the Light and of the increased self-knowledge and self-loathing resulting from it, to modify character.

In the Orient the systematization of mental prayer was carried out at some unknown but certainly very early date. Both in India and China spiritual exercises (accompanied or preceded by more or less elaborate physical exercises, especially breathing exercises) are known to have been used several centuries before the birth of Christ. In the West, the monks of the Thebaïd spent a good part of each day in meditation as a means to contemplation or the unitive knowledge of God; and at all periods of Christian history, more or less methodical mental prayer has been largely used to supplement the vocal praying of public and private worship. But the systematization of mental prayer into elaborate spiritual exercises was not undertaken, it would seem, until near the end of the Middle Ages, when reformers within the Church popularized this new form of spirituality in an effort to revivify a decaying monasticism and to reinforce the religious life of a laity that had been bewildered by the Great Schism and profoundly shocked by the corruption of the clergy. Among these early systematizers the most effective and influential were the canons of Windesheim, who were in close touch with the Brethren of the Common Life. During the later sixteenth and early seventeenth centuries spiritual exercises became, one might almost say, positively fashionable. The early Jesuits had shown what extraordinary transformations of character, what intensities of will and devotion, could be achieved by men systematically trained on the intellectual and imaginative exercises of St. Ignatius Loyola, and as the prestige of the Jesuits stood very high, at this time, in Catholic Europe, the prestige of spiritual exercises also stood high. Throughout the first century of the Counter-Reformation numerous systems of mental prayer (many of them, unlike the Ignatian exercises, specifically mystical) were composed, published and eagerly bought. After the Quietist controversy mysticism fell into disrepute and, along with mysticism, many of the once popular systems, which their authors had designed to assist the soul on the path towards contemplation. For more detailed information on this interesting and important subject the reader should consult Pourrat's *Christian Spirituality*, Bede Frost's *The Art of Mental Prayer*, Edward Leen's *Progress through Mental Prayer* and Aelfrida Tillyard's *Spiritual Exercises*. Here it is only possible to give a few characteristic specimens from the various religious traditions.

> Know that when you learn to lose yourself, you will reach the Beloved. There is no other secret to be learnt, and more than this is not known to me.
>
> *Ansari of Herat*

Six hundred years later, as we have seen, St. François de Sales was saying very much the same thing to young Camus and all the others who came to him in the ingenuous hope that he could reveal some easy and infallible trick for achieving the unitive knowledge of God. But to lose self in the Beloved—there is no other secret. And yet the Sufis, like their Christian counterparts, made ample use of spiritual exercises—not, of course, as ends in themselves, not even as proximate means, but as means to the proximate means of union with God, namely selfless and loving contemplation.

> For twelve years I was the smith of my soul. I put it in the furnace of austerity and burned it in the fire of combat, I laid it on the anvil of reproach and smote it with the hammer of blame until I made of my soul a mirror. Five years I was the mirror of myself and was ever polishing that mirror with divers acts of worship and piety. Then for a year I gazed in contemplation. On my waist I saw a girdle of pride and vanity and self-conceit and reliance on devotion and approbation of my works. I laboured for five years more until that girdle became worn out and I professed Islam anew. I looked and saw that all created things were dead. I pronounced four *akbirs* over them and returned from the funeral of them all, and without intrusion of creatures, through God's help alone, I attained unto God.
>
> *Bayazid of Bistun*

The simplest and most widely practised form of spiritual exercise is repetition of the divine name, or of some phrase affirming God's existence and the soul's dependence upon Him.

And therefore, when thou purposest thee to this work (of contemplation), and feelest by grace that thou are called by God, lift up thine heart unto God with a meek stirring of love. And mean God that made thee, and bought thee, and graciously called thee to thy degree, and receive none other thought of God. And yet not all these, except thou desirest; for a naked intent directed unto God, without any other cause than himself, sufficeth wholly.

And if thou desirest to have this intent lapped and folden in one word, so that thou mayest have better hold thereupon, take thee but a little word of one syllable, for so it is better than of two; for the shorter the word, the better it accordeth with the work of the spirit. And such a word is this word GOD or this word LOVE. Choose whichever thou wilt, or another; whatever word thou likest best of one syllable. And fasten this word to thy heart that so it may never go thence for anything that befalleth.

The word shall be thy shield and thy spear, whether thou ridest on peace or on war. With this word thou shalt beat on this cloud and this darkness above thee. With this word thou shalt smite down all manner of thought under the *cloud of forgetting*. Insomuch that, if any thought press upon thee to ask what thou wouldst have, answer with no more words than with this one word (GOD or LOVE). And if he offer of his great learning to expound to thee that word, say to him that thou wilt have it all whole, and not broken nor undone. And if thou wilt hold fast to this purpose, be sure that that thought will no while bide.

The Cloud of Unknowing

In another chapter the author of the *Cloud* suggests that the word symbolizing our final end should sometimes be alternated with a word denoting our present position in relation to that end. The words to be repeated in this exercise are SIN and GOD.

Not breaking or expounding these words with curiosity of wit, considering the qualities of these words, as if thou wouldst by that consideration increase thy devotion. I believe it should never be so in this case and in this work. But hold them all whole, these words; and mean by SIN a *lump*, thou knowest never what, none other thing but thyself. . . . And because ever the whiles thou livest in this wretched life, thou must always feel in some part this foul stinking lump of sin, as it were oned and congealed with the substance of thy being, therefore shalt thou alternately mean these two words—SIN and GOD. With this general understanding that, if thou hadst God, then shouldst thou lack sin; and mightest thou lack sin, then shouldst thou have God.

The Cloud of Unknowing

The shaykh took my hand and led me into the convent. I sat down in the portico, and the shaykh picked up a book and began to read. As is the way of scholars, I could not help wondering what the book was.

The shaykh perceived my thoughts. "Abu Sa'id," he said, "all the hundred and twenty-four thousand prophets were sent to preach one word. They bade the people say, 'Allah,' and devote themselves to Him. Those who heard this word by the ear alone let it go out by the other ear; but those who heard it with their souls imprinted it on their souls and repeated it until it penetrated their hearts and souls, and their whole beings became this word. They were made independent of the pronunciation of the word; they were released from the sound of the letters. Having understood the spiritual meaning of this word, they became so absorbed in it that they were no more conscious of their own non-existence."

Abu Sa'id

Take a short verse of a psalm, and it shall be shield and buckler to you against all your foes.

Cassian, quoting Abbot Isaac

In India the repetition of the divine name or the *mantram* (a short devotional or doctrinal affirmation) is called *japam* and is a favourite spiritual exercise among all the sects of Hinduism

and Buddhism. The shortest *mantram* is OM—a spoken sym
bol that concentrates within itself the whole Vedanta philosophy. To this and other *mantrams* Hindus attribute a kind
of magical power. The repetition of them is a sacramental act,
conferring grace *ex opere operato*. A similar efficacy was
and indeed still is attributed to sacred words and formulas
by Buddhists, Moslems, Jews and Christians. And, of course,
just as traditional religious rites seem to possess the power to
evoke the real presence of existents projected into psychic
objectivity by the faith and devotion of generations of worshippers, so too long-hallowed words and phrases may become
channels for conveying powers other and greater than those
belonging to the individual who happens at the moment to
be pronouncing them. And meanwhile the constant repetition
of "this word GOD or this word LOVE" may, in favourable circumstances, have a profound effect upon the subconscious
mind, inducing that selfless one-pointedness of will and
thought and feeling, without which the unitive knowledge of
God is impossible. Furthermore, it may happen that, if the
word is simply repeated "all whole, and not broken up or
undone" by discursive analysis, the Fact for which the word
stands will end by presenting itself to the soul in the form of
an integral intuition. When this happens, "the doors of the
letters of this word are opened" (to use the language of the
Sufis) and the soul passes through into Reality. But though
all this *may* happen, it need not necessarily happen. For there
is no spiritual patent medicine, no pleasant and infallible
panacea for souls suffering from separateness and the depri-
vation of God. No, there is no guaranteed cure; and, if used
improperly, the medicine of spiritual exercises may start a
new disease or aggravate the old. For example, a mere mechanical repetition of the divine name can result in a kind of
numbed stupefaction that is as much below analytical thought
as intellectual vision is above it. And because the sacred word
constitutes a kind of prejudgment of the experience induced
by its repetition, this stupefaction, or some other abnormal
state, is taken to be the immediate awareness of Reality and
is idolatrously cultivated and hunted after, with a turning of
the will towards what is supposed to be God before there has
been a turning of it away from the self.

The dangers which beset the practicer of *japam*, who is
insufficiently mortified and insufficiently recollected and aware,

are encountered in the same or different forms by those who make use of more elaborate spiritual exercises. Intense concentration on an image or idea, such as is recommended by many teachers, both Eastern and Western, may be very helpful for certain persons in certain circumstances, very harmful in other cases. It is helpful when the concentration results in such mental stillness, such a silence of intellect, will and feeling, that the divine Word can be uttered within the soul. It is harmful when the image concentrated upon becomes so hallucinatingly real that it is taken for objective Reality and idolatrously worshipped; harmful, too, when the exercise of concentration produces unusual psycho-physical results, in which the person experiencing them takes a personal pride, as being special graces and divine communications. Of these unusual psycho-physical occurrences the most ordinary are visions and auditions, foreknowledge, telepathy and other psychic powers, and the curious bodily phenomenon of intense heat. Many persons who practise concentration exercises experience this heat occasionally. A number of Christian saints, of whom the best known are St. Philip Neri and St. Catherine of Siena, have experienced it continuously. In the East techniques have been developed whereby the accession of heat resulting from intense concentration can be regulated, controlled and put to do useful work, such as keeping the contemplative warm in freezing weather. In Europe, where the phenomenon is not well understood, many would-be contemplatives have experienced this heat, and have imagined it to be some special divine favour, or even the experience of union, and being insufficiently mortified and humble, have fallen into idolatry and a God-eclipsing spiritual pride.

The following passage from one of the great Mahayana scriptures contains a searching criticism of the kind of spiritual exercises prescribed by Hinayanist teachers—concentration on symbolic objects, meditations on transience and decay (to wean the soul away from attachment to earthly things), on the different virtues which must be cultivated, on the fundamental doctrines of Buddhism. (Many of these exercises are described at length in *The Path of Purity*, a book which has been translated in full and published by the Pali Text Society. Mahayanist exercises are described in the Surangama Sutra, translated by Dwight Goddard and in the volume on *Tibetan Yoga*, edited by Dr. Evans-Wentz.)

In his exercise the Yogin sees (imaginatively) the form of the sun or moon, or something looking like a lotus, or the underworld, or various forms, such as sky, fire and the like. All these appearances lead him in the way of the philosophers; they throw him down into the state of Sravakahood, into the realm of the Pratyekabuddhas. When all these are put aside and there is a state of imagelessness, then a condition in conformity with Suchness presents itself, and the Buddhas will come together from all their countries and with their shining hands will touch the head of this benefactor.

Lankavatara Sutra

In other words intense concentration on any image (even if the image be a sacred symbol, like the lotus) or on any idea, from the idea of hell to the idea of some desirable virtue or its apotheosis in one of the divine attributes, is always concentration on something produced by one's own mind. Sometimes, in mortified and recollected persons, the act of concentration merges into the state of openness and alert passivity, in which true contemplation becomes possible. But sometimes the fact that the concentration is on a product of the concentrator's own mind results in some kind of false or incomplete contemplation. Suchness, or the divine Ground of all being, reveals itself to those in whom there is no ego-centredness (nor even any alter-ego-centredness) either of will, imagination, feeling or intellect.

I say, then, that introversion must be rejected, because extraversion must never be admitted; but one must live continuously in the abyss of the divine Essence and in the nothingness of things; and if at times a man finds himself separated from them (the divine Essence and created nothingness) he must return to them, not by introversion, but by annihilation.

Benet of Canfield

Introversion is the process condemned in the Lankavatara Sutra as the way of the Yogin, the way that leads at worst to idolatry, at best to a partial knowledge of God in the heights within, never to complete knowledge in the fulness without as well as within, Annihilation (of which Father Benet distinguishes two kinds, passive and active) is for the Mahayanist the "state of imagelessness" in contemplation and, in active life, the state of total non-attachment, in which eternity can be apprehended within time, and Samsara is known to be one with Nirvana.

And therefore, if thou wilt stand and not fall, cease never in thine intent, but beat overmore on this cloud of unknowing that is betwixt thee and thy God, with a sharp dart of longing love. And loathe to think of aught under God. And go not thence for anything that befalleth. For this only is that work that destroyeth the ground and the root of sin. . . .

Yea, and what more? Weep thou never so much for sorrow of thy sins, or of the passion of Christ, or have thou never so much thought of the joys of heaven, what may it do to thee? Surely much good, much help, much profit, much grace will it get thee. But in comparison of this blind stirring of love, it is but little that it doth, or may do, without this. This by itself is the *best part* of Mary, without these other. They without it profit but little or nought. It destroyeth not only the ground and the root of sin, as it may be here, but also it getteth virtues. For if it be truly conceived, all virtues shall be subtly and perfectly conceived, felt and comprehended in it, without any mingling of thine intent. And have a man never so many virtues without it, all they be mingled with some crooked intent, for the which they be imperfect. For virtue is nought else but an ordered and measured affection, plainly directed unto God for Himself.

The Cloud of Unknowing

If exercises in concentration, repetitions of the divine name, or meditations on God's attributes or on imagined scenes in the life of saint or Avatar help those who make use of them to come to selflessness, openness and (to use Augustine Baker's phrase) that "love of the pure divinity," which makes possible the soul's union with the Godhead, then such spiritual exercises are wholly good and desirable. If they have other results— well, the tree is known by its fruits.

Benet of Canfield, the English Capuchin who wrote *The Rule of Perfection* and was the spiritual guide of Mme.

Acarie and Cardinal Bérulle, hints in his treatise at a method by which concentration on an image may be made to lead up to imageless contemplation, "blind beholding," "love of the pure divinity." The period of mental prayer is to begin with intense concentration on a scene of Christ's passion; then the mind is, as it were, to abolish this imagination of the sacred humanity and to pass from it to the formless and attributeless Godhead which that humanity incarnates. A strikingly similar exercise is described in the *Bardo Thödol* or Tibetan Book of the Dead (a work of quite extraordinary profundity and beauty, now fortunately available in translation with a valuable introduction and notes by Dr. Evans-Wentz).

> Whosoever thy tutelary deity may be, meditate upon the form for much time—as being apparent, yet non-existent in reality, like a form produced by a magician. . . . Then let the visualization of the tutelary deity melt away from the extremities, till nothing at all remaineth visible of it; and put thyself in the state of the Clearness and the Voidness—which thou canst not conceive as something— and abide in that state for a little while. Again meditate upon the tutelary deity; again meditate upon the Clear Light; do this alternately. Afterwards allow thine own intellect to melt away gradually, beginning from the extremities.

> *The Tibetan Book of the Dead*

As a final summing up of the whole matter we may cite a sentence of Eckhart's. "He who seeks God under settled form lays hold of the form, while missing the God concealed in it." Here, the key word is "settled." It is permissible to seek God provisionally under a form which is from the first recognized as merely a symbol of Reality, and a symbol which must sooner or later be discarded in favour of what it stands for. To seek Him under a settled form—settled because regarded as the very shape of Reality—is to commit oneself to illusion and a kind of idolatry.

The chief impediments in the way of taking up the practice of some form of mental prayer are ignorance of the Nature of Things (which has never, of course, been more abysmal than in this age of free compulsory education) and the absorption in self-interest, in positive and negative emotions connected with the passions and with what is technically known as a "good time." And when the practice has been taken up, the chief impediments in the way of advance towards the goal of mental prayer are distractions.

Probably all persons, even the most saintly, suffer to some extent from distractions. But it is obvious that the distractions of one who, in the intervals of mental prayer, leads a dispersed, unrecollected, self-centred life will have more and worse distractions to contend with than a person who lives one-pointedly, never forgetting who he is and how related to the universe and its divine Ground. Some of the most profitable spiritual exercises actually make use of distractions, in such a way that these impediments to self-abandonment, mental silence and passivity in relation to God are transformed into means of progress.

But first, by way of preface to the description of these exercises, it should be remarked that all teachers of the art of mental prayer concur in advising their pupils never to use violent efforts of the surface will against the distractions which arise in the mind during periods of recollection. The reason for this has been succinctly stated by Benet of Canfield in his *Rule of Perfection*. "The more a man operates, the more he is and exists. And the more he is and exists, the less of God is and exists within him." Every enhancement of the separate personal self produces a corresponding diminution of that self's awareness of divine Reality. But any violent reaction of the surface will against distractions automatically enhances the separate, personal self and therefore reduces the individual's chances of coming to the knowledge and love of God. In the process of trying forcibly to abolish our God-eclipsing day-dreams, we merely deepen the darkness of our native ignorance. This being so, we must give up the attempt to fight distractions and find ways either of circumventing them, or of somehow making use of them. For example, if we have already achieved a certain degree of alert passivity in relation to Reality and distractions intervene, we can simply "look over the shoulder" of the malicious and concupiscent imbecile who stands between us and the object of our "simple regard." The distractions now appear in the foreground of consciousness; we take notice of their presence, then, lightly and gently, without any straining of the will, we shift the focus of attention to Reality which we glimpse, or divine, or (by past experience or an act of faith) merely know about, in the background. In many cases, this effortless shift of attention will cause the distractions to lose their obsessive "thereness" and, for a time at least, to disappear.

> If the heart wanders or is distracted, bring it back to the point quite gently and replace it tenderly in its Master's presence. And even if you did nothing during the whole of your hour but bring your heart back and place it again in Our Lord's presence, though it went away every time you brought it back, your hour would be very well employed.
>
> *St. François de Sales*

In this case the circumvention of distractions constitutes a valuable lesson in patience and perseverance. Another and more direct method of making use of the monkey in our heart is described in the Cloud of Unknowing.

> When thou feelest that thou mayest in no wise put them (distractions) down, cower then down under them as a caitiff and a coward overcome in battle, and think it is but folly to strive any longer with them, and therefore thou yieldest thyself to God in the hands of thine enemies. . . . And surely, I think, if this device be truly conceived, it is nought else but a true knowing and a feeling of thyself as thou art, a wretch and a filthy thing, far worse than nought; the which knowing and feeling is meekness (humility). And this meekness meriteth to have God mightily descending to venge thee on thine enemies, so as to take thee up and cherishingly dry thy ghostly eyes, as the father doth to the child that is at the point to perish under the mouths of wild swine and mad biting bears.
>
> *The Cloud of Unknowing*

Finally, there is the exercise, much employed in India, which consists in dispassionately examining the distractions as they arise and in tracing them back, through the memory of particular thoughts, feelings and actions, to their origins in temperament and character, constitution and acquired habit. This procedure reveals to the soul the true reasons for its separation from the divine Ground of its being. It comes to realize that its spiritual ignorance is due to the inert recalcitrance or positive rebelliousness of its selfhood, and it discovers, specifically, the points where that eclipsing selfhood congeals, as it were, into the hardest, densest clots. Then, having made the resolution to do what it can, in the course of daily living, to rid itself of these impediments to Light, it quietly puts aside the thought of them and, empty, purged and silent, passively exposes itself to whatever it may be that lies beyond and within.

"*Noverim me, noverim Te,*" St. Francis of Assisi used to repeat. Self-knowledge, leading to self-hatred and humility, is the condition of the love and knowledge of God. Spiritual exercises that make use of distractions have this great merit, that they increase self-knowledge. Every soul that approaches God must be aware of who and what it is. To practice a form of mental or vocal prayer that is, so to speak, above one's moral station is to act a lie: and the consequences of such lying are wrong notions about God, idolatrous worship of private and unrealistic phantasies and (for lack of the humility of self-knowledge) spiritual pride.

It is hardly necessary to add that this method has, like every other, its dangers as well as its advantages. For those who employ it there is a standing temptation to forget the end in the all too squalidly personal means—to become absorbed in a whitewashing or remorseful essay in autobiography to the exclusion of the pure Divinity, before whom the "angry ape" played all the fantastic tricks which he now so relishingly remembers.

We come now to what may be called the spiritual exercises of daily life. The problem, here, is simple enough—how to keep oneself reminded, during the hours of work and recreation, that there is a good deal more to the universe than that which meets the eye of one absorbed in business or pleasure? There is no single solution to this problem. Some kinds of work and recreation are so simple and unexactive that they permit of continuous repetition of sacred name or phrase, unbroken thought about divine Reality, or, what is still better, uninterrupted mental silence and alert passivity. Such occupations as were the daily task of Brother Lawrence (whose "practice of the presence of God" has enjoyed a kind of celebrity in circles otherwise completely uninterested in mental prayer or spiritual exercises) were almost all of this simple and unexacting kind. But there are other tasks too complex to admit of this constant recollectedness. Thus, to quote Eckhart, "a celebrant of the mass who is over-intent on recollection is liable to make mistakes. The best way is to try to concentrate the mind before and afterwards, but, when saying it, to do so quite straightforwardly." This advice applies to any occupation demanding undivided attention. But undivided attention is seldom demanded and is with difficulty sustained for long periods at a stretch. There are always intervals of relaxation. Everyone is free to choose whether these intervals shall be filled with day-dreaming or with something better.

Whoever has God in mind, simply and solely God, in all things, such a man carries God with him into all his works and into all places, and God alone does all his works. He seeks nothing but God, nothing seems good to him but God. He becomes one with God in every thought. Just as no multiplicity can dissipate God, so nothing can dissipate this man or make him multiple.

Eckhart

I do not mean that we ought voluntarily to put ourselves in the way of dissipating influences; God forbid! That would be tempting God and seeking danger. But such distractions as come in any way providentially, if met with due precaution and carefully guarded hours of prayer and reading, will turn to good. Often those things which make you sigh for solitude are more profitable to your humiliation and self-denial than the most utter solitude itself would be. . . . Sometimes a stimulating book of devotion, a fervent meditation, a striking conversation, may flatter your tastes and make you feel self-satisfied and complacent, imagining yourself far advanced towards perfection; and by filling you with unreal notions, be all the time swelling your pride and making you come from your religious exercises less tolerant of whatever crosses your will. I would have you hold fast to this simple rule: seek nothing dissipating, but bear quietly with whatever God sends without your seeking it, whether of dissipation or interruption. It is a great delusion to seek God afar off in matters perhaps quite unattainable, ignoring that He is beside us in our daily annoyances, so long as we bear humbly and bravely all those which arise from the manifold imperfections of our neighbours and ourselves.

Fénelon

Consider that your life is a perpetual perishing, and lift up your mind to God above all whenever the clock strikes, saying, "God, I adore your eternal being; I am happy that my being should perish every moment, so that at every moment it may render homage to your eternity."

J. J. Olier

When you are walking alone, or elsewhere, glance at the general will of God, by which He wills all the works of his mercy and justice in heaven, on earth, under the earth, and approve, praise and then love that sovereign will, all holy, all just, all beautiful. Glance next at the special will of God, by which He loves his own, and works in them in divers ways, by consolation and tribulation. And then you should ponder a little, considering the variety of consolations, but especially of tribulations, that the good suffer; and then with great humility approve, praise and love all this will. Consider that will in your own person, in all the good or ill that happens to you and may happen to you, except sin; then approve, praise and love all that, protesting that you will ever cherish, honour and adore that sovereign will, and submitting to God's pleasure and giving Him all who are yours, amongst whom am I. End in a great confidence in that will, that it will work all good for us and our happiness. I add that, when you have performed this exercise two or three times in this way, you can shorten it, vary it and arrange it, as you find best, for it should often be thrust into your heart as an aspiration.

St. François de Sales

Dwelling in the light, there is no occasion at all for stumbling, for all things are discovered in the light. When thou art walking abroad it is present with thee in thy bosom, thou needest not to say, Lo here, or Lo there; and as thou lyest in thy bed, it is present to teach thee and judge thy wandering mind, which wanders abroad,

and thy high thoughts and imaginations, and makes
them subject. For following thy thoughts, thou art
quickly lost. By dwelling in this light, it will discover to
thee the body of sin and thy corruptions and fallen estate,
where thou art. In that light which shows thee all this,
stand; go neither to the right nor to the left.

George Fox

The extract which follows is taken from the translation by
Waitao and Goddard of the Chinese text of *The Awakening
of Faith*, by Ashvaghosha—a work originally composed in Sanskrit during the first century of our era, but of which the
original has been lost. Ashvaghosha devotes a section of his
treatise to the "expedient means," as they are called in Buddhist terminology, whereby unitive knowledge of Thusness
may be achieved. The list of these indispensable means
includes charity and compassion towards all sentient beings,
sub-human as well as human, self-naughting or mortification.
personal devotion to the incarnations of the Absolute Buddha-
nature, and spiritual exercises designed to free the mind from
its infatuating desires for separateness and independent selfhood and so make it capable of realizing the identity of its
own essence with the universal Essence of Mind. Of these
various "expedient means" I will cite only the last two—the
Way of Tranquillity, and the Way of Wisdom.

The Way of Tranquillity. The purpose of this discipline
is twofold: to bring to a standstill all disturbing thoughts
(and all discriminating thoughts are disturbing), to quiet
all engrossing moods and emotions, so that it will be
possible to concentrate the mind for the purpose of meditation and realization. Secondly, when the mind is tranquillized by stopping all discursive thinking, to practise
'reflection' or meditation, not in a discriminating, analytical way, but in a more intellectual way (cp. the scholastic
distinction between reason and intellect), by realizing
the meaning and significances of one's thoughts and
experiences. By this twofold practice of 'stopping and
realizing' one's faith, which has already been awakened,
will be developed, and gradually the two aspects of this
practice will merge into one another—the mind perfectly
tranquil, but most active in realization. In the past one

naturally had confidence in one's faculty of discrimination (analytical thinking), but this is now to be eradicated and ended.

Those who are practising 'stopping' should retire to some quiet place and there, sitting erect, earnestly seek to tranquillize and concentrate the mind. While one may at first think of one's breathing, it is not wise to continue this practice very long, nor to let the mind rest on any particular appearances, or sights, or conceptions, arising from the senses, such as the primal elements of earth, water, fire and ether (objects on which Hinayanists were wont to concentrate at one stage of their spiritual training), nor to let it rest on any of the mind's perceptions, particularizations, discriminations, moods or emotions. All kinds of ideation are to be discarded as fast as they arise; even the notions of controlling and discarding are to be got rid of. One's mind should become like a mirror, reflecting things, but not judging them or retaining them. Conceptions of themselves have no substance; let them arise and pass away unheeded. Conceptions arising from the senses and lower mind will not take form of themselves, unless they are grasped by the attention; if they are ignored, there will be no appearing and no disappearing. The same is true of conditions outside the mind; they should not be allowed to engross one's attention and so to hinder one's practice. The mind cannot be absolutely vacant, and as the thoughts arising from the senses and the lower mind are discarded and ignored, one must supply their place by right mentation. The question then arises: what is right mentation? The reply is: right mentation is the realization of mind itself, of its pure undifferentiated Essence. When the mind is fixed on its pure Essence, there should be no lingering notions of the self, even of the self in the act of realizing, nor of realization as a phenomenon. . . .

The Way of Wisdom. The purpose of this discipline is to bring a man into the habit of applying the insight that has come to him as the result of the preceding disciplines. When one is rising, standing, walking, doing something, stopping, one should constantly concentrate one's mind on the act and the doing of it, not on one's relation to the act, or its character or value. One should think: there is walking, there is stopping, there is realizing; not, I am walking, I am doing this, it is a good thing, it is disagreeable, I am gaining merit, it is I who am realizing how wonderful it is. Thence come vagrant thoughts, feelings of elation or of failure and unhappiness. Instead of all this, one should simply practice concentration of the mind on the act itself, understanding it to be an expedient means for attaining tranquillity of mind, realization, insight and Wisdom; and one should follow the practice in faith, willingness and gladness. After long practice the bondage of old habits becomes weakened and disappears, and in its place appear confidence, satisfaction, awareness and tranquillity.

What is this Way of Wisdom designed to accomplish? There are three classes of conditions that hinder one from advancing along the path to Enlightenment. First, there are the allurements arising from the senses, from external conditions and from the discriminating mind. Second, there are the internal conditions of the mind, its thoughts, desires and mood. All these the earlier practices (ethical and mortificatory) are designed to eliminate. In the third class of impediments are placed the individual's instinctive and fundamental (and therefore most insidious and persistent) urges—the will to live and to enjoy, the will to cherish one's personality, the will to propagate, which give rise to greed and lust, fear and anger, infatuation, pride and egotism. The practice of the Wisdom Paramita is designed to control and eliminate these fundamental and instinctive hindrances. By means of it the mind gradually grows clearer, more luminous, more peaceful. Insight becomes more penetrating, faith deepens and broadens, until they merge into the inconceivable Samadhi of the Mind's Pure Essence. As one continues the practice of the Way of Wisdom, one yields less and less to thoughts of comfort or desolation; faith becomes surer, more pervasive, beneficent and joyous; and fear of retrogression vanishes. But do not think that the consummation is to be attained easily or quickly; many rebirths may be necessary, many aeons may have to elapse. So long as doubt, unbelief, slanders, evil conduct, hindrances of karma, weakness of faith, pride, sloth and mental agitation persist, so long as even their shadows linger, there can be no attainment of the Samadhi of the Buddhas. But he who has attained to the radiance of highest Samadhi, or unitive Knowledge, will be able to realize, with all the Buddhas, the perfect unity of all sentient beings with Buddhahood's Dharmakaya. In the pure Dharmakaya there is no dualism, neither shadow of differentiation. All sentient beings, if only they were able to realize it, are already in Nirvana. The Mind's pure Essence is Highest Samadhi, is *Anuttara-samyak-sambodhi*, is *Prajna Paramita*, is Highest Perfect Wisdom.

Ashvaghosha

CHAPTER XXVI

Perseverance and Regularity

He who interrupts the course of his spiritual exercises and prayer is like a man who allows a bird to escape from his hand; he can hardly catch it again.

St. John of the Cross

Si volumus non redire, currendum est. (If we wish not to go backwards, we must run.)

Pelagius

If thou shouldst say, "It is enough, I have reached perfection," all is lost. For it is the function of perfection to make one know one's imperfection.

St. Augustine

THE Buddhists have a similar saying to the effect that, if an arhat thinks to himself that he is an arhat, that is proof that he is not an arhat.

I tell you that no one can experience this birth (of God realized in the soul) without a mighty effort. No one can attain this birth unless he can withdraw his mind entirely from things.

Eckhart

If a sharp penance had been laid upon me, I know of none that I would not very often have willingly undertaken, rather than prepare myself for prayer by self-recollection. And certainly the violence with which Satan assailed me was so irresistible, or my evil habits were so strong, that I did not betake myself to prayer; and the sadness I felt on entering the oratory was so great that it required all the courage I had to force myself in. They say of me that my courage is not slight, and it is known that God has given me a courage beyond that of a woman; but I have made a bad use of it. In the end Our Lord came to my relief, and when I had done this violence to myself, I found greater peace and joy than I sometimes had when I had a desire to pray.

St. Teresa

To one of his spiritual children our dear father (St François de Sales) said, "Be patient with everyone, but above all with yourself. I mean, do not be disheartened by your imperfections, but always rise up with fresh courage. I am glad you make a fresh beginning daily; there is no better means of attaining to the spiritual life than by continually beginning again, and never thinking that we have done enough. How are we to be patient in bearing with our neighbour's faults, if we are impatient in bearing with our own? He who is fretted by his own failings will not correct them; all profitable correction comes from a calm, peaceful mind."

Jean Pierre Camus

There are scarce any souls that give themselves to internal prayer but some time or other do find themselves in great indisposition thereto, having great obscurities in the mind and great insensibility in their affections, so that if imperfect souls be not well instructed and prepared, they will be in danger, in case that such contradictions of inferior nature continue long, to be dejected, yea, and perhaps deterred from pursuing prayer, for they will be apt to think that their recollections are to no purpose at all, since, for as much as seems to them, whatsoever they think or actuate towards God is a mere loss of time and of no worth at all; and therefore that it would be more profitable for them to employ their time some other way.

Yea, some souls there are conducted by Almighty God by no other way, but only by such prayer of aridity, finding no sensible contentment in any recollection, but, on the contrary, continual pain and contradiction, and yet, by a privy grace and courage imprinted deeply in the spirit, cease not for all that, but resolutely break through all difficulties and continue, the best way they can, their internal exercises to the great advancement of their spirit.

Augustine Baker

CHAPTER XXVII

Contemplation, Action and Social Utility

IN ALL the historic formulations of the Perennial Philosophy it is axiomatic that the end of human life is contemplation, or the direct and intuitive awareness of God; that action is the means to that end; that a society is good to the extent that it renders contemplation possible for its members; and that the existence of at least a minority of contemplatives is necessary for the well-being of any society. In the popular philosophy of our own time it goes without saying that the end of human life is action; that contemplation (above all in its lower forms of discursive thought) is the means to that end; that a society is good to the extent that the actions of its members make for progress in technology and organization (a progress which is assumed to be causally related to ethical and cultural advance); and that a minority of contemplatives is perfectly useless and perhaps even harmful to the community which tolerates it. To expatiate further on the modern *Weltanschauung* is unnecessary; explicitly or by implication it is set forth on every page of the advertising sections of every newspaper and magazine. The extracts that follow have been chosen in order to illustrate the older, truer, less familiar theses of the Perennial Philosophy.

Work is for the purification of the mind, not for the perception of Reality. The realization of Truth is brought

about by discrimination, and not in the least by ten
millions of acts.

Shankara

Now, the last end of each thing is that which is intended
by the first author or mover of that thing; and the first
author and mover of the universe is an intellect. Consequently, the last end of the universe must be the good
of the intellect; and this is truth. Therefore truth must
be the last end of the whole universe, and the consideration thereof must be the chief occupation of wisdom. And
for this reason divine Wisdom, clothed in flesh declares
that He came into the world to make known the truth.
. . . Moreover Aristotle defines the First Philosophy as
being the knowledge of truth, not of any truth, but of
that truth which is the source of all truth, of that, namely,
which refers to the first principle of being of all things;
wherefore its truth is the principle of all truth, since the
disposition of things is the same in truth as in being.

St. Thomas Aquinas

A thing may belong to the contemplative life in two
ways, essentially or as a predisposition. . . . The moral
virtues belong to the contemplative life as a predisposition. For the act of contemplation, in which the contemplative life essentially consists, is hindered both by the
impetuosity of the passions and by outward disturbances.
Now the moral virtues curb the impetuosity of the passions and quell the disturbance of outward occupations.
Hence moral virtues belong to the contemplative life as a
predisposition.

St. Thomas Aquinas

These works (of mercy), though they be but active, yet
they help very much, and dispose a man in the beginning
to attain afterwards to contemplation.

Walter Hilton

In Buddhism, as in Vedanta and in all but the most recent
forms of Christianity, right action is the means by which the
mind is prepared for contemplation. The first seven branches
of the Eightfold Path are the active, ethical preparation for

unitive knowledge of Suchness. Only those who consistently practise the Four Virtuous Acts, in which all other virtues are included—namely, the requital of hatred by love, resignation, "holy indifference" or desirelessness, obedience to the *dharma* or Nature of Things—can hope to achieve the liberating realization that *samsara* and *nirvana* are one, that the soul and all other beings have as their living principle the Intelligible Light or Buddha-womb.

A question now, quite naturally, presents itself: Who is called to that highest form of prayer which is contemplation? The answer is unequivocally plain. All are called to contemplation, because all are called to achieve deliverance, which is nothing else but the knowledge that unites the knower with what is known, namely the eternal Ground or Godhead. The oriental exponents of the Perennial Philosophy would probably deny that everyone is called here and now; in this particular life, they would say, it may be to all intents and purposes impossible for a given individual to achieve more than a partial deliverance, such as personal survival in some kind of "heaven," from which there may be either an advance towards total liberation or else a return to those material conditions which, as all the masters of the spiritual life agree, are so uniquely propitious for taking the cosmic intelligence test that results in enlightenment. In orthodox Christianity it is denied that the individual soul can have more than one incarnation, or that it can make any progress in its posthumous existence. If it goes to hell, it stays there. If it goes to purgatory, it merely expiates past evil doing, so as to become capable of the beatific vision. And when it gets to heaven, it has just so much of the beatific vision as its conduct during its one brief life on earth made it capable of, and everlastingly no more. Granted these postulates, it follows that, if all are called to contemplation, they are called to it from that particular position in the hierarchy of being, to which nature, nurture, free will and grace have conspired to assign them. In the words of an eminent contemporary theologian, Father Garigou-Lagrange, "all souls receive a general remote call to the mystical life, and if all were faithful in avoiding, as they should, not only mortal but venial sins, if they were, each according to his condition, generally docile to the Holy Ghost, and if they lived long enough, a day would come when they would receive the proximate and efficacious vocation to a high perfection and to the mystical life properly so called." This view—that the life of mystical contemplation is the proper and normal development of the "interior life" of recollectedness and devotion to God—is then justified by the following considerations. First, the principle of the two lives is the same. Second, it is only in the life of mystical contemplation that the interior life finds its consummation. Third, their end, which is eternal life, is the same; moreover only the life of mystical contemplation prepares immediately and perfectly for that end.

> There are few contemplatives, because few souls are perfectly humble.
>
> *The Imitation of Christ*

> God does not reserve such a lofty vocation (that of mystical contemplation) to certain souls only; on the contrary, He is willing that all should embrace it. But He finds few who permit Him to work such sublime things for them. There are many who, when He sends them trials, shrink from the labour and refuse to bear with the dryness and mortification, instead of submitting, as they must, with perfect patience.
>
> *St. John of the Cross*

This assertion that all are called to contemplation seems to conflict with what we know about the inborn varieties of temperament and with the doctrine that there are at least three principal roads to liberation—the ways of works and devotion as well as the way of knowledge. But the conflict is more apparent than real. If the ways of devotion and works lead to liberation, it is because they lead into the way of knowledge. For total deliverance comes only through unitive knowledge. A soul which does not go on from the ways of devotion and works into the way of knowledge is not totally delivered, but achieves at the best the incomplete salvation of "heaven." Coming now to the question of temperament, we find that, in effect, certain individuals are naturally drawn to lay the main doctrinal and practical emphasis in one place, certain others elsewhere. But though there may be born devotees, born workers, born contemplatives, it is nevertheless true that even those at the extreme limits of temperamental eccentricity are capable of making use of other ways than that to which they are naturally drawn. Given the requisite degree of obedience to the leadings of the Light, the born contemplative can learn to purify his heart by work and direct his mind by one-pointed adoration; the born devotee and the born worker can learn to "be still and know that I am God." Nobody need be the victim of his peculiar talents. Few or many, of this stamp or of that, they are given us to be used for the gaining of one great end. We have the power to choose whether to use them well or badly—in the easier, worse way or the harder and better.

Those who are more adapted to the active life can prepare themselves for contemplation in the practice of the active life, while those who are more adapted to the contemplative life can take upon themselves the works of the active life so as to become yet more apt for contemplation.

St. Thomas Aquinas

He who is strong in faith, weak in understanding, will generally place his confidence in good-for-nothing people and believe in the wrong object. He who is strong in understanding, weak in faith, leans towards dishonesty and is difficult to cure, like a disease caused by medicine. One in whom both are equal believes in the right object.

He who is strong in concentration, weak in energy, is overcome by idleness, since concentration partakes of the nature of idleness. He who is strong in energy, weak in concentration, is overcome by distractions, since energy partakes of the nature of distraction. Therefore they should be made equal to one another, since from equality in both comes contemplation and ecstasy. . . .

Mindfulness should be strong everywhere, for mindfulness keeps the mind away from distraction, into which it might fall, since faith, energy and understanding partake of the nature of distraction: and away from idleness, into which it might fall, since concentration partakes of the nature of idleness.

Buddhaghosha

At this point it is worth remarking parenthetically that God is by no means the only possible object of contemplation. There have been and still are many philosophic, aesthetic and scientific contemplatives. One-pointed concentration on that which is not the highest may become a dangerous form of idolatry. In a letter to Hooker, Darwin wrote that "it is a cursed evil to any man to become so absorbed in any subject as I am in mine." It is an evil because such one-pointedness may result in the more or less total atrophy of all but one side of the mind. Darwin himself records that in later life he was unable to take the smallest interest in poetry, art or religion. Professionally, in relation to his chosen specialty, a man may be completely mature. Spiritually and sometimes even ethically, in relation to God and his neighbours, he may be hardly more than a foetus.

In cases where the one-pointed contemplation is of God there is also a risk that the mind's unemployed capacities may atrophy. The hermits of Tibet and the Thebaïd were certainly one-pointed, but with a one-pointedness of exclusion and mutilation. It may be, however, that if they had been more truly "docile to the Holy Ghost," they would have come to understand that the one-pointedness of exclusion is at best a preparation for the one-pointedness of inclusion—the realization of God in the fulness of cosmic being as well as in the interior height of the individual soul. Like the Taoist sage, they would at last have turned back into the world riding on their tamed and regenerate individuality; they would have "come eating and drinking," would have associated with "publicans and sinners" or their Buddhist equivalents, "winebibbers and butchers." For the fully enlightened, totally liberated person, *samsara* and *nirvana*, time and eternity, the phenomenal and the Real, are essentially one. His whole life is an unsleeping and one-pointed contemplation of the Godhead in and through the things, lives, minds and events of the world of becoming. There is here no mutilation of the soul, no atrophy of any of its powers and capacities. Rather, there is a general enhancement and intensification of consciousness, and at the same time an extension and transfiguration. No saint has ever complained that absorption in God was a "cursed evil."

In the beginning was the Word; behold Him to whom Mary listened. And the Word was made flesh; behold Him whom Martha served.

St. Augustine

> God aspires us into Himself in contemplation, and then we must be wholly His; but afterwards the Spirit of God expires us without, for the practice of love and good works.
>
> *Ruysbroeck*

Action, says Aquinas, should be something added to the life of prayer, not something taken away from it. One of the reasons for this recommendation is strictly utilitarian; action that is "taken away from the life of prayer" is action unenlightened by contact with Reality, uninspired and unguided; consequently it is apt to be ineffective and even harmful. "The sages of old," says Chuang Tzu, "first got Tao for themselves, then got it for others." There can be no taking of motes out of other people's eyes so long as the beam in our own eye prevents us from seeing the divine Sun and working by its light. Speaking of those who prefer immediate action to acquiring, through contemplation, the power to act well, St. John of the Cross asks, "What do they accomplish?" And he answers, *Poco mas que nada, y a veces nada, y aun a veces dano* ("Little more than nothing, and sometimes nothing at all, and sometimes even harm"). Income must balance expenditure. This is necessary not merely on the economic level, but also on the physiological, the intellectual, the ethical and the spiritual. We cannot put forth physical energy unless we stoke our body with fuel in the form of food. We cannot hope to utter anything worth saying, unless we read and inwardly digest the utterances of our betters. We cannot act rightly and effectively unless we are in the habit of laying ourselves open to leadings of the divine Nature of Things. We must draw in the goods of eternity in order to be able to give out the goods of time. But the goods of eternity cannot be had except by giving up at least a little of our time to silently waiting for them. This means that the life, in which ethical expenditure is balanced by spiritual income, must be a life in which action alternates with repose, speech with alertly passive silence. *Otium sanctum quaerit caritas veritatis; negotium justum suscipit necessitas caritatis* ("The love of Truth seeks holy leisure; the necessity of love undertakes righteous action"). The bodies of men and animals are reciprocating engines, in which tension is always succeeded by relaxation. Even the unsleeping heart rests between beat and beat. There is nothing in living Nature that even distantly resembles man's greatest technical invention, the continuously revolving wheel. (It is this fact, no doubt, which accounts for the boredom, weariness and apathy of those who, in modern factories, are forced to adapt their bodily and mental movements to circular motions of mechanically uniform velocity.) "What a man takes in by contemplation," says Eckhart, "that he pours out in love." The well-meaning humanist and the merely muscular Christian, who imagines that he can obey the second of the great commandments without taking time even to think how best he may love God with all his heart, soul and mind, are people engaged in the impossible task of pouring unceasingly from a container that is never replenished.

> Daughters of Charity ought to love prayer as the body loves the soul. And just as the body cannot live without the soul, so the soul cannot live without prayer. And in so far as a daughter prays as she ought to pray, she will do well. She will not walk, she will run in the ways of the Lord, and will be raised to a high degree of the love of God.
>
> *St. Vincent de Paul*

> Households, cities, countries and nations have enjoyed great happiness, when a single individual has taken heed of the Good and Beautiful. . . . Such men not only liberate themselves; they fill those they meet with a free mind.
>
> *Philo*

Similar views are expressed by Al-Ghazzali, who regards the mystics not only as the ultimate source of our knowledge of the soul and its capacities and defects, but as the salt which preserves human societies from decay. "In the time of the philosophers," he writes, "as at every other period, there existed some of these fervent mystics. God does not deprive this world of them, for they are its sustainers." It is they who, dying to themselves, become capable of perpetual inspiration and so are made the instruments through which divine grace is mediated to those whose unregenerate nature is impervious to the delicate touches of the Spirit.

A List of Recommended Books

AL-GHAZZALI. *Confessions*. Translated by Claud Field (London, 1909).

ANSARI OF HERAT. *The Invocations of Sheikh Abdullah Ansari of Herat*. Translated by Sardar Sir Jogendra Singh (London, 1939).

ATTAR. *Selections*. Translated by Margaret Smith (London, 1932).

AUGUSTINE, ST. *Confessions* (numerous editions).

AUROBINDO, SRI. *The Life Divine*, 3 vols. (Calcutta, 1939).

BAKER, AUGUSTINE. *Holy Wisdom* (London, 1876).

BEAUSOBRE, JULIA DE. *The Woman Who Could Not Die* (London and New York, 1938).

BERNARD OF CLAIRVAUX, ST. *The Steps of Humility* (Cambridge, Mass., 1940).

——. *On the Love of God* (New York, 1937).

——. *Selected Letters* (London, 1904) An admirably lucid account of St. Bernard's thought may be found in *The Mystical Doctrine of Saint Bernard*, by Professor Etienne Gilson (London and New York, 1940).

BERTOCCI, PETER A. *The Empirical Argument for God in Late British Philosophy* (Cambridge, Mass., 1938).

Bhagavad Gita. Among many translations of this Hindu scripture the best, from a literary point of view, is that of Swami Prabhavananda and Christopher Isherwood (Los Angeles, 1944). Valuable notes, based upon the commentaries of Shankara, are to be found in Swami Nikhilananda's edition (New York, 1944), and Professor Franklin Edgerton's literal translation (Cambridge, Mass., 1944) is preceded by a long and scholarly introduction.

BINYON, L. *The Flight of the Dragon* (London, 1911).

BOEHME, JAKOB. A good introduction to the work of this very difficult writer is *The Mystic Will*, by Howard H. Brinton (New York, 1930).

BRAHMANANDA, SWAMI. Records of his teaching and a biography by Swami Prabhavananda are contained in *The Eternal Companion* (Los Angeles, 1944).

CAMUS, JEAN PIERRE. *The Spirit of St. Francis de Sales* (London, n. d.).

CAUSSADE, J. P. DE. *Abandonment* (New York, 1887).

——. *Spiritual Letters*, 3 vols. (London, 1937).

CHANTAL, ST. JEANNE FRANÇOISE. *Selected Letters* (London and New York, 1918).

CHAPMAN, ABBOT JOHN. *Spiritual Letters* (London, 1935).

CHUANG TZU. *Chuang Tzu, Mystic, Moralist and Social Reformer*. Translated by Herbert Giles (Shanghai, 1936).

——. *Musings of a Chinese Mystic* (London, 1920).

——. *Chinese Philosophy in Classical Times*. Translated by E. R. Hughes (London, 1943).

The Cloud of Unknowing (with commentary by Augustine Baker). Edited with an introduction by Justin McCann (London, 1924).

COOMARASWAMY, ANANDA K. *Buddha and the Gospel of Buddhism* (New York, 1916).

——. *The Transformation of Nature in Art* (Cambridge, Mass., 1935).

——. *Hinduism and Buddhism* (New York, n. d.).

CURTIS, A. M. *The Way of Silence* (Burton Bradstock, Dorset, 1937).

DEUSSEN, PAUL. *The Philosophy of the Upanishads* (London, 1906).

DIONYSIUS THE AREOPAGITE. *On the Divine Names and the Mystical Theology*. Translated with an introduction by C. E. Rolt (London, 1920).

ECKHART, MEISTER. *Works*, translated by C. B. Evans (London, 1924).

——. *Meister Eckhart, A Modern Translation*. By R. B. Blakney (New York, 1941).

EVANS-WENTZ, W. Y. *The Tibetan Book of the Dead* (New York, 1927).

——. *Tibet's Great Yogi, Milarepa* (New York, 1928).

——. *Tibetan Yoga and Secret Doctrines* (New York, 1935).

The Following of Christ. Unknown author, but mistakenly attributed to Tauler in the first English edition (London, 1886).

FROST, BEDE. *The Art of Mental Prayer* (London, 1940).

——. *Saint John of the Cross* (London, 1937).

GARRIGOU-LAGRANGE, R. *Christian Perfection and Contemplation* (London and St. Louis, 1937).

GODDARD, DWIGHT. *A Buddhist Bible* (published by the editor, Thetford, Maine, 1938). This volume contains translations of several Mahayana texts not to be found, or to be found only with much difficulty, elsewhere. Among these are "The Diamond Sutra," "The Surangama Sutra," "The Lankavatara Sutra," "The Awakening of Faith" and "The Sutra of the Sixth Patriarch."

GUÉNON, RENÉ. *Man and His Becoming According to the Vedanta* (London, n. d.).

——. *East and West* (London, 1941).

——. *The Crisis of the Modern World* (London, 1942).

HEARD, GERALD. *The Creed of Christ* (New York, 1940).

——. *The Code of Christ* (New York, 1941).

——. *Preface to Prayer* (New York, 1944).

HILTON, WALTER. *The Scale of Perfection* (London, 1927).

HUGEL, FRIEDRICH VON. *The Mystical Element in Religion as Studied in Saint Catherine of Genoa and Her Friends* (London, 1923).

IBN TUFAIL. *The Awakening of the Soul*. Translated by Paul Bronnle (London, 1910).

The Imitation of Christ. Whitford's translation, edited by E. J. Klein (New York, 1941).

JOHN OF THE CROSS, ST. *Works,* 3 vols. (London, 1934-1935).

JONES, RUFUS. *The Spiritual Reformers in the 16th and 17th Centuries* (New York, 1914).

———. *The Flowering of Mysticism* (New York, 1939).

JORGENSEN, JOHANNES. *Saint Catherine of Sienna* (London, 1938).

LAO TZU. There are many translations of the Tao Teh King. Consult and compare those of Arthur Waley in *The Way and Its Power* (London, 1933), of F. R. Hughes in *Chinese Philosophy in Classical Times* (Everyman's Library) and of Ch'u Ta-Kao (London, 1927) reprinted in *The Bible of the World* (New York, 1939).

LAW, WILLIAM. Several modern editions of the *Serious Call* are available; but many of Law's finest works, such as *The Spirit of Love* and *The Spirit of Prayer,* have not been reprinted in recent years and are hard to come by. An excellent anthology of Law's writings, *Characters and Characteristics of William Law,* was compiled by Alexander Whyte towards the end of last century (3rd ed., London, 1898).

LEEN, EDWARD. *Progress through Mental Prayer* (London, 1940).

McKEON, RICHARD. Selections from Medieval Philosophers, 2 vols (New York, 1929).

The Mirror of Simple Souls. Author unknown (London, 1927).

NICHOLAS OF CUSA. *The Idiot* (San Francisco, 1940).

———. *The Vision of God* (London and New York), 1928).

NICHOLSON, R. *The Mystics of Islam* (London, 1914).

OMAN, JOHN. *The Natural and the Supernatural.* (London, 1938).

OTTO, RUDOLF. *India's Religion of Grace* (London, 1930).

———. *Mysticism East and West* (London, 1932).

PATANJALI. *Yoga Aphorisms.* Translated with a commentary by Swami Vivekananda (New York, 1899).

PONNELLE, L. and L. BORDET. *St. Philpi Neri and the Roman Society of His Time* (London, 1932).

POULAIN, A. *The Graces of Interior Prayer* (London, 1910).

POURRAT, P. *Christian Spirituality,* 3 vols. (London, 1922).

PRATT, J. B. *The Pilgrimage of Buddhism* (New York, 1928).

RADHAKRISHNAN, S. *The Hindu View of Life* (London and New York, 1927).

———. *Indian Philosophy* (London and New York, 1923-1927).

———. *Eastern Religions and Western Thought* (New York, 1939).

RAMAKRISHNA, SRI. *The Gospel of Sri Ramakrishna.* Translated from the Bengali narrative of "M" by Swami Nikhilananda (New York, 1942).

RUMI, JALAL-UDDIN. *Masnavi.* Translated by E. H. Whinfield (London, 1898).

RUYSBROECK, JAN VAN. *The Adornment of the Spiritual Marriage*

(London, 1916). Consult also the studies by Evelyn Underhill (London, 1915) and Wautier d'Aygalliers (London, 1925).

SALES, ST. FRANÇOIS DE. *Introduction to the Devout Life* (numerous editions).

——. *Treatise on the Love of God* (new edition, Westminster, Md., 1942).

——. *Spiritual Conferences* (London, 1868).

——. See also J. P. Camus.

The Secret of the Golden Flower. Translated from the Chinese by Richard Wilhelm. Commentary by Dr. C. G. Jung (London and New York, 1931).

STOCKS, J. L. *Time, Cause and Eternity* (London, 1938).

STOUT, G. F. *Mind and Matter* (London, 1931).

Sutra Spoken by the Sixth Patriarch, Hui Neng. Translated by Wung Mou-lam (Shanghai, 1930). Reprinted in *A Buddhist Bible* (Thetford, 1938).

SUZUKI, B. L. *Mahayana Buddhism* (London, 1938).

SUZUKI, D. T. *Studies in Zen Buddhism* (London, 1927).

——. *Studies in the Lankavatara Sutra* (Kyoto and London, 1935).

——. *Manual of Zen Buddhism* (Kyoto, 1935).

TAGORE, RABINDRANATH. *One Hundred Poems of Kabir* (London, 1915).

TAULER, JOHANN. *Life and Sermons* (London, 1907).

——. *The Inner Way* (London, 1909).

——. Consult Inge's *Christian Mysticism*, Rufus Jones's *Studies in Mystical Religion* and Pourrat's *Christian Spirituality*.

TENNANT, F. R. *Philosophical Theology* (Cambridge, 1923).

Theologia Germanica. Winkworth's translation (new edition, London, 1937).

TILLYARD, AELFRIDA. *Spiritual Exercises* (London, 1927).

TRAHERNE, THOMAS. *Centuries of Meditation* (London, 1908).

——. Consult *Thomas Traherne, A Critical Biography*, by Gladys I. Wade (Princeton, 1944).

UNDERHILL, EVELYN. *Mysticism* (London, 1924).

——. *The Mystics of the Church* (London, 1925).

Upanishads. *The Thirteen Principal Upanishads*. Translated by R. E. Hume (New York, 1931).

The Ten Principal Upanishads. Translated by Shree Purohit and W. B. Yeats (London, 1937).

The Himalayas of the Soul. Translated by J. Mascaro (London, 1938).

WATTS, ALAN W. *The Spirit of Zen* (London, 1936).

WHITNEY, JANET. *John Woolman, American Quaker* (Boston, 1942).

Elizabeth Fry, Quaker Heroine (Boston, 1936).

Index

About the author

About the book

Insights,
Interviews
& More...

Read on

Aldous Huxley
A Life of the Mind

POET, PLAYWRIGHT, NOVELIST, short story writer, travel writer, essayist, critic, philosopher, mystic, and social prophet, Aldous Huxley was one of the most accomplished and influential English literary figures of the mid-twentieth century. In the course of an extraordinary prolific writing career, which began in the early 1920s and continued until his death in 1963, Huxley underwent a remarkable process of self-transformation from a derisive satirist of England's chattering classes to a deeply religious writer preoccupied with the human capacity for spiritual transcendence. Yet in everything Huxley wrote, from the most frivolous to the most profound, there runs the common thread of his search to explain the meaning and possibilities of human life and perception.

Aldous Huxley was born in Surrey, England, in 1894, the son of Leonard Huxley, editor of the prestigious *Cornhill* magazine; and of Julia Arnold, niece of the poet and essayist Matthew Arnold, and sister of Mrs. Humphrey Ward. He was the grandson of T. H. Huxley, the scientist. Thus by "birth and disposition," as one biographer put it, Huxley belonged to England's intellectual aristocracy.

As Sybille Bedford writes in her fascinating biography, *Aldous Huxley* (Alfred A. Knopf / Harper & Row, 1974): "What we know about him as a young child is the usual residue of anecdote and snapshot. During his first years his head was proportionately enormous, so that he could not walk till he was two because

Courtesy of Man Ray/The Granger Collection

he was apt to topple over. 'We put father's hat on him and it fitted.' In another country, at a great distance in time and place, when he lay ill and near his end in southern California, a friend, wanting to distract him, said, 'Aldous, didn't you ever have a nickname when you were small?' and Aldous, who hardly ever talked about his childhood or indeed about himself (possibly because one did not ask) said promptly, 'They called me Ogie. Short for Ogre.'

"The Ogre was a pretty little boy, the photographs . . . show the high forehead, the (then) clear gaze, the tremulous mouth and a sweetness of expression, an alertness beyond that of other angelic little boys looking into a camera. Aldous, his brother, Julian, tells us, sat quietly a good deal of the time 'contemplating the strangeness of things.'

" 'I used to watch him with a pencil,' said his cousin and contemporary Gervas Huxley, 'you see, he was always drawing. . . . My earliest memory of him is sitting— absorbed—to me it was magic, a little boy of my own age drawing so beautifully.'

"He was delicate; he had mischievous moods; he could play. He carried his rag doll about him for company until he was eight. He was fond of grumbling. They gave him a milk mug which bore the inscription: *Oh, isn't the world extremely flat / With nothing whatever to grumble at.*

". . . And Aldous aged six being taken with all the Huxleys to the unveiling of the statue of his grandfather at the Natural History Museum by the Prince of Wales, and his mother trying, in urgent whispers, to persuade Julian, then a young Etonian, to give up his top hat—a very young Etonian and a very new top hat—to Aldous, queasy, overcome, to be sick in."

When Huxley was a sixteen-year-old student at Eton, he contracted a disease ▶

> 'They called me Ogie. Short for Ogre.'

3

Aldous Huxley *(continued)*

that left him almost totally blind for two years and seriously impaired his vision for years to come. The loss of sight was an "event," Huxley later wrote, "which prevented me from becoming a complete public school English-gentleman." It also ended his early dreams of becoming a doctor. Yet, in a curious way, though he abandoned science for literature, Huxley's outlook remained essentially scientific. As his brother, the zoologist Julian Huxley, wrote, science and mysticism were overlapping and complementary realms in Aldous Huxley's mind: "The more [science] discovers and the more comprehension it gives us of the mechanisms of existence, the more clearly does the mystery of existence itself stand out."

Huxley took his undergraduate degree in literature at Balliol College, Oxford, in 1916, and spent several years during World War I working in a government office. After teaching briefly at Eton, he launched his career as a professional writer in 1920 by taking a job as a drama critic for the *Westminster Gazette*, and a staff writer for *House and Garden* and *Vogue*. Possessed of seemingly infinite literary energy, he wrote poetry, essays, and fiction in his spare time, publishing his first novel, *Crome Yellow*, in 1921. This bright, sharp, mildly shocking satire of upper-class artists won Huxley an immediate reputation as a dangerous wit. He swiftly composed several more novels in a similar vein, including *Antic Hay* (1923) and *Those Barren Leaves* (1925).

In *Point Counter Point* (1928), considered by many critics his strongest novel, Huxley broke new ground, both stylistically and thematically. In a narrative that jumps abruptly from scene to scene and character to character, Huxley confronts modern man's disillusionment with religion, art, sex, and politics. The character Philip Quarles, a novelist intent on "transform[ing] a detached intellectual skepticism into a way of harmonious all-round living," is the closest Huxley came to painting his own portrait in fiction. *Brave New World* (1932), though less experimental in style than *Point Counter Point*, is more radical in its pessimistic view of human nature. Huxley's antiutopia, with its eerie combination of totalitarian government and ubiquitous feel-good drugs and sex, disturbed many readers of his day; but it has proven to be his most enduring and influential work.

During the 1930s, Huxley turned increasingly toward an exploration of fundamental questions of philosophy, sociology, politics, and ethics. In his 1936 novel *Eyeless in Gaza* he wrote of a man's transformation from cynic to mystic, and as war threatened Europe once again, he allied himself with the pacifist movement and began lecturing widely on peace and internationalism.

For a number of years Huxley lived in Italy, where he formed a close relationship with D. H. Lawrence, whose letters he edited in 1933. In 1937, Huxley and his Belgian-born wife, Maria Nys, and their son, Matthew, left Europe to live in Southern California for the rest of his life. Maria Huxley died of cancer in 1955, and the following year Huxley married the Italian violinist and psychotherapist Laura Archera.

In the 1940s and 1950s, Huxley changed direction yet again as he became fascinated by the spiritual life, in particular with the possibility of direct communication between people and the divinity. Huxley read widely in the writings of the mystics and assembled an anthology of mystical writing called *The Perennial Philosophy* (1945). Around this time he began experimenting with mind-altering drugs like mescaline and LSD, which he came to believe gave users essentially the same experiences that mystics attained through fasting, prayer, and meditation. *The Doors of Perception* (1954) and *Heaven and Hell* (1956), Huxley's books about the effects of what he termed psychedelic drugs, became essential texts for the counterculture during the 1960s. Yet Huxley's brother Julian cautions against the image of Aldous as a kind of spiritual godfather to hippies: "One of Aldous's major preoccupations was how to achieve self-transcendence while yet remaining a committed social being—how to escape from the prison bars of self and the pressures of here and now into realms of pure goodness and pure enjoyment."

Huxley pursued his quest for "pure goodness and pure enjoyment" right up to the end of his life on November 22, 1963. Today he is remembered as one of the great explorers of twentieth-century literature, a writer who continually reinvented himself as he pushed his way deeper and deeper into the mysteries of human consciousness. ∽

"Beliefs"
An Essay by
Aldous Huxley

No ACCOUNT of the scientific picture of the world and its history would be complete unless it contained a reminder of the fact, frequently forgotten by scientists themselves, that this picture does not even claim to be comprehensive. From the world we actually live in, the world that is given by our senses, our intuitions of beauty and goodness, our emotions and impulses, our moods and sentiments, the man of science abstracts a simplified private universe of things possessing only those qualities which used to be called "primary." Arbitrarily, because it happens to be convenient, because his methods do not allow him to deal with the immense complexity of reality, he selects from the whole of experience only those elements which can be weighed, measured, numbered, or which lend themselves in any other way to mathematical treatment. By using this technique of simplification and abstraction, the scientist has succeeded to an astonishing degree in understanding and dominating the physical environment. The success was intoxicating and, with an illogicality which, in the circumstances, was doubtless pardonable, many scientists and philosophers came to imagine that this useful abstraction from reality was reality itself. Reality as actually experienced contains intuitions of value and significance, contains love, beauty, mystical ecstasy, intimations of godhead. Science did not and still does not possess intellectual instruments with which to deal with these aspects of reality. Consequently it ignored them and concentrated its attention upon such aspects of the world as it could deal with by means of arithmetic, geometry and the various branches of higher mathematics. Our conviction that the world is meaningless is due in part to the fact (discussed in a later paragraph) that the philosophy of meaninglessness lends itself very effectively to furthering the ends of erotic or political passion; in part to a genuine intellectual error—the error of identifying the world of science, a world from which all meaning and value has been deliberately excluded, with ultimate reality. It is worthwhile to quote in this context the words with which Hume closes his *Enquiry*. "If we take in our hand any volume; of divinity or school metaphysics, for instance; let us ask, Does it contain any abstract reasoning concerning quantity or number? No. Does it contain any experimental reasoning concerning matter of fact or evidence? No. Commit it then to the flames; for it can contain nothing but sophistry and illusion." Hume mentions only divinity and school metaphysics; but his argument would apply just as cogently to poetry, music, painting, sculpture and all ethical and religious teaching. Hamlet contains no abstract reasoning concerning quantity or number and no experimental reason concerning evidence; nor does the Hammerklavier Sonata, nor Donatello's David, nor the *Tao Te Ching*, nor the *Following of Christ*. Commit them therefore to the flames: for they can contain nothing but sophistry and illusion.

We are living now, not in the delicious intoxication induced by the early successes of science, but in a rather grisly morning-after, when it has become apparent that what triumphant science has done hitherto is to improve the means for achieving unimproved or actually deteriorated ends. In this condition of apprehensive sobriety ▶

"Beliefs" *(continued)*

we are able to see that the contents of literature, art, music—even in some measure of divinity and school metaphysics—are not sophistry and illusion, but simply those elements of experience which scientists chose to leave out of account, for the good reason that they had no intellectual methods for dealing with them. In the arts, in philosophy, in religion men are trying—doubtless, without complete success—to describe and explain the non-measurable, purely qualitative aspects of reality. Since the time of Galileo, scientists have admitted, sometimes explicitly but much more often by implication, that they are incompetent to discuss such matters. The scientific picture of the world is what it is because men of science combine this incompetence with certain special competences. They have no right to claim that this product of incompetence and specialization is a complete picture of reality. As a matter of historical fact, however, this claim has constantly been made. The successive steps in the process of identifying an arbitrary abstraction from reality with reality itself have been described, very fully and lucidly, in Burtt's excellent "Metaphysical Foundations of Modern Science"; and it is therefore unnecessary for me to develop the theme any further. All that I need add is the fact that, in recent years, many men of science have come to realize that the scientific picture of the world is a partial one—the product of their special competence in mathematics and their special incompetence to deal systematically with aesthetic and moral values, religious experiences and intuitions of significance. Unhappily, novel ideas become acceptable to the less intelligent members of society only with a very considerable time-lag. Sixty or seventy years ago the majority of scientists believed—and the belief often caused them considerable distress—that the product of their special incompetence was identical with reality as a whole. Today this belief has begun to give way, in scientific circles, to a different and obviously truer conception of the relation between science and total experience. The masses, on the contrary, have just reached the point where the ancestors of today's scientists were standing two generations back. They are convinced that the scientific picture of an arbitrary abstraction from reality is a picture of reality as a whole and that therefore the world is without meaning or value. But nobody likes living in such a world. To satisfy their hunger for meaning and value, they turn to such doctrines as nationalism, fascism and revolutionary communism. Philosophically and scientifically, these doctrines are absurd; but for the masses in every community, they have this great merit: they attribute the meaning and value that have been taken away from the world as a whole to the particular part of the world in which the believers happen to be living.

These last considerations raise an important question, which must now be considered in some detail. Does the world as a whole possess the value and meaning that we constantly attribute to certain parts of it (such as human beings and their works); and, if so, what is the nature of that value and meaning? This is a question which, a few years ago, I should not even have posed. For, like so many of my contemporaries, I took it for granted that there was no meaning. This was partly due to the fact that I shared the common belief that the scientific picture of an abstraction from reality was a true picture of reality as a whole; partly also to other, non-intellectual reasons. I had motives for not wanting the world to have a meaning; consequently assumed that it had none, and was able without any difficulty to find satisfying reasons for this assumption.

Most ignorance is vincible ignorance. We don't know because we don't want to know. It is our will that decides how and upon what subjects we shall use our intelligence. Those who detect no meaning in the world generally do so because, for one reason or another, it suits their books that the world should be meaningless.

The behavior of the insane is merely sane behavior, a bit exaggerated and distorted. The abnormal casts a revealing light upon the normal. Hence the interest attaching, among other madmen, to the extravagant figure of the Marquis de Sade. The marquis prided himself upon being a thinker. His books, indeed, contain more philosophy than pornography. The hungry smut-hound must plough through long chapters of abstract speculation in order to find the cruelties and obscenities for which he hungers. De Sade's philosophy was the philosophy of meaninglessness carried to its logical conclusion. Life was without significance. Values were illusory and ideals merely the inventions of cunning priests and kings. Sensations and animal pleasures alone possessed reality and were alone worth living for. There was no reason why any one should have the slightest consideration for any one else. For those who found rape and murder amusing, rape and murder were fully legitimate activities. And so on.

Why was the Marquis unable to find any value or significance in the world? Was his intellect more piercing than that of other men? Was he forced by the acuity of his vision to look through the veils of prejudice and superstition to the hideous reality behind them? We may doubt it. The real reason why the Marquis could see no meaning or value in the world is to be found in those descriptions of fornications, sodomies and tortures which alternate with the philosophizings of *Justine* and *Juliette*. In the ordinary circumstances of life, the Marquis was not particularly ▶

"Beliefs" *(continued)*

cruel; indeed, he is said to have got into serious trouble during the Terror for his leniency toward those suspected of anti-revolutionary sentiments. His was a strictly sexual perversion. It was for flogging actresses, sticking pen-knives into shop girls, feeding prostitutes on sugar-plums impregnated with cantharides, that he got into trouble with the police. His philosophical disquisitions, which, like the pornographic day-dreams, were mostly written in prisons and asylums, were the theoretical justification of his erotic practices. Similarly his politics were dictated by the desire to avenge himself on those members of his family and his class who had, as he thought, unjustly persecuted him. He was enthusiastically a revolutionary—at any rate in theory; for, as we have seen, he was too gentle in practice to satisfy his fellow Jacobins. His books are of permanent interest and value because they contain a kind of *reductio ad absurdum* of revolutionary theory. Sade is not afraid to be a revolutionary to the bitter end. Not content with denying the particular system of values embodied in the *ancien régime*, he proceeds to deny the existence of any values, any idealism, any binding moral imperatives whatsoever. He preaches violent revolution not only in the field of politics and economics, but (logical with the appalling logicality of the maniac) also on that of personal relations, including the most intimate of all, the relations between lovers. And, after all, why not? If it is legitimate to torment and kill in one set of circumstances, it must be equally legitimate to torment and kill in all other circumstances. De Sade is the one completely consistent and thorough-going revolutionary of history.

If I have lingered so long over a maniac, it is because his madness illuminates the dark places of normal behavior. No philosophy is completely disinterested. The pure love of truth is always mingled to some extent with the need, consciously or unconsciously felt by even the noblest and the most intelligent philosophers, to justify a given form of personal or social behavior, to rationalize the traditional prejudices of a given class or community. The philosopher who finds meaning in the world is concerned, not only to elucidate that meaning, but also to prove that it is most clearly expressed in some established religion, some accepted code of morals. The philosopher who finds no meaning in the world is not concerned exclusively with a problem in pure metaphysics. He is also concerned to prove that there is no valid reason why he personally should not do as he wants to do, or why his friends should not seize political power and govern in the way that they find most advantageous to themselves. The voluntary, as opposed to the intellectual, reasons for holding the doctrines of materialism, for example, may be predominantly erotic, as they were in the case of Lamettrie (see his lyrical account of the pleasures of the bed in *La Volupté* and at the end of *L'Homme Machine*), or predominantly political, as they were in the case of Karl Marx. The desire to justify a particular form of political organization and, in some cases, of a personal will to power has played an equally large part in the formulation of philosophies postulating the existence of a meaning in the world. Christian philosophers have found no difficulty in justifying imperialism, war, the capitalistic system, the use of torture, the censorship of the press, and ecclesiastical tyrannies of every sort from the tyranny of Rome to the tyrannies of Geneva and New England. In all these cases they have shown that the meaning of the world was such as to be compatible with, or actually most completely expressed by, the iniquities I have mentioned above—iniquities which happened, of course, to serve the personal or sectarian interests of the philosophers concerned. In due course, there arose philosophers who denied not only the right of these Christian special pleaders to justify iniquity by an appeal to the meaning of the world, but even their right to find any such meaning whatsoever. In the circumstances, the fact was not surprising. One unscrupulous distortion of the truth tends to beget other and opposite distortions. Passions may be satisfied in the process; but the disinterested love of knowledge suffers eclipse.

For myself as, no doubt, for most of my contemporaries, the philosophy of meaninglessness was essentially an instrument of liberation. The liberation we desired was simultaneously liberation from a certain political and economic system and liberation from a certain system of morality. We objected to the morality because it interfered with our sexual freedom; we objected to the political and economic system because it was unjust. The supporters of these systems claimed that in some way they embodied the meaning (a Christian meaning, they insisted) of the world. There was one admirably simple method of confuting these people and at the same time justifying ourselves in our political and erotic revolt: we could deny that the world had any meaning whatsoever. Similar tactics had been adopted during the eighteenth century and for the same reasons. From the popular novelists of the period, such as Crébillon and Andréa de Nerciat, we learn that the chief reason for being "philosophical" was that one might be free from prejudices—above all prejudices of a sexual nature. More serious writers associated political with sexual prejudice and recommended philosophy (in practice, the philosophy of meaninglessness) as a preparation for social reform or revolution. ▶

"Beliefs" *(continued)*

The early nineteenth century witnessed a reaction toward meaningful philosophy of a kind that could, unhappily, be used to justify political reaction. The men of the new Enlightenment, which occurred in the middle years of the nineteenth century, once again used meaninglessness as a weapon against the reactionaries. The Victorian passion for respectability was, however, so great that, during the period when they were formulated, neither Positivism nor Darwinism was used as a justification for sexual indulgence. After the War the philosophy of meaninglessness came once more triumphantly into fashion. As in the days of Lamettrie and his successors the desire to justify a certain sexual looseness played a part in the popularization of meaninglessness at least as important as that played by the desire for liberation from an unjust and inefficient form of social organization. By the end of the twenties a reaction had begun to set in—away from the easy-going philosophy of general meaninglessness toward the hard, ferocious theologies of nationalistic and revolutionary idolatry. Meaning was reintroduced into the world, but only in patches. The universe as a whole still remained meaningless, but certain of its parts, such as the nation, the state, the class, the party, were endowed with significance and the highest value. The general acceptance of a doctrine that denies meaning and value to the world as a whole, while assigning them in a supreme degree to certain arbitrarily selected parts of the totality, can have only evil and disastrous results. "All that we are (and consequently all that we do) is the result of what we have thought." We have thought of ourselves as members of supremely meaningful and valuable communities—deified nations, divine classes and what not—existing within a meaningless universe. And because we have thought like this, rearmament is in full swing, economic nationalism becomes ever more intense, the battle of rival propagandas grows ever fiercer, and general war becomes increasingly more probable.

It was the manifestly poisonous nature of the fruits that forced me to reconsider the philosophical tree on which they had grown. It is certainly hard, perhaps impossible, to demonstrate any necessary connection between truth and practical goodness. Indeed it was fashionable during the Enlightenment of the middle nineteenth century to speak of the need for supplying the masses with "vital lies" calculated to make those who accepted them not only happy, but well behaved. The truth—which was that there was no meaning or value in the world—should be revealed only to the few who were strong enough to stomach it. Now, it may be, of course, that the nature of things has fixed a great gulf between truth about the world on the one hand and practical goodness on the other.

Meanwhile, however, the nature of things seems to have so constituted the human mind that it is extremely reluctant to accept such a conclusion, except under the pressure of desire or self-interest. Furthermore those who, to be liberated from political or sexual restraint, accept the doctrine of absolute meaninglessness tend in a short time to become so much dissatisfied with their philosophy (in spite of the services it renders) that they will exchange it for any dogma, however manifestly nonsensical, which restores meaning if only to a part of the universe. Some people, it is true, can live contentedly with a philosophy of meaninglessness for a very long time. But in most cases it will be found that these people possess some talent or accomplishment that permits them to live a life which, to a limited extent, is profoundly meaningful and valuable. Thus an artist, or a man of science can profess a philosophy of general meaninglessness and yet lead a perfectly contented life. The reason for this must be sought in the fact that artistic creation and scientific research are absorbingly delightful occupations, possessing, moreover, a certain special significance in virtue of their relation to truth and beauty. Nevertheless, artistic creation and scientific research may be, and constantly are, used as devices for escaping from the responsibilities of life. They are proclaimed to be ends absolutely good in themselves—ends so admirable that those who pursue them are excused from bothering about anything else. This is particularly true of contemporary science. The mass of accumulated knowledge is so great that it is now impossible for any individual to have a thorough grasp of more than one small field of study. Meanwhile, no attempt is made to produce a comprehensive synthesis of the general results of scientific research. Our universities possess no chair of synthesis. All endowments, moreover, go to special subjects—and almost always to subjects which have no need of further endowment, such as physics, chemistry and mechanics. In our institutions of higher learning about ten times as much is spent on the natural sciences as on the sciences of man. All our efforts are directed, as usual, to producing improved means to unimproved ends. Meanwhile intensive specialization tends to reduce each branch of science to a condition almost approaching meaninglessness. There are many men of science who are actually proud of this state of things. Specialized meaninglessness has come to be regarded, in certain circles, as a kind of hall mark of true science. Those who attempt to relate the small particular results of specialization with human life as a whole and its relation to the universe at large are accused of being bad scientists, charlatans, self-advertisers. The people who make such accusations do so, of course, because they do not wish ▶

"Beliefs" (continued)

to take any responsibility for anything, but merely to retire to their cloistered laboratories, and there amuse themselves by performing delightfully interesting researches. Science and art are only too often a superior kind of dope, possessing this advantage over booze and morphia: that they can be indulged in with a good conscience and with the conviction that, in the process of indulging, one is leading the "higher life." Up to a point, of course, this is true. The life of the scientist or the artist is a higher life. Unfortunately, when led in an irresponsible, one-sided way, the higher life is probably more harmful for the individual than the lower life of the average sensual man and certainly, in the case of the scientist, much worse for society at large....

We are now at the point at which we discover that an obviously untrue philosophy of life leads in practice to disastrous results; the point where we realize the necessity of seeking an alternative philosophy that shall be true and therefore fruitful of good. A critical consideration of the classical arguments in favor of theism would reveal that some carry no conviction whatever, while the rest can only raise a presumption in favor of the theory that the world possesses some integrating principle that gives it significance and value. There is probably no argument by which the case for theism, or for deism, or for pantheism in either its pancosmic or acosmic form, can be convincingly proved. The most that "abstract reasoning" (to use Hume's phrase) can do is to create a presumption in favor of one or other hypothesis; and this presumption can be increased by means of "experimental reasoning concerning matter of fact or evidence." Final conviction can only come to those who make an act of faith. The idea is one which most of us find very distressing. But it may be doubted whether this particular act of faith is intrinsically more difficult than those which we have to make, for example, every time we frame a scientific hypothesis, every time that, from the consideration of a few phenomena, we draw inference concerning all phenomena, past, present and future. On very little evidence, but with no qualms of intellectual conscience, we assume that our craving for explanation has a real object in an explicable universe, that the aesthetic satisfaction we derive from certain arguments is a sign that they are true, that the laws of thought are also laws of things. There seems to be no reason why, having swallowed this camel, we should not swallow another, no larger really than the first. Once recognized, the reasons why we strain at the second camel cease to exist and we become free to consider on their merits the evidence and arguments that would reasonably justify us in making the final act of faith and assuming the truth of a hypothesis that we are unable fully to demonstrate.

"Abstract reasoning" must now give place to "experimental reasoning concerning matter of fact or evidence." Natural science, as we have seen, deals only with those aspects of reality that are amenable to mathematical treatment. The rest it merely ignores. But some of the experiences thus ignored by natural science—aesthetic experiences, for example, and religious experiences—throw much light upon the present problem. It is with the fact of such experiences and the evidence they furnish concerning the nature of the world that we have now to concern ourselves.

To discuss the nature and significance of aesthetic experience would take too long. It is enough, in this place, merely to suggest that the best works of literary, plastic and musical art give us more than mere pleasure; they furnish us with information about the nature of the world. The *Sanctus* in Beethoven's Mass in D, Seurat's *Grande Jatte*, *Macbeth*— works such as these tell us, by strange but certain implication, something significant about the ultimate reality behind appearances. Even from the perfection of minor masterpieces—certain sonnets of Mallarmé, for instance, certain Chinese ceramics—we can derive illuminating hints about the "something far more deeply interfused," about "the peace of God that passeth all understanding." But the subject of art is enormous and obscure, and my space is limited, I shall therefore confine myself to a discussion of certain religious experiences which bear more directly upon the present problem than do our experiences as creators and appreciators of art.

Meditation, in Babbitt's words, is a device for producing a "super-rational concentration of the will." But meditation is more than a method of self-education; it has also been used, in every part of the world and from the remotest periods, as a method for acquiring knowledge about the essential nature of things, a method for establishing communion between the soul and the integrating principle of the universe. Meditation, in other words, is the technique of mysticism. Properly practiced, with due preparation, physical, mental and moral, meditation may result in a state of what has been called "transcendental consciousness"—the direct intuition of, and union with, an ultimate spiritual reality that is perceived as simultaneously beyond the self and in some way within it. ("God in the depths of us," says Ruysbroeck, "receives God who comes to us; it is God contemplating God.") Non-mystics have denied the validity of the mystical experience, describing it as merely subjective and illusory. But it should be remembered that to those who have never actually had it, any direct intuition must seem subjective and illusory. It is impossible for the deaf to form any idea of the nature or ▶

"Beliefs" *(continued)*

significance of music. Nor is physical disability the only obstacle in the way of musical understanding. An Indian, for example, finds European orchestral music intolerably noisy, complicated, over-intellectual, inhuman. It seems incredible to him that any one should be able to perceive beauty and meaning, to recognize an expression of the deepest and subtlest emotions in this elaborate cacophony. And yet, if he has patience and listens to enough of it, he will come at last to realize, not only theoretically but also by direct, immediate intuition, that this music possesses all the qualities which Europeans claim for it. Of the significant and pleasurable experiences of life only the simplest are open indiscriminately to all. The rest cannot be had except by those who have undergone a suitable training. One must be trained even to enjoy the pleasures of alcohol and tobacco; first whiskies seem revolting, first pipes turn even the strongest of boyish stomachs. Similarly first Shakespeare sonnets seem meaningless; first Bach fugues, a bore; first differential equations, sheer torture. But training changes the nature of our spiritual experiences. In due course, contact with an obscurely beautiful poem, an elaborate piece of counterpoint or of mathematical reasoning, causes us to feel direct intuitions of beauty and significance. It is the same in the moral world. A man who has trained himself in goodness comes to have certain direct intuitions about character, about the relations between human beings, about his own position in the world—intuitions that are quite different from the intuitions of the average sensual man. Knowledge is always a function of being. What we perceive and understand depends upon what we are; and what we are depends partly on circumstances, partly, and more profoundly, on the nature of the efforts we have made to realize our ideal and the nature of the ideal we have tried to realize. The fact that knowing depends upon being leads, of course, to an immense amount of misunderstanding. The meaning of words, for example, changes profoundly according to the character and experiences of the user. Thus, to the saint, words like "love," "charity," "compassion" mean something quite different from what they mean to the ordinary man. Again, to the ordinary man, Spinoza's statement that "blessedness is not the reward of virtue, but is virtue itself" seems simply untrue. Being virtuous is, for him, a most tedious and distressing process. But it is clear that to some one who has trained himself in goodness, virtue really is blessedness, while the life of the ordinary man, with its petty vices and its long spells of animal thoughtlessness and insentience, seems a real torture. In view of the fact that knowing is conditioned by being and that being can be profoundly modified by training, we are justified in ignoring most of the arguments by which non-mystics have sought to discredit the experience of mystics. The being of a color-blind man is such that he is not competent to pass judgment on a painting. The color-blind man cannot be educated into seeing colors, and in this respect he is different from the Indian musician, who begins by finding European symphonies merely deafening and bewildering, but can be trained, if he so desires, to perceive the beauties of this kind of music. Similarly, the being of a non-mystical person is such that he cannot understand the nature of the mystic's intuitions. Like the Indian musician, however, he is at liberty, if he so chooses, to have some kind of direct experience of what at present he does not understand. This training is one which he will certainly find extremely tedious; for it involves, at first, the leading of a life of constant awareness and unremitting moral effort; second, steady practice in the technique of meditation, which is probably about as difficult as the technique of violin playing. But, however tedious, the training can be undertaken by any one who wishes to do so. Those who have not undertaken the training can have no knowledge of the kind of experiences open to those who have undertaken it and are as little justified in denying the validity of those direct intuitions of an ultimate spiritual reality, at once transcendent and immanent, as were the Pisan professors who denied, on *a priori* grounds, the validity of Galileo's direct intuition (made possible by the telescope) of the fact that Jupiter has several moons. . . .

Systematic training in recollection and meditation makes possible the mystical experience, which is a direct intuition of ultimate reality. At all times and in every part of the world, mystics of the first order have always agreed that this ultimate reality, apprehended in the process of meditation, is essentially impersonal. This direct intuition of an impersonal spiritual reality, underlying all being, is in accord with the findings of the majority of the world's philosophers.

"There is," writes Professor Whitehead, in *Religion in the Making*, "a large concurrence in the negative doctrine that the religious experience does not include any direct intuition of a definite person, or individual. . . . The evidence for the assertion of a general, though not universal, concurrence in the doctrine of no direct vision of a personal God, can only be found by a consideration of the religious thought of the civilized world. . . . Throughout India and China, religious thought, so far as it has been interpreted in precise form, disclaims the intuition of ultimate personality substantial to the universe. This is true of Confucian philosophy, Buddhist philosophy and Hindu philosophy. There may be personal embodiments, but the substratum is impersonal. Christian theology has also, in the main, adopted the position that ▸

"Beliefs" *(continued)*

there is no direct intuition of such a personal substratum for the world. It maintains the doctrine of a personal God as a truth, but holds that our belief in it is based upon inference." There seems, however, to be no cogent reason why, from the existing evidence, we should draw such an inference. Moreover, the practical results of drawing such an inference are good only up to a point; beyond that point they are very often extremely bad.

We are now in a position to draw a few tentative and fragmentary conclusions about the nature of the world and our relation to it and to one another. To the casual observer, the world seems to be made up of great numbers of independent existents, some of which possess life and some consciousness. From very early times philosophers suspected that this common-sense view was in part at least, illusory. More recently investigators, trained in the discipline of mathematical physics and equipped with instruments of precision, have made observations from which it could be inferred that all the apparently independent existents in the world were built up of a limited number of patterns of identical units of energy. An ultimate physical identity underlies the apparent physical diversity of the world. Moreover, all apparently independent existents are in fact interdependent. Meanwhile the mystics had shown that investigators, trained in the discipline of recollection and meditation, could obtain direct experience of a spiritual unity underlying the apparent diversity of independent consciousness. They made it clear that what seemed to be the ultimate fact of personality was in reality not an ultimate fact and that it was possible for individuals to transcend the limitations of personality and to merge their private consciousness into a greater, impersonal consciousness underlying the personal mind. . . .

The physical world of our daily experience is a private universe quarried out of a total reality which the physicists infer to be far greater than it. This private universe is different, not only from the real world, whose existence we are able to infer, even though we cannot directly apprehend it, but also from the private universe inhabited by other animals—universes which we can never penetrate, but concerning whose nature we can, as Von Uexkull has done, make interesting speculative guesses. Each type of living creature inhabits a universe whose nature is determined and whose boundaries are imposed by the special inadequacies of its sense organs and its intelligence. In man, intelligence has been so far developed that he is able to infer the existence and even, to some extent, the nature of the real world outside his private universe. The nature of the sense organs and intelligence of living beings is imposed by biological necessity or convenience. The instruments of knowledge are good enough to enable their owners to survive. Less inadequate instruments of knowledge might not only lead to no biological advantage but might actually constitute a biological handicap. Individual human beings have been able to transcend the limitations of man's private universe only to the extent that they are relieved from biological pressure. An individual is relieved from biological pressure in two ways: from without, thanks to the efforts of others, and from within, thanks to his own efforts. If he is to transcend the limitations of man's private universe he must be a member of a community which gives him protection against the inclemencies of the environment and makes it easy for him to supply his physical wants. But this is not enough. He must also train himself in the art of being dispassionate and disinterested, must cultivate intellectual curiosity for its own sake and not for what he, as an animal, can get out of it.

The modern conception of man's intellectual relationship to the universe was anticipated by the Buddhist doctrine that desire is the source of illusion. To the extent that it has overcome desire, a mind is free from illusion. This is true not only of the man of science, but also of the artist and the philosopher. Only the disinterested mind can transcend commonsense and pass beyond the boundaries of animal or average-sensual human life. The mystic exhibits disinterestedness in the highest degree possible to human beings and is therefore able to transcend ordinary limitations more completely than the man of science, the artist or the philosopher. That which he discovers beyond the frontiers of the average sensual man's universe is a spiritual reality underlying and uniting all apparently separate existents—a reality with which he can merge himself and from which he can draw moral and even physical powers which, by ordinary standards, can only be described as super-normal.

The ultimate reality discoverable by those who choose to modify their being, so that they can have direct knowledge of it, is not, as we have seen, a personality. Since it is not personal, it is illegitimate to attribute to it ethical qualities. "God is not good," said Eckhart. "I am good." Goodness is the means by which men and women can overcome the illusion of being completely independent existents and can raise themselves to a level of being upon which it becomes possible, by recollection and meditation, to realize the fact of their oneness with ultimate reality, to know and in some measure actually associate themselves with it. The ultimate reality is "the peace of God which passeth all understanding"; goodness is the way by which it can be approached. "Finite beings," in the words of Royce, "are always such ▶

as they are in virtue of an inattention which at present blinds them to their actual relations to God and to one another." That inattention is the fruit, in Buddhist language, of desire. We fail to attend to our true relations with ultimate reality and, through ultimate reality, with our fellow beings, because we prefer to attend to our animal nature and to the business of getting on in the world. That we can never completely ignore the animal in us or its biological needs is obvious. Our separateness is not wholly an illusion. The element of specificity in things is a brute fact of experience. Diversity cannot be reduced to complete identity even in scientific and philosophical theory, still less in life which is lived with bodies, that is to say, with particular patternings of the ultimately identical units of energy. It is impossible in the nature of things, that no attention should be given to the animal in us; but in the circumstances of civilized life, it is certainly unnecessary to give all or most of our attention to it. Goodness is the method by which we divert our attention from this singularly wearisome topic of our animality and our individual separateness. Recollection and meditation assist goodness in two ways: by producing, in Babbitt's words, "a supra-rational concentration of will," and by making it possible for the mind to realize, not only theoretically, but also by direct intuition, that the private universe of the average sensual man is not identical with the universe as a whole. Conversely, of course, goodness aids meditation by giving detachment from animality and so making it possible for the mind to pay attention to its actual relationship with ultimate reality and to other individuals. Goodness, meditation, the mystical experience and the ultimate impersonal reality discovered in mystical experience are organically related. This fact disposes of the fears expressed by Dr. Albert Schweitzer in his recent book on Indian thought. Mysticism, he contends, is the correct world view; but, though correct, it is unsatisfactory in ethical content. The ultimate reality of the world is not moral ("God is not good") and the mystic who unites himself with ultimate reality is uniting himself with a non-moral being, therefore is not himself moral. But this is mere verbalism and ignores the actual facts of experience. It is impossible for the mystic to pay attention to his real relation to God and to his fellows, unless he has previously detached his attention from his animal nature and the business of being socially successful. But he cannot detach his attention from these things except by the consistent and conscious practice of the highest morality. God is not good; but if I want to have even the smallest knowledge of God, I must be good at least in some slight measure; and if I want as full a knowledge of God as it is possible for human beings to have, I must be as good as it is possible for human beings to be. Virtue is the essential preliminary to the mystical experience. And this is not all. There is not even any theoretical incompatibility between an ultimate reality, which is impersonal and therefore not moral, and the existence of a moral order on the human level. Scientific investigation has shown that the world is a diversity underlain by an identity of physical substance; the mystical experience testifies to the existence of a spiritual unity underlying the diversity of separate consciousnesses. Concerning the relation between the underlying physical unity and the underlying spiritual unity it is hard to express an opinion. Nor is it necessary, in the present context, that we should express one. For our present purposes the important fact is that it is possible to detect a physical and a spiritual unity underlying the independent existents (to some extent merely apparent, to some extent real, at any rate for beings on our plane of existence), of which our commonsense universe is composed. Now, it is a fact of experience that we can either emphasize our separateness from other beings and the ultimate reality of the world or emphasize our oneness with them and it. To some extent at least, our will is free in this matter. Human beings are creatures who, in so far as they are animals and persons tend to regard themselves as independent existents, connected at most by purely biological ties, but who, in so far as they rise above animality and personality, are able to perceive that they are interrelated parts of physical and spiritual wholes incomparably greater than themselves. For such beings the fundamental moral commandment is: You shall realize your unity with all being. But men cannot realize their unity with others and with ultimate reality unless they practice the virtue of love and understanding. Love, compassion and understanding or intelligence—these are the primary virtues in the ethical system, the virtues organically correlated with what may be called the scientific-mystical conception of the world. Ultimate reality is impersonal and non-ethical; but if we would realize our true relations with ultimate reality and our fellow beings, we must practice morality and (since no personality can learn to transcend itself unless it is reasonably free from external compulsion) respect the personality of others. Belief in a personal, moral God has led only too frequently to theoretical dogmatism and practical intolerance—to a consistent refusal to respect personality and to the commission in the name of the divinely moral person of every kind of iniquity.

"The fact of the instability of evil," in Professor Whitehead's words, "is the moral order of the world." Evil is that which makes for separateness; and that which makes for separateness is self-destructive. This self-destruction of evil may be sudden and violent, as when ▶

"Beliefs" *(continued)*

murderous hatred results in a conflict that
leads to the death of the hater; it may be
gradual, as when a degenerative process
results in impotence or extinction; or it may
be reformative, as when a long course of
evil-doing results in all concerned becoming
so sick of destruction and degeneration that
they decide to change their ways, thus
transforming evil into good.

The evolutionary history of life clearly
illustrates the instability of evil in the sense
in which it has been defined above. Biological
specialization may be regarded as a tendency
on the part of a species to insist on its
separateness; and the result of specialization,
as we have seen, is either negatively
disastrous, in the sense that it precludes
the possibility of further biological progress,
or positively disastrous, in the sense that it
leads to the extinction of the species. In the
same way intra-specific competition may be
regarded as the expression of a tendency on
the part of related individuals to insist on
their separateness and independence; the
effects of intraspecific competition are, as we
have seen, almost wholly bad. Conversely, the
qualities which have led to biological progress
are the qualities which make it possible for
individual beings to escape from their
separateness—intelligence and the tendency
to co-operate. Love and understanding are
valuable even on the biological level. Hatred,
unawareness, stupidity and all that makes for
increase of separateness are the qualities that,
as a matter of historical fact, have led either
to the extinction of a species, or to its
becoming a living fossil, incapable of
making further biological progress. ◖

Selected from Collected Essays *by Aldous
Huxley, Harper & Brothers, 1958.*

The Complete Aldous Huxley Bibliography

Dates are the year of first publication.

The Burning Wheel	1916
Jonah	1917
The Defeat of Youth and Other Poems	1918
Leda	1920
Limbo: Notes and Essays	1920
Crome Yellow	1921
Mortal Coils: Five Stories	1922
On the Margin	1923
Antic Hay	1923
Little Mexican	1924
Those Barren Leaves	1925
Along the Road: Notes and Essays	1925
Two or Three Graces: Four Stories	1926
Jesting Pilate: An Intellectual Holiday (The Diary of a Journey)	1926
Essays New and Old (U.S. title: Essays Old and New)	1926
Proper Studies	1927
Point Counter Point	1928
Do What You Will: Essays	1929
Brief Candles	1930
Vulgarity in Literature and Other Essays: Digressions from a Theme	1930
The World of Light	1931
The Cicadas and Other Poems	1931
Music at Night and Other Essays	1931
Brave New World	1932
Texts and Pretexts: An Anthology of Commentaries	1932
Beyond the Mexique Bay	1934

The Complete Aldous Huxley Bibliography
(continued)

Eyeless in Gaza	1936
The Olive Tree and Other Essays	1936
What Are You Going to Do About It?: The Case for Constructive Peace	1936
Ends and Means: An Enquiry into the Nature of Ideals and into the Methods Employed for Their Realization	1937
After Many a Summer Dies the Swan	1939
Gray Eminence: A Study in Religion and Politics	1941
The Art of Seeing	1942
Time Must Have a Stop	1944
The Perennial Philosophy	1946
Science, Liberty and Peace	1946
Ape and Essence	1948
The Gioconda Smile	1948
Themes and Variations	1950
The Devils of Loudun	1952
The Doors of Perception	1954
The Genius and the Goddess	1955
Heaven and Hell	1956
Adonis and the Alphabet and Other Essays (U.S. title: *Tomorrow and Tomorrow and Tomorrow*)	1956
Brave New World Revisited	1958
Island	1962
Literature and Science	1963

Have You Read?
More by Aldous Huxley

**THE DOORS OF PERCEPTION
AND HEAVEN AND HELL**

Two classic complete books in which Huxley
explores, as only he can, the mind's remote
frontiers and the unmapped areas of human
consciousness. These two books became
essential for the counterculture during the
1960s and influenced a generation's
perception of life.

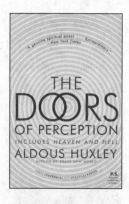

"A challenge is forcibly put, ideas are freshly
and prodigally presented."
—*San Francisco Chronicle*

THE DEVILS OF LOUDUN

First published in 1952, *The Devils of Loudun*
is Aldous Huxley's thrilling account of one
of history's most sensational cases of mass
demonic possession. The year 1643: When
an entire convent is apparently possessed by
the devil, a charismatic priest is accused of
being in league with Satan and seducing the
nuns—both spiritually and sexually. After a
celebrated trial, the priest, Urban Grandier,
was burnt at the stake for witchcraft. Here is
the gripping true history of Grandier and the
nuns of Loudun, as told by one of the master
storytellers of the twentieth century.

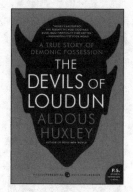

"Huxley's masterpiece and perhaps the most
enjoyable book about spirituality ever written.
In telling the grotesque, bawdy and true story
of a seventeenth-century convent of cloistered
French nuns who contrived to have a priest
they never met burned alive as a warlock . . .
Huxley painlessly conveys a wealth of
information about mysticism and the
unconscious." —*Washington Post Book World*

BRAVE NEW WORLD

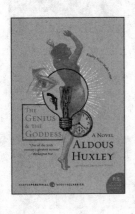

The astonishing novel *Brave New World*, originally published in 1932, presents Aldous Huxley's vision of the future— of a world utterly transformed. Through the most efficient scientific and psychological engineering, people are genetically designed to be passive and therefore consistently useful to the ruling class. This powerful work of speculative fiction sheds a blazing critical light on the present and is considered to be Aldous Huxley's most enduring masterpiece.

"Mr. Huxley is eloquent in his declaration of an artist's faith in man, and it is his eloquence, bitter in attack, noble in defense, that, when one has closed the book, one remembers." —*Saturday Review of Literature*

"Huxley never went out of style. Something about his work seem[s] to tug at our consciousness. . . . There is no escape from anxiety and struggle, and Huxley assists us in attaining this valuable glimpse of the obvious, precisely because it was a conclusion that was in many ways unwelcome to him."
—Christopher Hitchens

THE GENIUS AND THE GODDESS

Talking with a friend on Christmas Eve while a small grandson sleeps upstairs, John Rivers is moved to set the record straight about his mentor—the legendary scientific genius in whose home, thirty years before, ecstasy and torment had laid hold of Rivers, shocking him out of "half-baked imbecility into something more nearly resembling the human form." Fatefully, Rivers had an affair with the famous man's young wife, bringing the couple to ruin. Now back in print, *The*